# Formal and Methodological Approaches to Applied Linguistics

# Formal and Methodological Approaches to Applied Linguistics

Special Issue Editors

**Sonja Mujcinovic**
**Eduardo Gómez Garzarán**

MDPI • Basel • Beijing • Wuhan • Barcelona • Belgrade • Manchester • Tokyo • Cluj • Tianjin

*Special Issue Editors*
Sonja Mujcinovic
University of Valladolid
Spain

Eduardo Gómez Garzarán
University of Valladolid
Spain

*Editorial Office*
MDPI
St. Alban-Anlage 66
4052 Basel, Switzerland

This is a reprint of articles from the Special Issue published online in the open access journal *Languages* (ISSN 2226-471X) (available at: https://www.mdpi.com/journal/languages/special_issues/AESLA_2019).

For citation purposes, cite each article independently as indicated on the article page online and as indicated below:

LastName, A.A.; LastName, B.B.; LastName, C.C. Article Title. *Journal Name* **Year**, *Article Number*, Page Range.

**ISBN 978-3-03928-322-4 (Pbk)**
**ISBN 978-3-03928-323-1 (PDF)**

Cover image courtesy of Juan Carlos Guerra Velasco

© 2020 by the authors. Articles in this book are Open Access and distributed under the Creative Commons Attribution (CC BY) license, which allows users to download, copy and build upon published articles, as long as the author and publisher are properly credited, which ensures maximum dissemination and a wider impact of our publications.

The book as a whole is distributed by MDPI under the terms and conditions of the Creative Commons license CC BY-NC-ND.

# Contents

About the Special Issue Editors . . . . . . . . . . . . . . . . . . . . . . . . . . . . . . . . . . . vii

Preface to "Formal and Methodological Approaches to Applied Linguistics" . . . . . . . . . . ix

**Sonja Mujcinovic and Eduardo Gómez Garzarán**
Formal and Methodological Approaches to Applied Linguistics (*Languages* Special Issue)
Reprinted from: *Languages* **2019**, *4*, 94, doi:10.3390/languages4040094 . . . . . . . . . . . . . . . . 1

**Amaia Fernández, Pilar Sagasta and Nagore Ipiña**
Communicative Acts Used by Emergent Trilingual Pupils in English Classrooms in the Basque Autonomous Community
Reprinted from: *Languages* **2019**, *4*, 60, doi:10.3390/languages4030060 . . . . . . . . . . . . . . . . 5

**Mireia Ortega and M. Luz Celaya**
Lexical Crosslinguistic Influence and Study Abroad: Do Learners Use L1-Based Resources Less?
Reprinted from: *Languages* **2019**, *4*, 55, doi:10.3390/languages4030055 . . . . . . . . . . . . . . . . 15

**Irina Khomchenkova, Polina Pleshak and Natalia Stoynova**
Nonstandard Use of the "Reflexive" Affix -s$^j$a in Russian Speech of Bilingual Speakers of Northern Siberia and the Russian Far East
Reprinted from: *Languages* **2019**, *4*, 39, doi:10.3390/languages4020039 . . . . . . . . . . . . . . . . 25

**Amal Haddad Haddad and Silvia Montero-Martínez**
The 'Carbon Capture' Metaphor: An English-Arabic Terminological Case Study
Reprinted from: *Languages* **2019**, *4*, 77, doi:10.3390/languages4040077 . . . . . . . . . . . . . . . . 35

**Isabel Negro**
Metaphor and Metonymy in Food Idioms
Reprinted from: *Languages* **2019**, *4*, 47, doi:10.3390/languages4030047 . . . . . . . . . . . . . . . . 49

**Jorge R. Valdés Kroff, Frederieke Rooijakkers and M. Carmen Parafita Couto**
Spanish Grammatical Gender Interference in Papiamentu
Reprinted from: *Languages* **2019**, *4*, 78, doi:10.3390/languages4040078 . . . . . . . . . . . . . . . . 57

**Lucía Bellés-Calvera**
The Linguistic Landscape of the Valencian Community: A Comparative Analysis of Bilingual and Multilingual Signs in Three Different Areas
Reprinted from: *Languages* **2019**, *4*, 38, doi:10.3390/languages4020038 . . . . . . . . . . . . . . . . 69

**Rosana Villares**
The Role of Language Policy Documents in the Internationalisation of Multilingual Higher Education: An Exploratory Corpus-Based Study
Reprinted from: *Languages* **2019**, *4*, 56, doi:10.3390/languages4030056 . . . . . . . . . . . . . . . . 89

**Isabel Moskowich and Begoña Crespo**
"Arguments That Could Possibly Be Urged": Modal Verbs and Tentativeness in the *Coruña Corpus*
Reprinted from: *Languages* **2019**, *4*, 57, doi:10.3390/languages4030057 . . . . . . . . . . . . . . . . 99

**Candela Contero Urgal**
Law and Business Students' Attitudes towards Learning English for Specific Purposes within CLIL and Non-CLIL Contexts
Reprinted from: *Languages* **2019**, *4*, 45, doi:10.3390/languages4020045 . . . . . . . . . . . . . . . . . **111**

**Juan Rojas-Garcia and Pamela Faber**
Extraction of Terms Related to Named Rivers
Reprinted from: *Languages* **2019**, *4*, 46, doi:10.3390/languages4030046 . . . . . . . . . . . . . . . . . **121**

# About the Special Issue Editors

**Sonja Mujcinovic** holds a degree in English Philology and a second degree in Spanish Philology both from the University of Valladolid. She obtained her Master's Degree in Advanced English Studies from the joint program of the universities of Valladolid and Salamanca. She is currently working on her doctoral dissertation on second language acquisition focused on bilingual morphosyntactic analysis and cross-linguistic influence. She also works as a part-time professor at the University of Valladolid.

**Eduardo Gómez Garzarán** is a full time English and content subjects teacher and the coordinator of the English-Spanish bilingual section at Colegio Ave María in Valladolid (Spain). He is a PhD student in the Valladolid-Salamanca interuniversity PhD Program in Advanced English Studies: Languages and Cultures in Contact at the University of Valladolid. His doctoral research revolves around cross-linguistic influence and word order within the determiner phrase domain in structures presenting nominal modification by adjectives and by nouns.

# Preface to "Formal and Methodological Approaches to Applied Linguistics"

This Special Issue, entitled Formal and Methodological Approaches to Applied Linguistics, brings together recently published papers on various aspects of applied linguistics presented at the AESLA37 (Spanish Society of Applied Linguistics) conference in Valladolid held on 27–29 March 2019. This issue aims to provide a better understanding of different aspects of language and to share new insights into theoretical and practical aspects in the field. It does so by addressing the study of language in its different dimensions and areas of applicability through the use of multiple methodologies and formal accounts as used by researchers in the field.

This Special Issue contains contributions from the following areas related to applied linguistics: language acquisition and language learning; language for specific purposes; language psychology, child language and psycholinguistics; sociolinguistics; discourse analysis; corpus linguistics; and lexicology and lexicography.

We are certain that the papers published in this volume offer a clear insight into the topics currently being dealt with, both from a theoretical and practical perspective, within the field of applied linguistics. Together, they provide a good example of how research on language and languages in contact are developing at present.

Sonja Mujcinovic, Eduardo Gómez Garzarán
*Special Issue Editors*

*Editorial*

# Formal and Methodological Approaches to Applied Linguistics (*Languages* Special Issue)

### Sonja Mujcinovic * and Eduardo Gómez Garzarán *

Department of English, University of Valladolid, 47002 Valladolid, Spain
* Correspondence: sonja@fing.uva.es (S.M.); eduardo.gomez@vedruna.es (E.G.G.)

Received: 6 November 2019; Accepted: 13 November 2019; Published: 21 November 2019

## 1. Prologue

This Special Issue, entitled Formal and Methodological Approaches to Applied Linguistics, brings together recently published papers on various aspects of applied linguistics presented at the AESLA37 (Spanish Society of Applied Linguistics) conference in Valladolid held on 27–29 March 2019. This issue aims to provide a better understanding of different aspects of language and to share new insights into theoretical and practical aspects in the field. It does so by addressing the study of language in its different dimensions and areas of applicability through the use of multiple methodologies and formal accounts as used by researchers in the field.

This Special Issue contains contributions from the following areas related to applied linguistics: language acquisition and language learning; language for specific purposes; language psychology, child language and psycholinguistics; sociolinguistics; discourse analysis; corpus linguistics; and lexicology and lexicography.

We are certain that the papers published in this volume offer a clear insight into the topics currently being dealt with, both from a theoretical and practical perspective, within the field of applied linguistics. Together, they provide a good example of how research on language and languages in contact are developing at present.

We would like to thank everyone who has made this Special Issue possible: authors, panel directors, and a special mention to the reviewers whose dedication has contributed considerably to this publication.

## 2. Organizing Committee

Chair: Raquel Fernández Fuertes
(English department)
Susana Álvarez Álvarez
(Spanish department)
Esther Álvarez de la Fuente
(English department)
Carmen Cuellar Lázaro
(French and German department)
Goretti Faya Ornia
(English department)
Alejandro Martínez González
(English department)

Laura Filardo Llamas
(English department)
Pedro Fuertes Olivera
(English department)
Tamara Gómez Carrero
(English department)
Eduardo Gómez Garzarán
(English department)
Lorena Hurtado Malillos
(French and German department)
Elena Jiménez García
(Didactics of language and literature department)

Nieves Mendizábal de la Cruz
(Spanish department)
Susana Merino Mañueco
(Spanish department)
Leticia Moreno Pérez
(English department)
Sonja Mujcinovic
(English department)

Silvia Sánchez Calderón
(English department)
Francisco Javier Sanz Trigueros
(Didactics of language and literature department)
Mª Ángeles Sastre Ruano
(Spanish department)
Radoslava Stankova Laykova
(English department)
Qianting Yuan
(English department)

## 3. Coordinators of AESLA's Scientific Panels

Ana Llinares
Universidad Autónoma de Madrid
Irina Argüelles Álvarez
Universidad Politécnica de Madrid Campus Sur
María Belén Díez BedmarUniversidad de Jaén
Isabel Alonso Belmonte
Universidad Autónoma de Madrid
Paloma López Zurita
Universidad de Cádiz
María del Carmen Horno Chéliz
Universidad de Zaragoza

Elena Fernández de Molina Ortés
Universidad de Granada
Francisco Alonso Almeida
Universidad de Las Palmas de Gran Canaria
Begoña Bellés FortuñoUniversitat Jaume I, Castellón
Moisés Almela Sánchez
Universidad de Murcia
Iraide Ibarretxe Antuñano
Universidad de Zaragoza
Miguel Ángel Candel Mora
Universitat Politècnica de València

## 4. Reviewers

María Pilar Agustín Llach, Ana Maria Anderson, Vincent Beltrán-Palanques, Jelena Bobkina, Feng Cao, Ricardo Casaño Pitach, Joseph Casillas, M. Luz Celaya, María Enriqueta Cortés de los Ríos, Do Coyle, Klaus-Dieter Rossade, María Fernández Agüero, Esther Gómez Lacabex, Diana González Pastor, Dinda L. Gorlée, Anton Granvik, Bryan Koronkiewicz, Avizia Yim Long, Silvia Molina Plaza, Natascha Müller, Jesús Manuel Nieto García, Inés Olza, Ana Isabel Otto Cantón, Vicky Papachristou, Isabel Pérez Jiménez, Paula Pérez Sobrino, M.ª, Dolores Porto Requejo, Anna Rufat, Efthymia Tsaroucha, Sarah Turner, Chelo Vargas-Sierra, and several other anonymous reviewers.

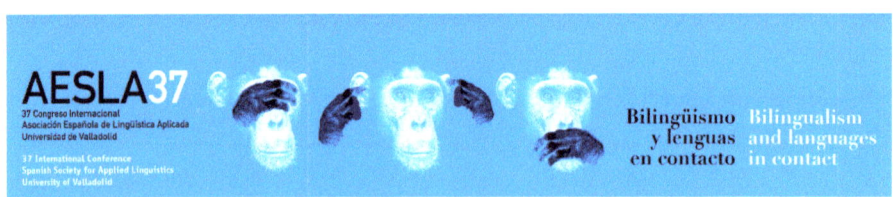

The AESLA 2019 international conference was held as part of the UVALAL (University of Valladolid Language Acquisition Lab) research activities within the framework of two research projects funded by the Castile and León Regional Government and FEDER (ref. VA009P17), and the Spanish Ministry of Science, Innovation and Universities and FEDER (ref. PGC2018-097693-B-I00).

 © 2019 by the authors. Licensee MDPI, Basel, Switzerland. This article is an open access article distributed under the terms and conditions of the Creative Commons Attribution (CC BY) license (http://creativecommons.org/licenses/by/4.0/).

Article

# Communicative Acts Used by Emergent Trilingual Pupils in English Classrooms in the Basque Autonomous Community

Amaia Fernández, Pilar Sagasta and Nagore Ipiña *

Faculty of Humanities and Educational Sciences, Mondragon Unibertsitatea, 20540 Eskoriatza, Spain
* Correspondence: nipina@mondragon.edu

Received: 13 May 2019; Accepted: 26 July 2019; Published: 30 July 2019

**Abstract:** This research aims at examining the communicative acts (CA) performed by Grade 5 emergent trilingual pupils in the Basque Autonomous Community (BAC) in northern Spain when interacting in the English classroom. Likewise, it examines translanguaging practices when performing CA to analyze whether pupils deploy similar linguistic resources (LR) regardless of the CA they enact. Moreover, it investigates whether pupils from different sociolinguistic contexts behave similarly. Preliminary results suggest that Grade 5 pupils taking part in this study enact CA related to inviting elaboration or reasoning, expressing or inviting ideas, guiding direction of dialogue or activity, positioning and coordination, and showing understanding by using LR coming from different linguistic systems (mostly English and Basque) when interacting in the English classroom across sociolinguistic areas.

**Keywords:** spontaneous translanguaging; discourse practices; language acquisition

## 1. Introduction

Translanguaging is a relatively new term that was first used by Cen Williams in 1994 in Wales concerning a pedagogical strategy observed in the Welsh classrooms. Baker (2011) defined translanguaging as a process to make meaning, shape experiences, acquire understanding and knowledge through the use of two languages, and Cenoz and Gorter (2017) drew the difference between pedagogical and spontaneous translanguaging. This paper focuses on spontaneous translanguaging and examines the discursive practices (Cenoz and Gorter 2017) of emergent trilinguals in the English classroom, because as Canagarajah (2011) states, research is needed to investigate how multilingual speakers combine codes in their discursive practices. Moreover, these trilingual pupils have three languages in the curriculum: Basque, Spanish, and English, and their schools are situated in two different sociolinguistic areas. Therefore, this paper considers the social context to better understand these pupils' discursive practices, because as Cenoz and Gorter (2019, p. 133) claim, "the social context is crucial when discussing translanguaging, particularly in communities that involved minority languages".

Cenoz and Gorter (2017) analyzed translanguaging in the context of minority regional languages and examined whether it could be a threat or an opportunity for minority languages. They state that spontaneous translanguaging is common practice in the case of bilingual speakers. Nevertheless, they claim that people involved in the maintenance of these regional languages may fear that their language will lose prominence and they advocate to soften borders between languages in a sustainable way. Linguistic separation, they assert (Cenoz and Gorter 2019), may have benefited minority languages in the past, but today that separation may be counterproductive, because as Gorter et al. (2014, p. 217) affirm, "Basque, Spanish and English reinforce each other". Five principles have been suggested by Cenoz and Gorter (2017) for promoting sustainable translanguaging in school contexts in which minority languages are used; creating breathing spaces for the minority language; fostering the use of the minority language in translanguaging practices; developing metalinguistic awareness through the use of the emergent multilinguals' entire linguistic repertoire; reinforcing language awareness; and linking spontaneous translanguaging to pedagogical tasks.

Nonetheless, as Otheguy and García (2019, p. 10) claim, educators who foster a translanguaging pedagogy realize that named languages are socio-cultural constructions; but they also recognize that "named languages do not correspond to a psycholinguistic reality of dual systems". That is, bilinguals have access to their whole linguistic repertoire in communicative situations in which the use of linguistic features is not restricted to named languages. On the contrary, bilinguals need to monitor the selection of linguistic features when the interlocutor does not share their linguistic repertoire, as in the case of a monolingual speaker, or in situations in which strict language separation is required. Hence, as Otheguy et al. (2015, p. 297) claim, translanguaging focuses on the individual, it views the speaker from the inside, whereas named languages adopt "the view from the outside".

Concerning research conducted on translanguaging, positive results have been highlighted as regards language learning opportunities and metalinguistic (Fuller 2015; St. John 2018; Rosiers 2018). Fuller (2015) examined the discursive practices of nine-year-old students enrolled in a German–English bilingual school placed in Berlin. She found that the children's choices to deploy bilingual discourse were personal choices with interactional motivations; when they played the role of good students, they used English, the language of the classroom. Nonetheless, they knew that German was the language of the wider community, and that its status as a symbol of youth culture was more powerful; so they often used it for creating solidarity with their classmates. St. John (2018) studied the multilingual interactions among subject teachers, newly arrived Somali pupils, and mother tongue tutors in oral examinations in Sweden, and found that translanguaging is a situated practice and language choice and its use depends on both the communicative situation and the participants' idiolects. Therefore, it should be analyzed within an interactional framework. Rosiers (2018) investigated the interactional engagement of primary pupils with their linguistic repertoire in two multilingual Belgian schools and claimed that translanguaging practices are influenced by factors such as the topic, the group, as well as cognitive and linguistic factors.

Considering all the above-mentioned studies, it is evident that further research is necessary to find out how emergent multilinguals use their linguistic repertoire in their classrooms, because as Wei (2015, p. 196) asserts, translanguaging can have an important impact on "the development of identity, social relationships and values amongst their users". Moreover, studies that examine spontaneous practices in classrooms where three languages are included in the curriculum, and one of them is a regional minority language are needed, and that is precisely the main goal of this study. This research aims at examining the communicative acts (CA) performed by emergent trilingual pupils in the BAC when interacting in the English classroom. Likewise, it examines translanguaging practices to study whether pupils deploy similar linguistic resources (LR) regardless of the CA they enact. Moreover, it investigates whether pupils from different sociolinguistic contexts behave similarly, because, as mentioned above, the social context may have an impact on translanguaging practices (Cenoz and Gorter 2019).

Regarding the aforementioned literature, this study raises the following questions:

1. Which CA do emergent trilingual pupils perform when communicating in the English classroom?
2. Do they use similar LR regardless of the CA being performed?
3. Does the sociolinguistic area make a difference?

## 2. Materials and Methods

The BAC is a bilingual community with Basque and Spanish as co-official languages and this study was conducted in two schools; School A located in Araba (Spanish sociolinguist area) and School B in Gipuzkoa (Basque sociolinguistic area). Both schools follow a D linguistic model, with Basque as the main language of instruction and Spanish and English taught as a subject. It must be clarified that this is part of an ongoing study we are carrying out with 153 Grade 5 pupils. Nonetheless, for the purpose of this study, fourteen pupils have been randomly selected, as depicted in Table 1.

Table 1. Participants.

| School A (Spanish Area) | | School B (Basque Area) | |
| --- | --- | --- | --- |
| Grade 5 (n:6) | S1 | Grade 5 (n:6) | S19 |
| | S2 | | S20 |
| | S3 | | S21 |
| | | | S22 |
| | S4 | | S23 |
| | S5 | | S24 |
| | S6 | | S25 |
| | | | S26 |

Participants.

Fourteen Grade 5 emergent trilingual pupils from two different sociolinguistic areas took part in this study. Six pupils were randomly selected in the Spanish sociolinguistic area and eight pupils in the Basque area.

All participants are Basque and Spanish bilinguals and English is an L3 and they all started learning English at the age of four. It is an ethnographic case study (Gay et al. 2006) in which these fourteen emergent trilingual pupils were observed in the English classroom during the school year 2016/2017, and their spontaneous interactions were audio-recorded. Altogether, 25 h and 48 min of study were analyzed; 13 h and 14 min in School A and 12 h and 33 min in School B.

Data collected were transcribed and analyzed using the SEDA scheme (Hennessy et al. 2016), which was previously adapted to take into account the particular context of study. This scheme is a tool used to examine the CA enacted in classroom dialogue, which are grouped into clusters according to the function of the act. A CA is defined by Hennessy et al. (2016, p. 20) as "the minimum number of utterances or actions needed to reflect its function".

Based on the research work conducted by these authors, the CA performed by the fourteen participants were identified. Subsequently, the CA were coded and clustered, taking into account the communicative function fulfilled. Afterwards, the translanguaging practices observed in the CA were detected and categorized following this code: LR1 (Basque); LR2 (Spanish); LR3 (English); LR4 (Basque/Spanish); LR5 (Basque/English); LR6 (Spanish/English); LR7 (Other/English); and LR8 (Basque/Spanish/English). Finally, data corresponding to each sociolinguistic area were detected and analyzed separately in order to compare and contrast the results.

### 3. Results

#### 3.1. Results Concerning Research Question One and Two

Regarding the first research question, Grade 5 pupils articulated 4523 utterances and enacted 4365 CA, which were coded, clustered, and analyzed, as Table 2 shows.

Table 2 depicts that these participants mostly performed CA to focus the dialogue on key aspects of the activity (G5), 12%. They also uttered CA to state (dis)agreement or position (P6), 11.1% or propose solution (P3), 11%. Similarly, they enacted CA to ask for elaboration or clarification (I6), 9.8%.

Table 2. Performed communicative acts (CA).

| Cluster | | | CA PERFORMED | FREQUENCY | PERCENTAGE |
|---|---|---|---|---|---|
| | | | Interactional Function | | |
| I | Invite elaboration or reasoning | I1 | Ask for explanation or justification of another's contribution | 7 | 0.2% |
| | | I2 | Invite build on/elaboration/(Dis)agreement/evaluation of another's contribution or view | 30 | 0.7% |
| | | I3 | Invite possibility thinking based on another's contribution | 5 | 0.1% |
| | | I4 | Ask for explanation or justification | 58 | 1.3% |
| | | I5 | Invite possibility thinking or prediction | 4 | 0.1% |
| | | I6 | Ask for elaboration or clarification | 427 | 9.8% |
| R | Make reasoning explicit | R1 | Explain or justify another's contribution | 13 | 0.3% |
| | | R2 | Explain or justify own contribution | 17 | 0.4% |
| | | R3 | Speculate or predict on the basis of another's contribution | 39 | 0.9% |
| | | R4 | Speculate or predict | 72 | 1.6% |
| B | Build on ideas | B1 | Build on/Explain/clarify other's contribution | 72 | 1.6% |
| | | B2 | Clarify/elaborate own contribution | 74 | 1.7% |
| | | B3 | Synthesize ideas | 7 | 0.2% |
| E | Express or invite ideas | E1 | Invite opinion/beliefs/ideas | 229 | 5.2% |
| | | E2 | Make other (relevant) contribution | 279 | 6.4% |
| G | Guide direction of dialogue or activity | G1 | Encourage dialogue | 56 | 1.3% |
| | | G2 | Propose action or activity | 237 | 5.4% |
| | | G3 | Introduce authoritative perspective | 8 | 0.2% |
| | | G4 | Provide informative feedback | 57 | 1.3% |
| | | G5 | Focus the dialogue on key aspects of the activity (guiding) | 523 | 12.0% |
| | | G6 | Allow thinking time | 4 | 0.1% |
| | | G7 | organization of group activities | 201 | 4.6% |
| P | Positioning and coordination | P1 | Synthesize ideas | 4 | 0.1% |
| | | P2 | Compare/evaluate alternative views | 21 | 0.5% |
| | | P3 | Propose solution | 480 | 11.0% |
| | | P4 | Acknowledge shift in position | 1 | 0.0% |
| | | P5 | Challenge viewpoint | 5 | 0.1% |
| | | P6 | State (dis)agreement/position | 485 | 11.1% |
| | | P7 | Gap of knowledge | 4 | 0.1% |
| C | Connect | C1 | Refer back to prior contributions | 1 | 0.0% |
| | | C2 | Make learning trajectory explicit | 0 | 0.0% |
| | | C3 | Link learning with other contexts | 0 | 0.0% |
| | | C4 | Invite inquiry beyond the lesson | 0 | 0.0% |
| RD | Reflect on dialogue or activity | RD1 | Talk about talk | 0 | 0.0% |
| | | RD2 | Reflect on learning process/purpose/value | 0 | 0.0% |
| | | RD3 | Invite reflection about process/purpose/value of learning | 0 | 0.0% |
| EE | Express emotions | EE1 | Happiness | 19 | 0.4% |
| | | EE2 | Excitement | 73 | 1.7% |
| | | EE3 | Gratitude | 7 | 0.2% |
| | | EE4 | Expectation/hope | 16 | 0.4% |
| | | EE5 | Astonishment | 81 | 1.9% |
| | | EE6 | Dubious | 43 | 1.0% |
| | | EE7 | Tedium | 18 | 0.4% |
| | | EE8 | Irritation | 26 | 0.6% |
| | | EE9 | Frustration | 78 | 1.8% |
| | | EE10 | Anger | 28 | 0.6% |

Table 2. Cont.

| Cluster | CA PERFORMED | | | FREQUENCY | PERCENTAGE |
|---|---|---|---|---|---|
| | | | Interactional Function | | |
| | | CU | Check understanding | 78 | 1.8% |
| | | SU | Show understanding | 227 | 5.2% |
| | | AH | Ask for help | 39 | 0.9% |
| | | AP | Ask for permission | 41 | 0.9% |
| | | Apr | Ask for participation | 22 | 0.5% |
| NRC | | | Non Relevant Contribution | 149 | 3.4% |
| | | | TOTAL: | 4365 | 100% |

Performed CA.

Concerning the second research question, Table 3 below displays the most common CA enacted by all the participants and the resources they used. It is evident that English resources (LR3) are by far the most common means used to perform the CA in the English classroom: I6 (208 utterances), E1 (89 utterances), E2 (138 utterances), G2 (63 utterances), G5 (333 utterances), G7 (52 utterances), P3 (374 utterances), P6 (271 utterances), and SU (158 utterances).

Table 3. Linguistic resources (LR) used in the most frequently performed CA.

| | CA Performed | | | LR Used | | | | | | | | |
|---|---|---|---|---|---|---|---|---|---|---|---|---|
| | Cluster | | Interactional Function | LR1 | LR2 | LR3 | LR4 | LR5 | LR6 | LR7 | LR8 | - |
| I | Invite elaboration or reasoning | I6 | Ask for elaboration or clarification | 104 | 19 | 208 | 22 | 30 | 28 | 0 | 9 | 7 |
| E | Express or invite ideas | E1 | Invite opinion/beliefs/ideas | 44 | 31 | 89 | 24 | 17 | 20 | 0 | 2 | 2 |
| | | E2 | Make other (relevant) contribution | 47 | 22 | 138 | 21 | 17 | 25 | 0 | 5 | 4 |
| G | Guide direction of dialogue or activity | G2 | Propose action or activity | 77 | 30 | 63 | 35 | 10 | 12 | 0 | 10 | 0 |
| | | G5 | Focus the dialogue on key aspects of the activity (guiding) | 49 | 18 | 333 | 28 | 28 | 52 | 0 | 9 | 6 |
| | | G7 | Organization of group activities | 68 | 16 | 52 | 34 | 12 | 16 | 0 | 2 | 0 |
| P | Positioning and coordination | P3 | Propose solution | 25 | 15 | 374 | 7 | 17 | 33 | 0 | 6 | 3 |
| | | P6 | State (dis)agreement/position | 101 | 40 | 271 | 24 | 27 | 19 | 0 | 2 | 0 |
| SU | | | Show understanding | 12 | 26 | 158 | 3 | 6 | 10 | 0 | 0 | 12 |

LR used in the most frequently performed CA.

Nonetheless, Basque resources (LR1) were used more often than English resources (LR3) to propose action or activity (G2), 77 utterances. Basque means were also frequently observed when participants asked for elaboration or clarification (I6), 104 utterances or stated (dis)agreement/position (P6), 101 utterance, although they frequently used English means for those CA. When showing understanding (SU), even though they deployed English means (LR3) more often, Spanish resources (LR2) were frequently observed, 26 utterances. Participants also made use of Spanish and English resources (LR6) when focusing the dialogue on key aspects of the activity (G5), 52 utterances, or when proposing a solution (P3), 33 utterances, although the use of English was predominant. Finally, the number of Basque, Spanish, and English means (LR8) were rather low, but they were observed in eight out of nine most frequent CA: I6 (9 utterances), E1 (2 utterances), E2 (5 utterances), G2 (10 utterances), G5 (9 utterances), G7 (2 utterances), P3 (6 utterances), P6 (2 utterances).

Here is a sample interaction (Table 4) to exemplify the aforementioned CA performed and the use of LR:

Table 4. Sample interaction.

| | | |
|---|---|---|
| 26. S3-Then pour, *ze pour da botatzea* [because pour means spill] | P3 | LR5 |
| 27. S1-*Eta gero* [and then]? | I6 | LR1 |
| 28. S3-Take one::::  | P3 | LR3 |
| *A ver* [let's see], ... the monkeys ... coma, daisy's petal, no daisy's petal no ... | P3 | LR6 |
| 29. S-And ... | | |
| 30. S1-*Y ponemos* [and we write ] and, and. *Bai zer da koma bat*:::[Yes because it is a comma] | E2 | LR8 |
| 31. S2-*A ver* [Let's see ] ... all the monkeys .... On a spoon ... *venga* [come on]! on a spoon | P3 | LR6 |
| Spoon, *he dicho* [I said], spoon ... on a spoon, comma, two centiliters, comma ... | G3 | LR6 |
| 32. S1-E two *centilits* [centilitres] of | I6 | LR3 |
| 33. S2-Spoon! | P3 | LR3 |
| 34. S1-*Bai* [yes], spoon. | P6 | LR5 |
| Two *centilits* [centilitres] ... *dos centilitros* [two centilitres]. | B2 | LR6 |

Sample interaction.

### 3.2. Results Concerning Research Question Three

In order to analyze the impact sociolinguistic area could have on the performance of CA, utterances from each area were identified: 2408 in School A and 2115 in School B. A total amount of 2318 CA in School A and 1970 in School B were detected, coded, and clustered. Table 5 below displays a summary of the most frequently enacted CA in each sociolinguistic area:

Table 5. Most frequently performed CA in each sociolinguistic area.

| | Cluster | | Interactional Function | Frequency | Percentage |
|---|---|---|---|---|---|
| **CA Performed in School A** | | | | | |
| I | Invite elaboration or reasoning | I6 | Ask for elaboration or clarification | 226 | 9.7% |
| G | Guide direction of dialogue or activity | G2 | Propose action or activity | 141 | 6.1% |
| | | G5 | Focus the dialogue on key aspects of the activity (guiding) | 263 | 11.3% |
| P | Positioning and coordination | P3 | Propose solution | 263 | 11.3% |
| | | P6 | State (dis)agreement/position | 223 | 9.6% |
| **CA performed in School B** | | | | | |
| I | Invite elaboration or reasoning | I6 | Ask for elaboration or clarification | 201 | 10.2% |
| E | Express or invite ideas | E2 | Make other (relevant) contribution | 182 | 9.2% |
| G | Guide direction of dialogue or activity | G5 | Focus the dialogue on key aspects of the activity (guiding) | 260 | 13.2% |
| P | Positioning and coordination | P3 | Propose solution | 217 | 11% |
| | | P6 | State (dis)agreement/position | 262 | 13.3% |

Most frequently performed CA in each sociolinguistic area.

Results show that participants in both sociolinguistic areas performed similar CA when interacting in the English classroom. However, in the Spanish sociolinguist area (School A), participants mostly enacted CA to focus the dialogue on key aspects of the activity (G5), 11.3%, or to propose solutions (P3), 11.3%. Nonetheless, pupils from the Basque sociolinguistic area (School B) enacted more CA to make contributions (E2), 9.2%. The frequency was also higher in School B when enacting CA to state (dis)agreement/position (P6), 13.3%, or focusing the dialogue on key aspect of the activity (G5), 13.2%. Therefore, the impact of the sociolinguistic area cannot be confirmed.

Concerning LR identified when performing the five most frequent CA, Table 6 below depicts that participants in the Spanish sociolinguistic area mostly used English resources (LR3), except for proposing actions or activity (G2), CA which were pupils frequently performed in Basque (LR1). Nonetheless, pupils from the Basque sociolinguistic area mostly deployed English resources (LR3) in the enacted five CA. However, it can also be observed that the use of Basque resources (LR1) in both areas is more frequent than the use of Spanish ones (LR2), even in the Spanish sociolinguistic area. Therefore, the impact of the sociolinguistic area cannot be confirmed.

Table 6. LR used in the most frequently performed CA in each sociolinguistic area.

| | Cluster | | Interactional Function | LR1 | LR2 | LR3 | LR4 | LR5 | LR6 | LR7 | LR8 | - |
|---|---|---|---|---|---|---|---|---|---|---|---|---|
| | | | **CA Performed School A** | | | | | | | | | |
| I | Invite elaboration or reasoning | I6 | Ask for elaboration or clarification | 66 | 17 | 100 | 13 | 10 | 14 | 0 | 3 | 3 |
| G | Guide direction of dialogue or activity | G2 | Propose action or activity | 48 | 25 | 23 | 30 | 6 | 5 | 0 | 4 | 0 |
| | | G5 | Focusing the dialogue on key aspects of the activity (guiding) | 15 | 10 | 189 | 9 | 11 | 26 | 0 | 2 | 1 |
| P | Positioning and coordination | P3 | Propose solution | 19 | 10 | 181 | 5 | 13 | 27 | 0 | 6 | 2 |
| | | P6 | State (dis)agreement/position | 63 | 31 | 82 | 18 | 14 | 12 | 0 | 2 | 1 |
| | | | **CA performed School B** | | | | | | | | | |
| I | Invite elaboration or reasoning | I6 | Ask for elaboration or clarification | 38 | 2 | 108 | 9 | 20 | 14 | 0 | 6 | 4 |
| E | Express or invite ideas | E2 | Make other (relevant) contribution | 31 | 12 | 91 | 12 | 10 | 21 | 0 | 2 | 3 |
| G | Guide direction of dialogue or activity | G5 | Focusing the dialogue on key aspects of the activity (guiding) | 34 | 8 | 144 | 19 | 17 | 26 | 0 | 7 | 5 |
| P | Positioning and coordination | P3 | Propose solution | 6 | 5 | 193 | 2 | 4 | 6 | 0 | 0 | 1 |
| | | P6 | State (dis)agreement/position | 38 | 9 | 189 | 6 | 13 | 7 | 0 | 0 | 0 |

LR used in the most frequently performed CA in each sociolinguistic area.

Here are two sample interactions (Tables 7 and 8) to exemplify the aforementioned use of CA and the LR deployed:

Table 7. Example from School A.

| | | |
|---|---|---|
| 340. S3-*Zuek jaten badituzue txuriak ... niri eman una de cada ... porque si no yo me quedo sin txuri.* [If you it the white ones ... give one of each ... because the other way I won't have white] | P3 | LR4 |
| 341. S1-*Si uno no come ...* [If one of us don't eat ... ] | G5 | LR2 |
| 342. S2-*A ver ... nahastu behar ditugu ...* [let's see ... we have to mix them] | G7 | LR4 |
| 343. S3-*Zuek jan behar dituzue hau eta hau ...* [you have to eat this and this] | G5 | LR1 |
| 344. S1-*A ver ... bat jaten du ... bi hau, a ver, bi jaten du bi con leche ... eta* [Let's see ... you eat one ... second this. Let's see ... she eats two with milk ... and] one, one. | G7 | LR8 |
| 345. S3-*A ver, zuk jango duzu hau eta Maiderrek hau ... Orduan nik ez dudanez jaten txuria.* [Let's see, you will eat this and Maider this ... So, as I don't eat White ... ] | G7 | LR4 |
| 346. S2-*Nik ez dut jaten* [I don't eat] black. | E1 | LR5 |
| 347. S3-*Pues hori ... nik ez dudanez jaten txuria, eman behar didazue bat de* [So that ... as I don't eat White, you have to give me a piece of] black ... - | G2 | LR8 |

Example from School A.

Table 8. Example from School B.

| | | |
|---|---|---|
| 201. S26-And the cauldron we?-.-No … | I6 | LR3 |
| 202. S19- … and put it in the caldron … | P3 | LR3 |
| 203. S22-Pour it *ez* [no]! | P6 | LR5 |
| 204. S20-*Zer eingo deu* [what are we going to do]? | I6 | LR1 |
| 205. S22-Simmer and mix with … | P3 | LR3 |
| 206. S21-Simmer?-The ingredients are into the caldron. | I6 | LR3 |
| 207. S22-And simmer it-*Punto* [dot]. Meanwhile … -Meanwhile … | P3 | LR5 |
| 208. S20-*A ver* [let's see] … *in daikeu* [we can do] … Mix together in a bowl … a dragon head … | G5 | LR8 |
| 209. S19- … and a bit of … | P3 | LR3 |
| 210. S22-*Jarri daikeu* [we can put] dry … | P3 | LR5 |
| 211. S20-Mix together … mix together. | P3 | LR3 |
| 212. S19-*TH, T, H, E* [in Basque] | E2 | LR1 |
| 213. S22-R | E2 | LR3 |

Example from School B.

## 4. Discussion

The aim of the present study was twofold: on the one hand, to examine the communicative acts (CA) performed and the linguistic resources (LR) used by Grade 5 emergent trilingual pupils in the BAC while interacting in the English classroom. Also, on the other hand, to investigate the possible impact the sociolinguist area could have on the use of linguistic resources.

Addressing our first research question, the analysis suggests that participants in this study mostly performed CA concerning inviting elaboration or reasoning, expressing or inviting ideas, guiding direction of dialogue or activity, positioning and coordination, and showing understanding. All these CA are closely related to the type of activities performed in the English classroom and the patterns of interaction involved in such activities. Looking at our classroom data and observations carried out throughout the academic year 2016/2017, it can be said that the pupils had plenty of opportunities for meaningful interaction with their peers due to the great amount of activities done in groups, small groups, and whole class activities in which pupils needed to organize themselves, negotiate meaning, and take a stance in order to perform the task. This pedagogical approach seems to be suitable in order to observe the translanguaging practices of these emergent trilinguals, as can be seen in the following paragraph. As Otheguy and García (2019) state, bilinguals, in this case emergent trilinguals, have access to their whole linguistic repertoire in communicative situations in which the use of linguistic features is not restricted to named languages. These were exactly the communicative situations created in the English classroom. Rosiers (2018) and St. John (2018) also found that translanguaging practices should be analyzed in an interactional framework, because factors such as communicative situations, the topic, the group, as well as cognitive and linguistic features, may impact such practices.

Turning to the second research question, it was observed that pupils used similar linguistic resources (LR) regardless of the communicative acts (CA) being performed. These emergent trilinguals deployed English resources (LR3) more often than Basque (LR1) or Spanish ones (LR2) in the English classroom. Likewise, as reported by other researchers concerning bilingual students (Baker 2011; Cenoz 2017; García 2017; García-Mateus and Palmer 2017; Lewis et al. 2012), participants in the study frequently used linguistic resources coming from two systems, in this study, Basque and Spanish, in order to make meaning, share ideas, acquire understanding, and knowledge. Hence, this study confirms that spontaneous translanguaging is common practice in bilingual speakers, in our case, emergent trilingual speakers, as Cenoz and Gorter (2017) affirm. Equally, it reinforces the idea put forward by Wei (2015, p. 180), in the sense that translanguaging is not merely a combination of linguistic structures, "but also a creative strategy by the language user".

Results also showed that participants tended to deploy resources from Basque when they asked for elaboration or clarification, stated (dis)agreement or position, or when they proposed an action or activity. It seems that due to the status of Basque in both schools, as it is the main language of instruction, participants could have acquired more resources in that language than the ones developed in Spanish or English. Likewise, these emergent trilingual pupils deployed Spanish means (LR2) more often than Basque ones (LR1) when showing understanding, focusing the dialogue on key aspects of the activity, or when they proposed a solution. This tendency may be related to the fact that Basque is the main language of instruction in both schools, and Spanish and English are taught as subjects. Nonetheless, further research is needed to find out the possible impact of individual differences. It may well be that the home language of these emergent trilingual pupils and the use of Basque and Spanish resources in the different language domains have an impact on the use of their whole linguistic repertoire.

Finally, concerning the third and last research question, a comparison between both sociolinguistic areas suggest that pupils from both schools performed similar CA related to inviting elaboration or reasoning, guiding direction of dialogue or activity, and positioning and coordination. However, in the Basque sociolinguistic area, CA related to expressing or inviting ideas are also frequent. Our finding also reveals that the use of linguistic resources (LR) was similar in both sociolinguist areas. It seems that the possible impact of the sociolinguist area in the translanguaging practices of these Grade 5 emergent trilingual pupils cannot be confirmed. This could be due to the fact that the main language of instruction in both schools is Basque. In addition, the use of the same material during the English lessons could have an impact in the CA enacted by participants in both areas, as they followed the same methodology and they had similar classroom and task organization. Nevertheless, as aforementioned, individual differences should be analyzed to fine-tune these results.

Given the limited size of our sample, it is evident that further research is needed to study how these emergent trilingual pupils in the BAC communicate spontaneously to make themselves understood in the English classroom over the academic year. The present study is only an exploratory study in which fourteen pupils from two different sociolinguistic areas were randomly selected, observed, and recorded, with the aim of examining the enacted CA and LR used in the English classroom. In that line, the ongoing longitudinal study we are conducting will help us contribute to this field of research. As researchers such as Lewis et al. (2012) claim, a sociolinguistic approach is also needed in this field of research. Equally, Cenoz and Gorter (2017) highlight the possible impact of the social context when studying translanguaging practices.

**Author Contributions:** Conceptualization, A.F. and P.S.; Investigation, A.F.; Methodology, A.F., P.S., and N.I.; Formal Analysis, A.F. and N.I.; Data curation, A.F.; Writing original draft and presentation, A.F.; Writing, review and editing, A.F., P.S., and N.I.

**Funding:** This research received no external funding.

**Conflicts of Interest:** The authors declare no conflict of interest.

## References

Baker, Colin. 2011. Language development and language allocation in bilingual education. In *Foundations of Bilingual Education and Bilingualism*, 3rd ed. Clevedon: Multilingual Matters LTD, pp. 269–94.

Canagarajah, Suresh. 2011. Translanguaging in the Classroom: Emerging Issues for Research and Pedagogy. *Applied Linguistics Review* 2: 1–28.

Cenoz, Jasone. 2017. Translanguaging in school contexts: International perspectives. *Journal of Language, Identity & Education* 16: 193–98. [CrossRef]

Cenoz, Jasone, and Durk Gorter. 2017. Minority languages and sustainable translanguaging: Threat or opportunity? *Journal of Multilingual and Multicultural Development*. [CrossRef]

Cenoz, Jasone, and Durk Gorter. 2019. Multilingualism, translanguaging, and minority languages in SLA. *The Modern Language Journal* 103. [CrossRef]

Fuller, Janet M. 2015. Language choices and ideology in the bilingual classroom. In *Multilingual Education: Between Language Learning and Translanguaging*. Cambridge: Cambridge University Press, pp. 137–58. ISBN 978-1-107-47751-3.

García, Ofelia. 2017. Translanguaging in Schools: Subiendo y Bajando, Bajando y Subiendo as Afterword. *Journal of Language, Identity & Education* 16: 256–63.

García-Mateus, Suzanne, and Deborah Palmer. 2017. Translanguaging Pedagogies for Positive Identities in Two-Way Dual Language Bilingual Education. *Journal of Language, Identity & Education* 16: 245–55.

Gay, Lorraine R., Mills Geoffrey, and Airasian Peter. 2006. *Educational Research: Competencies for Analysis and Applications*. New York: Pearson Merrill Prentice Hall.

Gorter, Durk, Victoria Zenotz, and Jasone Cenoz. 2014. Multilingualism and European minority languages: The case of Basque. In *Minoriy Languages and Multilingual Education*. Dordrecht: Springer Science + Business Media, pp. 201–20. ISBN 978-94-007-7316-5.

Hennessy, Sara, Sylvia Rojas-Drummond, Rupert Higham, Ana María Márquez, Fiona Maine, Rosa María Ríos, Rocío García-Carrión, Omar Torreblanca, and María JoséBarrera. 2016. Developing coding scheme for classroom dialogue across educational contexts. *Learning, Culture and Social Interaction* 9: 16–44. [CrossRef]

Lewis, Gwyn, Bryn Jones, and Colin Baker. 2012. Translanguaging: Origins and development from school to street and beyond. *Educational Research and Evaluation: An International Journal on Theory and Practice* 18: 641–54. [CrossRef]

Otheguy, Ricardo, and Ofelia García. 2019. Plurilingualism and translanguaging: Commonalities and divergences. *International Journal of Bilingual Education and Bilingualism*. [CrossRef]

Otheguy, Ricardo, Ofelia García, and Wallis Reid. 2015. Clarifying translanguaging and deconstructing named languages: A new perspective from linguistics. *Applied Linguistics Review* 6: 281–307. [CrossRef]

Rosiers, Kirsten. 2018. Translanguaging revisited Challenges for research, policy and pedagogy based on an inquiry in two Belgian classrooms. In *Translation and Translanguaging in Multilingual Contexts*. Amsterdam: John Benjamins Publishing Company, pp. 361–83. [CrossRef]

St. John, Oliver. 2018. Between question and answer Mother tongue tutoring and translanguaging as dialogic action. In *Translation and Translanguaging in Multilingual Contexts*. Amsterdam: John Benjamins Publishing Company, pp. 334–60. [CrossRef]

Wei, Li. 2015. Complementary classrooms for multilingual minority ethnic children as a translanguaging space. In *Multilingual Education: Between Language Learning and Translanguaging*. Cambridge: Cambridge University Press, pp. 177–98. ISBN 978-1-107-47751-3.

© 2019 by the authors. Licensee MDPI, Basel, Switzerland. This article is an open access article distributed under the terms and conditions of the Creative Commons Attribution (CC BY) license (http://creativecommons.org/licenses/by/4.0/).

*Article*

# Lexical Crosslinguistic Influence and Study Abroad: Do Learners Use L1-Based Resources Less?

### Mireia Ortega * and M. Luz Celaya

Department of Modern Languages and Literatures and English Studies, University of Barcelona, 08007 Barcelona, Spain
* Correspondence: m.ortega@ub.edu

Received: 14 May 2019; Accepted: 6 July 2019; Published: 15 July 2019

**Abstract:** Research in Crosslinguistic Influence (CLI) has traditionally addressed two broad types of lexical CLI—*transfer of form* and *transfer of meaning* (Ringbom 1987)—which were reconceptualized by Jarvis (2009) as *lexemic* and *lemmatic transfer*, respectively. Whereas the former considers the phonological and graphemic structure of words, the latter is related to semantic and syntactic properties. These types of lexical CLI have been analysed in relation to L2 proficiency, but not in relation to factors such as Study Abroad (SA), which the present study aims to investigate. The oral production by 107 Catalan/Spanish learners of English as a Foreign Language (EFL) was analysed in terms of lexical CLI and the amount of input received during their SA. Results show an inverse relationship between the amount of input in SA and lexical CLI; that is, the higher the number of hours abroad, the fewer cases of lexical CLI. Statistical differences were found for *lemmatic* CLI and for one type of *lexemic* CLI. In light of these findings, it is suggested that learners that take part in SA programmes do not rely on L1-based resources when gaps in their knowledge arise.

**Keywords:** English as a Foreign Language; lexemic transfer; lemmatic transfer; Lexical Crosslinguistic Influence; Study Abroad

---

## 1. Introduction

As defined by Jarvis (2009, p. 99), Crosslinguistic Influence (CLI) is "the influence that a person's knowledge of one language has on that person's recognition, interpretation, processing, storage and production of words in another language." Since the number of multilingual speakers has drastically increased all over the world since the 1960s, research in CLI has been recently gaining momentum, as evident from the number of publications in the last ten years (e.g., Alonso 2016; Angelovska and Hahn 2017; De Angelis and Dewaele 2011; Martínez-Adrián et al. 2019; Peukert 2015). Therefore, many terms and concepts from the first wave of experimental studies have been redefined under new paradigms. Such is the case of lexical CLI, which has traditionally addressed two broad types, *transfer of form* and *transfer of meaning* (Ringbom 1987, 2001). Jarvis (2009) reconceptualised these types as *lexemic* and *lemmatic transfer*, respectively, following Kempen and Hoenkamp's (1987) distinction between *lexeme* and *lemma*. *Lexeme* is related to the phonological and graphemic forms of words, whereas *lemma* specifies semantic and syntactic properties. Thus, *lexemic* transfer reflects "lexeme-level links and processes, in the sense that they appear to be induced largely by formal cross-linguistic lexemic similarities and/or by levels of lexeme activation" (Jarvis 2009, p. 112); it includes cases of *borrowings*, *false cognates* and *coinages*, among others. While the former two types involve the use of an inappropriate word, the latter refers to the modification of the word stem to make the word similar to a word in the Target Language (TL) or to the blending of two morphemes or words from different languages. *Lemmatic* transfer is realized as *semantic extensions* (polysemy is represented in different ways in the languages involved), *calques* (directly translated compound words, idioms and fixed expressions), and *collocational transfer* and *subcategorization transfer*, which are related to the collocational and syntactic constraints on words.

Several studies on CLI have shown that these two types of lexical CLI seem to appear at different stages in the acquisition of the second language (L2)[1] (Celaya 2006; Celaya and Navés 2009; Ortega and Celaya 2013; Navés et al. 2005; Ringbom 2001), since types of lexical CLI are related to a gradual change from organization by form to organization by meaning as learners become more competent in the TL (Ringbom 2001). However, as acknowledged by Ecke (2015), instances of *form-based CLI* might still affect the production of advanced learners. This is one of the results that Lindqvist (2010) found in her study with 14 very advanced learners of L3 French. That is, although her participants presented more instances of *meaning-based transfer* (54%), especially of *semantic extensions*, they still produced a high amount of *form-based CLI* (46%). Nevertheless, the impact of factors other than L2 competence on lexical CLI is still in need of research. A case in point is the relationship between Study Abroad (SA) and lexical CLI, a line of research which very few studies have dealt with so far and which the present study aims to investigate through the analysis of *lexemic* and *lemmatic* transfer. Among the few studies that have addressed the issue of the relationship between CLI and SA, Andria and Serrano (2013) and Andria (2014) investigated L1 Catalan/Spanish learners of Greek and the transfer of thinking-for-speaking patterns of experiential verbs. The results of these studies suggest that both proficiency and time spent abroad have an effect on the appearance of the type of conceptual transfer under analysis. Although CLI was more evident in beginner and intermediate learners, advanced learners still presented cases of transfer, in line with previous studies on proficiency and CLI. On the other hand, the effect of SA was more salient in pattern recognition than in pattern production, as test scores were positively correlated between the results of the test performed and time spent in Greece.

The importance of SA learning contexts has been emphasized by several scholars (e.g., Collentine 2009; Freed 1995, 1998), who have considered it a very efficient way to learn an L2. Recent research on the effects of SA programmes on L2 acquisition has highlighted the improvements that learners make while abroad, especially, but not solely, in the area of oral production—as it is the area considered to improve the most (see Tullock and Ortega (2017) for a recent synthesis of studies on multilingualism and SA). This is due to both the quantity and quality of input that learners obtain in this type of setting, as compared to traditional classroom contexts. SA experiences give language learners the opportunity to increase their amount of exposure to the TL, as well as to experience different types of language discourses. That is, learners in a naturalistic environment are more prone to receive both a higher *amount of input* and a more varied and interactive type of input in comparison to the limited language contact that has traditionally characterized instructional settings (Lightbown 2000). In this respect, the *input* that learners receive while abroad is richer. Thus, the increase of both quantity and quality of the *input* leads to language improvement (i.e., DeKeyser 2007; DuFon and Churchill 2006; Freed 1995, 1998; Lafford 2004; Llanes and Muñoz 2009, 2013; Pérez-Vidal 2014; Sasaki 2007; Serrano et al. 2011), although recent research has also highlighted the importance of L2 use, especially in relation to proficiency before departure, (see Faretta-Stutenberg and Morgan-Short 2018). This access to rich *input*, as well as plenty of opportunities to practice the learnt items, enables learners to automatize and proceduralise new knowledge. As a consequence, learners do not need to rely on their previously learnt languages as frequently, since gaps in their knowledge have been filled but also because, as shown in Linck et al. (2009), the L1 seems to be inhibited in immersion contexts. In this study, the researchers analysed a group of L1 English learners of L2 Spanish in a semester abroad in Spain and compared it against a group from the same American university that followed regular classes at home during the same time period. The participants who were abroad produced fewer category exemplars in the L1 in the verbal-fluency task as well as no sensitivity to L1-related distractors in the translation task, thus suggesting that L1 influence was attenuated while abroad.

---

[1] L2 is used in this paper as standing for any language acquired subsequent to the first (L1).

Apart from an increase in the *amount of input* while abroad, learners are also exposed to different types of input. It is a good opportunity for them to interact with native speakers of the language, which guarantees a high-quality type of input. The need for native-like input has been acknowledged by some researchers, (e.g., Piske et al. 2001) as a key determinant in learning a foreign language. In fact, in the study by Muñoz (2014) the number of hours abroad of her EFL learners positively correlated with measures of lexical diversity.

The above findings lead us to pose the following research question: Does SA have an effect on amount and type of lexical (*lexemic* and *lemmatic*) CLI in L2 oral production? It is hypothesized that those learners who have spent more hours abroad will present a lower amount of lexical CLI, which will especially affect lemmatic CLI.

## 2. Materials and Methods

The participants in the present study are part of the "Age, input and aptitude. Effects in the long run in the acquisition of English in formal contexts Project" from which 107 students of EFL (87 females, 20 males) at two different universities in Barcelona were selected. All subjects gave their informed consent for inclusion before they participated in the study. The study was conducted in accordance with the Declaration of Helsinki, and the protocol was approved by the Ethics Committee of Project HUM2007-64302. They are all adult bilingual (Spanish/Catalan) EFL learners, with ages that range from 18 to 32 years of age (mean age 22.6). Their level of proficiency in English is mainly from intermediate to advanced; proficiency was controlled for, and is used as a control variable in the present study. The impact of SA was explored through hours spent in an English-speaking country; in this line, the participants spent between 0 h and a maximum of 4320 h in SA, with a mean of 965.6 h in an English-speaking country.

Participants in the study performed a series of tests, which aimed to test the learners' general proficiency in English, and answered a background questionnaire and an interview to gather data on the *amount* and *type of input* received during their English learning history, including their SA, if any. A film retelling task (an eight-minute segment, called "Alone and Hungry," from Charles Chaplin's silent film "Modern Times") was used to elicit oral production by the learners, from which instances of lexical CLI were identified for analysis. The scene features Charles Chaplin and Paulette Goddard and shows how a poor young girl tries to steal a loaf of bread, is then arrested and finally escapes with the help of Chaplin. This elicitation task "provides [learners] with a uniform prompt from which to speak" (Gass and Mackey 2007, p. 136), and it has already been used in transfer studies by Jarvis (1998, 2000).

Instances of lexical CLI were classified into subtypes of *lexemic* and *lemmatic* transfer, the former divided into 7 types and the latter into 6 (see categorization and examples from the data in Tables 1 and 2 below). The data analysis was data-driven and consisted of the search for forms that exhibited traces of L1 influence. Interrater measures were used in the coding of the narratives. Interrater reliability agreement of 10% of the data reached 86.4%. Due to the great deal of variance in the number of tokens produced by the participants, the percentage of tokens that did not present L1 influence was obtained and its logarithm was used in the analysis as the distribution of residuals was close to normal.

**Table 1.** Classification of *lexemic* Crosslinguistic Influence (CLI) and examples from the data.

|  |  |  |
|---|---|---|
| Language switches | Borrowing | There's a woman that saw all the *escena* [scene] |
|  | Editing terms | She ran away but she *bueno* she stopped with a man [well] |
|  | Meta-comments | A man sees her and follows her and she *no sé com es diu xoca* and she finds with another man [I don't know how to say crash] |
|  | Insert implicit elicit | In this time the man that was catch the first time goes to a *cafeteria* and takes a lot of food [cafeteria] |
| Lexical invention |  | They're eating huge piece of meat a *bisteak* [steak] |
| False cognates |  | And then he *presents* himself [introduces] |
| Lexemic self-repairs |  | He doesn't pay the *com com* I don't know [how how] |

Table 2. Classification of *lemmatic* CLI and examples from the data.

| | |
|---|---|
| Semantic extensions | Then the man enters in a *coffee* and eat a lot of things [café/cafeteria] |
| Calque | Both the woman and the man meet in *the van of the police* [the police van] |
| Collocational transfer | She *makes the meal* [cooks/prepares the meal] |
| Subcategorization—Preposition | Then he sees no the police phones *to the police department* [phones the police department] |
| Subcategorization—Type of complement | They are sitting *in the table* [at the table] |
| Lemmatic self-repair | There is a girl that *he has hungry who is hungry* |

NVivo was used for qualitative analysis and data were afterwards submitted to statistical treatment (Multiple Linear Regression) with SPSS (Statistical Package for the Social Sciences) v20; alpha was set at 0.05. "Lexical CLI occurrences" was established as the dependent variable and "hours abroad" as the independent one; a control variable—proficiency—was also introduced in the analysis, since it has been found to be directly related to lexical CLI in previous research. A backward method through blocks was used. Normality of the data was tested through the Kolmogorov-Smornov Test.

## 3. Results

The total number of lexical CLI occurrences was 604 out of a total of 48,748 words. As regards the two broad types of lexical CLI, *lemmatic* transfer (480 occurrences, 79.5%) was much more frequent than *lexemic* transfer (124 occurrences, 20.5%) (see Table 3 below). However, it is important to note here that the number of occurrences was not equally distributed across the different participants. Thus, while 9 of the participants did not produce any instances of CLI, up to 22 instances of transfer were identified in one of the learner's oral production. When the data were analysed according to each of the subcategories, *lexemic* transfer appeared as *language switches* in 88 instances (71%), followed by *lexical inventions* (21 instances, 17%), *false cognates* (13, 10%), and, finally, *lexemic self-repair* (2, 2%).

Table 3. Tokens and percentages of lemmatic and lexemic transfer.

| | | |
|---|---|---|
| Lemmatic transfer Total: 480 (79.5%) | semantic extensions | 244 (50.8%) |
| | subcategorization transfer | 82 (17.1%) |
| | subcategorization CLI | 52 (10.8%) |
| | calques | 58 (12.1%) |
| | lemmatic self-repairs | 30 (6.25%) |
| | collocational transfer | 14 (2.9%) |
| Lexemic transfer Total: 124 (20.5%) | language switches | 88 (71%) |
| | lexical inventions | 21 (17%) |
| | false cognates | 13 (10%) |
| | lexemic self-repair | 2 (2%) |

In the case of *lemmatic* transfer, 244 (50.8%) instances of *semantic extensions* were traced back. The second most frequent subcategory was *subcategorization transfer* that involved the choice of the wrong complement, as 82 occurrences (17.1%) were singled out in the corpus. The type of *subcategorization CLI* that involved the choice of the wrong preposition within the prepositional phrase was fewer in number—52 cases (10.8%). A similar number—58 occurrences (12.1%)—were identified as *calques*, and 30 cases of *lemmatic self-repairs* (6.25%) appeared in the data. Finally, the less frequent type of *lemmatic* CLI was *collocational transfer*, which has been identified on 14 occasions (2.9%). However, it is important to highlight that the high number of *semantic extensions* in the data can be explained by the appearance of the word "police" instead of "policeman" or 'police officer," which accounts for 40% of the total number of semantic extensions in the data. Learners used the term 'police' when they want to refer to a single policeman or police officer, since "policia" in Spanish or Catalan (although with different pronunciation) can refer to both the officer and the department; the learner, thus, extends these two uses in English.

Table 4 below presents the results of the multiple linear regression. The adjusted R square shows the amount of variance in each dependent variable that can be explained by hours abroad. As can be observed in the table, hours abroad explain 24% of lexical CLI (see Figure 1 for the distribution of values). Regarding lemmatic CLI and language switches, hours abroad account for 27% and 13% of the variance respectively.

**Table 4.** Multiple Linear Regression. Predictor variable: Hours abroad. Dependent variables: lexical CLI, lemmatic CLI, language switches.

| Predictor Variable | Dependent Variable | R Square | Adjusted R Square | Std. Error of the Estimate |
|---|---|---|---|---|
| Hours Abroad | Lexical CLI | 0.25 | 0.24 | 0.01 |
| | Lemmatic CLI | 0.29 | 0.27 | 0.008 |
| | Language switches | 0.16 | 0.13 | 0.004 |

The results of the statistical analysis performed on the data yielded statistically significant differences between lexical CLI and hours abroad for one of the types of *lexemic* CLI, namely, *language switches* ($p = 0.008$), and for *lemmatic* transfer overall ($p < 0.001$). In both cases, there exists an inverse relationship between hours abroad and amount of lexical CLI; in other words, a higher number of hours spent in an SA programme implies a decrease in *language switches* and in *lemmatic* transfer. The statistical analysis performed with the different subtypes of *lemmatic* transfer appeared to be nonsignificant.

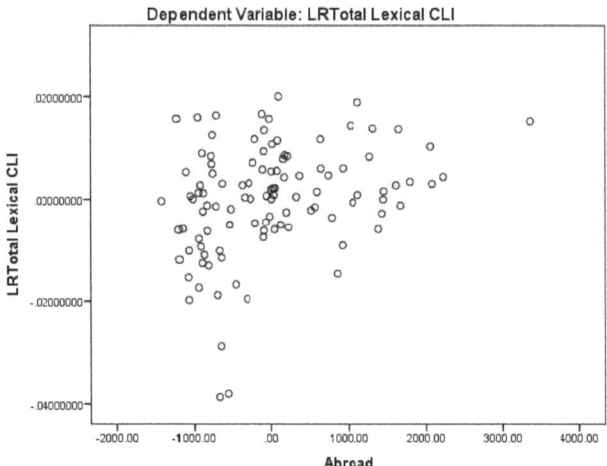

**Figure 1.** Scatterplot: Lexical CLI—Hours Abroad.

## 4. Discussion

As explained above, our findings show that *lemmatic* CLI appeared more frequently than *lexemic* transfer in the learners' oral productions. It is suggested here that the difference in the occurrence of both types of lexical CLI can be accounted for by the fact that *lemmatic* CLI is a more complex type that extends, in most cases, to the word unit. These results are in line with previous studies on lexical CLI; as Ringbom (2001) pointed out, there seems to be a change from organization by form to organization by meaning as the learners' language proficiency develops. In other words, while *transfer of form* or *lexemic* CLI might be most predominant at the earliest stages of acquisition, *transfer of meaning* or *lemmatic CLI* seems to develop at a later proficiency stage. This suggests that CLI might work in different ways at different levels of proficiency and due to the different needs that learners have. Both factors are intrinsic to the definition of SA contexts. Similar findings appear in studies on CLI and proficiency, such as Celaya's (2006) longitudinal study of the written productions of Catalan/Spanish learners of EFL, where the researcher found that whereas *borrowings* and *coinages* (two types of *lexemic* CLI in her study) decreased as L2 proficiency increased, *calques* (one type of *lemmatic* CLI) increased with higher levels of proficiency. This suggests that not all types of lexical CLI develop in the same way, as also evident in Navés et al.'s (2005) study where the researchers found a statistically significant decrease of *borrowings* as proficiency increased. Lindqvist's (2010) study with 14 very advanced learners of L3 French points in the same direction, as her participants presented more instances of *meaning-based* transfer (54%), especially of *semantic extensions*, than of *form-based* CLI (46%). The difference appeared to be more striking in the present study, which can be accounted for by the fact of having used a slightly different classification of *meaning-based* transfer and, thus, including the categories of *collocational CLI* and *subcategorization CLI*, as suggested by Jarvis (2009).

Furthermore, our findings suggest an impact of SA on the amount of lexical CLI, as in previous studies, (see Collentine and Freed 2004), that is, the more hours spent abroad, the less L1-based lexical CLI, as in the case of the lower number of *language switches* (*lexemic* transfer), and also the less *lemmatic* transfer overall. It also has to be highlighted that language switches were the type of *lexemic* transfer that occurred more frequently in the data, whereas the other types were scarce. This could account for the fact that no other statistically significant results were found with the other subtypes. Furthermore, such findings may also be due to the fact that, as claimed by Kroll and Stewart (1994, p. 168), "cross-language connections between lexical representations, and between lexical representations and concepts, are asymmetric" in bilingual memory.

Access to rich input and plenty of opportunities to practise the TL are put forward as the reasons for such an outcome, since as claimed by Bolibaugh and Foster (2013), immersion settings provide a better environment for learning the more subtle aspects of the language. In other words, SA allows for both the automatization and proceduralisation of new knowledge, (e.g., DeKeyser 2007; Llanes and Muñoz 2009; Pérez-Vidal 2014) and for the inhibition of the L1 (Linck et al. 2009) and this is why we suggest that SA especially determines the occurrence of *lemmatic* transfer and one type of *lexemic* transfer, namely, *language switches*, which decrease with a higher number of hours abroad (see Hammarberg 2001); that is, when gaps in learners' knowledge arise, they draw on their L1 less (*lexemic* transfer). As Tremblay (2006) has argued, exposure to the L2 is needed for the L2 to become automatized, since high proficiency in the L2 alone is not enough. Cortés's (2005) study with L1 English learners of Spanish also confirms the importance of language exposure in a naturalistic setting for the decrease in occurrences of transfer. She pinpointed that the learners in her study that had studied the language for a longer time, as well as in a naturalistic environment, presented fewer cases of CLI. Pavlenko and Jarvis (2002) further argued that the level of socialization in the source language is important for transfer to take place from this language. Therefore, as Andria and Serrano (2013) and Andria (2014) claimed, more research is needed to analyse the impact of SA contexts on the acquisition of second languages, since factors other than total time abroad might be reliable predictors of pattern restructuring, for example, the concentration of the stays, the type and amount of contact with the L2 while abroad, or whether the learners also receive formal instruction in the host country. In other words, more detailed information of actual contact with the language is needed in further research.

## 5. Conclusions

The present study suggests that, since SA programmes provide more hours of contact and a more varied type of input than regular instruction, the use of L1-based resources in learners' oral production is impacted upon; in other words, there seems to exist an inverse relationship between amount of input in SA and lexical CLI: the more hours of SA, the fewer the cases of L1-based resources, as in the case of *language switches* in the present study, and also the fewer the cases of *lemmatic* CLI. However, for further research it is essential to obtain very precise information about the learners' use of the L2 before and after the SA so as to be able to carry out detailed analyses of the impact of SA on CLI, since in many cases the amount of input during the SA might be limited due to the lack of opportunities to interact with native speakers, as Muñoz and Singleton (2011) have thoroughly discussed.

**Author Contributions:** Both authors were in charge of collecting data together with the rest of the members in the GRAL research group (www.ubgral.com). The study presented here is a revised version of part of the first author's Ph.D. dissertation, which was supervised by the second author of this paper. For the present paper the second author has updated the review of the literature, the first author has revised the analysis of the data, worked with the statistical analysis again and prepared the corresponding tables and figures and, finally, we have carried out the discussion of the findings together.

**Funding:** This research was funded by Ministerio de Ciencia y Tecnología of the Spanish Government, grant number HUM2007-64302 to the GRAL research group.

**Acknowledgments:** The authors acknowledge support from the GRAL research group. Our special thanks to Ferran Carrascosa and Joan Carles Mora for their invaluable help with statistics. We are also grateful to the three anonymous reviewers for their valuable feedback. Any mistakes remain our own.

**Conflicts of Interest:** The authors declare no conflict of interest.

## References

Alonso, Rosa, ed. 2016. *Crosslinguistic Influence in Second Language Acquisition*. Bristol: Multilingual Matters.

Andria, Maria. 2014. Crosslinguistic influence in the acquisition of Greek as a foreign language by Spanish/Catalan L1 Learners: The Role of Proficiency and Stays Abroad. Unpublished Ph.D. dissertation, Universitat de Barcelona, Barcelona, Spain.

Andria, Maria, and Raquel Serrano. 2013. Developing new 'thinking-for-speaking' patterns in Greek as a foreign language: The role of proficiency and stays abroad. *The Language Learning Journal* 45: 66–80. [CrossRef]

Angelovska, Tanja, and Angela Hahn, eds. 2017. *L3 Syntactic Transfer. Models, New Developments and Implications*. Amsterdam: John Benjamins.

Bolibaugh, Cylcia, and Pauline Foster. 2013. Memory-based aptitude for nativelike selection. The role of phonological short-term memory. In *Sensitive Periods, Language Aptitude, and Ultimate Attainment*. Edited by Gisela Granena and Michael H. Long. Amsterdam: John Benjamins, pp. 205–30.

Celaya, M. Luz. 2006. Lexical transfer and L2 proficiency: A longitudinal analysis of EFL written production. In *Proceedings of the 29th AEDEAN Conference*. Edited by Alejandro Alcaraz-Sintes, Concepción Soto-Palomo and M. Cinta Zunido-Garrido. Jaén: Pubicaciones de la Universidad de Jaén. CD format.

Celaya, M. Luz, and M. Teresa Navés. 2009. Written production in English as a Foreign Language: Age-related differences and associated factors. In *Writing in Foreign Language Contexts. Learning, Teaching and Research*. Edited by Rosa M. Manchón. Clevedon: Multilingual Matters, pp. 130–55.

Collentine, Joseph G. 2009. Study abroad research: Findings, implications and future directions. In *Handbook of Language Teaching*. Edited by Catherine Doughty and Michael Long. Malden: Blackwell Publishing, pp. 218–33.

Collentine, Joseph G., and Barbara F. Freed. 2004. Learning contexts and its effects on second language acquisition. *Studies in Second Language Acquisition* 26: 153–71. [CrossRef]

Cortés, Nuria Calvo. 2005. Negative language transfer when learning Spanish as a foreign language. *Interlingüística* 16: 237–48.

De Angelis, Gessica, and Jean-Marc Dewaele, eds. 2011. *New Trends in Crosslinguistic Influence and Multilingualism Research*. Bristol: Multilingual Matters.

DeKeyser, Robert M. 2007. Study abroad as foreign language practice. In *Practice in a Second Language. Perspectives from Applied Linguistics and Cognitive Psychology*. Edited by Robert M. DeKeyser. Cambridge: Cambridge University Press, pp. 208–26.

DuFon, Margaret A., and Eton Churchill, eds. 2006. *Language Learners in Study Abroad Contexts*. Clevedon: Multilingual Matters.

Ecke, Peter. 2015. Parasitic vocabulary acquisition, cross-linguistic influence, and lexical retrieval in multilingual. *Bilingualism: Language and Cognition* 18: 145–62. [CrossRef]

Faretta-Stutenberg, Mandy, and Kara Morgan-Short. 2018. Contributions of initial proficiency and language use to second-language development during Study Abroad: Behavioral and event-related potential evidence. In *The Routledge Handbook of Study Abroad Research and Practice*. Edited by Cristina Sanz and Alfonso Morales-Front. New York: Routledge.

Freed, Barbara F. 1995. What makes us think that students who study abroad become fluent? In *Second Language Acquisition in a Study Abroad Context*. Edited by Barbara F. Freed. Amsterdam: John Benjamins, pp. 138–48.

Freed, Barbara F. 1998. An overview of issues and research in language learning in a study abroad setting. *Frontiers: The Interdisciplinary Journal of Study Abroad* 4: 31–60.

Gass, Susan M., and Alison Mackey. 2007. *Data Elicitation for Second and Foreign Language Research*. New York: Routledge.

Hammarberg, Björn. 2001. Roles of L1 and L2 in L3 production and acquisition. In *Cross-linguistic Influence in Third Language Acquisition: Psycholinguistic Perspectives*. Edited by Jasone Cenoz, Britta Hufeisen and Ulrike Jessner. Clevedon: Multilingual Matters, pp. 21–41.

Jarvis, Scott. 1998. *Conceptual Transfer in the Interlingual Lexicon*. Bloomington: Indiana University Linguistics Club Publications.

Jarvis, Scott. 2000. Methodological rigor in the study of transfer: Identifying L1 influence in the interlanguage lexicon. *Language Learning* 50: 245–309. [CrossRef]

Jarvis, Scott. 2009. Lexical transfer. In *The Bilingual Mental Lexicon*. Edited by Aneta Pavlenko. Bristol: Multilingual Matters, pp. 99–124.

Kempen, Gerard, and Edward Hoenkamp. 1987. An incremental procedural grammar for sentence formulation. *Cognitive Science* 11: 201–58. [CrossRef]

Kroll, Judith F., and Erika Stewart. 1994. Category interference in translation and picture naming: Evidence for asymmetric conncetions between bilingual memory representations. *Journal of Memory and Language* 33: 149–74. [CrossRef]

Lafford, Barbara A. 2004. The effect of the context of learning on the use of communication strategies by learners of Spanish as a second language. *Studies in Second Language Acquisition* 26: 201–25. [CrossRef]

Lightbown, Patsy M. 2000. Anniversary article: Classroom SLA research and second language teaching. *Applied Linguistics* 21: 431–62. [CrossRef]

Linck, Jared A., Judith F. Kroll, and Gretchen Sunderman. 2009. Losing Access to the Native Language While Immersed in a Second Language Evidence for the Role of Inhibition in Second-Language Learning. *Psychological Science* 20: 1507–15. [CrossRef] [PubMed]

Lindqvist, Christina. 2010. Inter- and intralingual lexical influences in advanced learners' French L3 oral production. *International Review of Applied Linguistics* 48: 131–57. [CrossRef]

Llanes, Angels, and Carmen Muñoz. 2009. A short stay abroad: Does it make a difference? *System* 37: 353–65. [CrossRef]

Llanes, Àngels, and Carmen Muñoz. 2013. Age effects in a study abroad context: Children and adults studying abroad and at home. *Language Learning* 63: 63–90. [CrossRef]

Martínez-Adrián, María, M. Juncal Gutiérrez-Mangado, and Francisco Gallardo-del-Puerto. 2019. L1 use in content-based and CLIL settings. *International Journal of Bilingual Education and Bilingualism* 22: 1–4. [CrossRef]

Muñoz, Carmen. 2014. Contrasting effects of starting age and input on the oral performance of foreign language learners. *Applied Linguistics* 35: 463–82. [CrossRef]

Muñoz, Carmen, and David Singleton. 2011. A critical review of age-related research on L2 ultimate attainment. *Language Teaching* 44: 1–35. [CrossRef]

Navés, M. Teresa, Imma Miralpeix, and M. Luz Celaya. 2005. Who transfers more... and what? Cross-linguistic influence in relation to school grade and and language dominance in EFL. *International Journal of Multilingualism* 2: 113–34. [CrossRef]

Ortega, Mireia, and M. Luz Celaya. 2013. "El gos és a dins del basket": Lexical CLI in L3 Catalan by L1 English-speaking learners. *Revista Española de Lingüística Aplicada (RESLA)* 26: 409–32.

Pavlenko, Aneta, and Scott Jarvis. 2002. Bidirectional transfer. *Applied Linguistics* 23: 190–214. [CrossRef]

Pérez-Vidal, Carmen, ed. 2014. *Language Acquisition in Study Abroad and Formal Instruction Contexts*. Amsterdam: John Benjamins.

Peukert, Hagen, ed. 2015. *Transfer Effects in Multilingual Language Development*. Amsterdam: John Benjamins.

Piske, Thorsten, Ian R. A. MacKay, and James E. Flege. 2001. Factors affecting degree of foreign accent in an L2: A review. *Journal of Phonetics* 29: 191–215. [CrossRef]

Ringbom, Håkan. 1987. *The Role of the First Language in Foreign Language Learning*. Clevedon: Multilingual Matters.

Ringbom, Håkan. 2001. Lexical transfer in L3 production. In *Cross-linguistic Influence in Third Language Acquisition: Psycholinguistic Perspectives*. Edited by Jasone Cenoz, Britta Hufeisen and Ulrike Jessner. Clevedon: Multilingual Matters, pp. 59–68.

Sasaki, Miyuki. 2007. Effects of study-abroad experiences on EFL writers: A multiple-data analysis. *The Modern Language Journal* 91: 602–20. [CrossRef]

Serrano, Raquel, Àngels Llanes, and Elsa Tragant. 2011. Analyzing the effect of second language learning: Domestic intensive and semi-intensive courses vs. study abroad in Europe. *System* 39: 133–43. [CrossRef]

Tremblay, Marie-Claude. 2006. Cross-linguistic influence in third language acquisition: The role of L2 proficiency and L2 exposure. *CLO/OPL* 34: 109–19.

Tullock, Brandon, and Lourdes Ortega. 2017. Fluency and multilingualism in study abroad: Lessons from a scoping review. *System* 71: 7–21. [CrossRef]

© 2019 by the authors. Licensee MDPI, Basel, Switzerland. This article is an open access article distributed under the terms and conditions of the Creative Commons Attribution (CC BY) license (http://creativecommons.org/licenses/by/4.0/).

Article

# Nonstandard Use of the "Reflexive" Affix -$s^j a$ in Russian Speech of Bilingual Speakers of Northern Siberia and the Russian Far East

Irina Khomchenkova [1,2,3], Polina Pleshak [1,2,*] and Natalia Stoynova [1,3,*]

1. Institute of Linguistics, Russian Academy of Sciences, 1 bld. 1 Bolshoi Kislovsky lane, 125009 Moscow, Russia; irina.khomchenkova@yandex.ru
2. Lomovosov Moscow State University, GSP-1, Leninskie Gory, 119991 Moscow, Russia
3. Vinogradov Russian Language Institute, Russian Academy of Sciences, Volkhonka str., 18/2, 119019 Moscow, Russia
* Correspondence: polinapleshak@yandex.ru (P.P.); stoynova@yandex.ru (N.S.)

Received: 16 May 2019; Accepted: 14 June 2019; Published: 17 June 2019

**Abstract:** One of the features of the oral Russian speech of bilingual speakers of the indigenous languages of Russia is the omission/the overuse of the "reflexive" affix -$s^j a$ (a "middle voice" marker with a wide range of uses including reflexive, reciprocal, anticausative, passive, and some others). We discuss the data on the nonstandard use of -$s^j a$ in the Russian speech of bilingual speakers of two language groups that differ both from Russian and from each other in this grammatical domain: Samoyedic (Forest Enets, Nganasan, and Nenets) and Tungusic (Nanai and Ulch). The data come from the corpus of contact-influenced Russian speech, which is being created by our team. We show that the mismatches in standard and nonstandard usage cannot be explained by direct structural copying from the donor language (indigenous) to the recipient one (the local variety of Russian). Nor is there a consistent system which differs from standard Russian since there are many more usages that follow the rules of standard Russian. The influence of the indigenous languages explains some overuses and omissions; the others can be explained by other factors, e.g., difficulties in the acquisition of verb pairs with non-transparent semantic or syntactic relations.

**Keywords:** bilingualism; language contact; pattern borrowing; Russian; Samoyedic languages; Tungusic languages; reflexive; valency changing; middle voice

---

## 1. Introduction

One of the features of the oral Russian speech of bilingual speakers of the indigenous languages of Russia is the nonstandard use of the "reflexive" affix -$s^j a$, which can occur as an overuse (1) or as an omission (2).

1. davaj    ne      propadaj-$s^j$a
   let's    NEG     disappear.IMP-SJA
   'Don't disappear'. (L1 Nganasan)[1]

2. ty       duma-ješ        živoj,       čto       li      **osta-l-$s^j$a**
   2SG      think-PRS.2SG   alive.SG.M   what      Q       stay-PST.SG.M-SJA
   'Do you think that he stayed alive?' (L1 Nanai)

---

[1] Abbreviations: 2, 3—2nd, 3rd person, ABL—ablative, ACC—accusative, ADJZ—adjectivized, ANT—anteriorsuffix, DAT—dative, DRV—derived, EX—existential predicate, F—feminine, GEN—genitive, IMP—imperative, IMPS—impersonal,

The nonstandard use of -sʲa is not just a characteristic of the Russian speech of the speakers of the Samoyedic and Tungusic languages. It was also mentioned in some other contact-influenced varieties of Russian, see (Daniel et al. 2010, p. 82) on Daghestanian Russian and (Shagal 2016) Erzya Russian. In addition, it is attested in some Russian dialects (Kasatkin 2005, p. 154).

The "reflexive" -sʲa (-sʲa/-sʲ) in Russian is a derivational affix (earlier a clitic), which is attached after inflectional affixes (a "postfix"). It is a "middle voice" marker, see (Kemmer 1993), which has a wide range of uses. It has the following main meanings: reflexive (*mytʲ*—*mytʲsʲa*, 'wash'—'wash-self'), reciprocal (*celovatʲ*—*celovatʲsʲa*, 'kiss'—'kiss each other'), passive (*stroitʲ*—*stroitʲsʲa*, 'build'—'be built'), modal-passive (*ne otkryvajetsʲa*, 'won't open'), passive-impersonal (*ukazyvatʲ*—*ukazyvaetsʲa*, 'point'—'be pointed out'), anticausative, or anticausative (*razbitʲ*—*razbitʲsʲa*, 'break (transitive)'—'break (intransitive)'), benefactive reflexive (*zakupatʲ*—*zakupatʲsʲa*, 'buy in'—'buy in', intransitive), objective-impersonal (*kusatʲ*—*kusatʲsʲa*, 'bite'—'bite everybody'), and modal-impersonal (*ne spitsʲa* 'not able to sleep'), for a more detailed classification see e.g., (Letuchiy 2016, pp. 268–340).

Apart from regular formations, -sʲa is also used with bound reflexive stems (verba deponentia, i.e., verbs without unsuffixed correlates): verbs of emotion (*bojatʲsʲa*, 'be afraid'), behaviour (*lenitʲsʲa*, 'be lazy'), natural phenomena (*smerkatʲsʲa*, 'get dark'), and some modal verbs (*nuždatʲsʲa*, 'have a need'). The affix -sʲa cannot be used with some transitive semelfactives (*kapnutʲ*, 'drop') and intransitive uncontrolled situations (*umeretʲ*, 'die'), but there are no restrictions on transitivity.

In Samoyedic languages (Enets, Nenets, and Nganasan), there is a reflexive (-medial) conjugation, which is used only with intransitive verbs or labile verbs (in the intransitive use). In other words, what is parallel to Russian -sʲa in these languages is a paradigm of inflectional suffixes (Siegl 2013; Nikolaeva 2014; Tereschenko 1979), which is not productive and which is used with a lexically determined set of verbs, e.g., only approximately 65 verbs in Forest Enets corpus (Khanina and Shluinsky 2019). It is hard to generalize the conditions of its use, but there are some tendencies, for example, these are mostly change-of-posture verbs (ad-e-zʔ [sit_down.PFV-REFL-3SG.REFL], 'sat down', Forest Enets), motion verbs (sɔʔ-e-zʔ [jump.PFV-REFL-3SG.REFL], 'jumped (somewhere)', Forest Enets), and some spontaneous events and emotions. However, having one of these meanings does not imply that the verb will obligatorily take the "reflexive" affixes. Another tendency is that the reflexive conjugation is frequently used with inchoatives (ɔzi-ʔ [be.visible.IPFV-3PL.S]—ɔzi-rio-zoʔ [be.visible.IPFV-INCH-3SG.REFL], 'was visible'—'appeared', Forest Enets) and passives (tɔza-d [bring.PFV-2SG.S]—tɔza-r-e-zʔ [bring.PFV-PASS-REFL-3SG.REFL], 'you bring'—'was brought', Forest Enets).

In Southern Tungusic languages (Nanai, Ulch), there are two derivational suffixes that share some functions with -sʲa. The first one is the "passive" -p (Avrorin 1961, pp. 41–42), which has passive, anticausative, and modal-passive uses, cf. *xoǯe-p-* 'to be finished' [finish-PASS-], *xuədə-p-* 'to be lost' [lose-PASS-] (Nanai). The second one is the reciprocal -*mači* (Avrorin 1961, pp. 42–43), cf. *sore-mači-* 'to fight to each other' [fight-RECIP-] (Nanai). The productivity of these suffixes is comparable to that of -sʲa. Moreover, there are labile verbs (however, this class is not very large), cf. *təpčiu-* 'to start (transitive, itransitive)', (Nanai), and the impersonal construction, which has an accusative object and no overt subject (Avrorin 1961, pp. 84–92; Stoynova 2016).

Thus, both Samoyedic and Tungusic markers overlap with -sʲa in the mediopassive semantic domain, but not in the reflexive one. Within this domain, the anticausative suffix -p in Tungusic is similar to the Russian -sʲa in terms of productivity, while the Samoyedic reflexive conjugation is much more restricted and it overlaps with -sʲa only for a closed set of verbs.

---

INCH—inchoative, INS—instrumental case, IPFV—imperfective, LIM—limitative, LOC—locative, M—masculine, N—neuter, NEG—negative, PASS—passive, PFV—perfective, PL—plural, PP—prepositional case, PRON—pronominal stem, PRS—present tense, PST—past tense, PTCL—particle, RECIP—reciprocal, REFL—reflexive conjugation, Q—question particle, S—subject conjugation, SEM—semelfactive, SJA—sja suffix, SG—singular, STAT—stative.

Since there are Samoyedic and Tungusic parallels to -$s^j a$, the following questions arise: (i) whether the attested nonstandard use of reflexives is triggered by the influence of indigenous languages, and (ii) whether the different overlap between functions of Russian -$s^j a$ and Samoyedic or Tungusic morphemes creates differences in the nonstandard uses of the former.

According to the facts above, the following differences are predicted: In Tungusic Russian, the nonstandard uses of -$s^j a$ are expected within the mediopassive (and especially anticausative) domain, in which -$s^j a$ and -$p$ considerably, but not fully, overlap. In Samoyedic Russian, deviations from standard Russian are expected to concern a closed set of particular verbs and not the entire semantic class.

In this paper, we compare the nonstandard use of -$s^j a$ in Samoyedic Russian and Tungusic Russian in order to check whether the indigenous language influences the use of -$s^j a$ and whether there is a difference between Samoyedic and Tungusic influence on -$s^j a$.

## 2. Materials and Methods

As the data source, we used the corpus of contact-influenced Russian speech of Northern Siberia and the Russian Far East, which is being created by our team. This is a small spoken corpus of narratives in Russian recorded from speakers of indigenous languages of the area. The texts are transcribed in standard Russian orthography in ELAN[2] and manually annotated of grammatical and lexical contact-induced features (one of them is the nonstandard use or omission of the reflexive affix). In the study, we used the transcribed and annotated part of the Tungusic and Samoyedic subcorpora, which contained approximately 17 h (29,283 clauses). The whole collection of the records from the speakers of the Tungusic and Samoyedic languages contained approximately 96 h; see Table 1 for the details.

**Table 1.** Text collection.

|  | All (in hours) | Annotated (in clauses) |
|---|---|---|
| Enets (Forest and Tundra) | 26.5 | 12,282 |
| Nenets | 9 | 2323 |
| Nganasan | 10 | 4768 |
| all Samoyedic | 45.5 | 19,373 |
| Nanai | 42 | 7269 |
| Ulch | 8.5 | 2641 |
| all Tungusic | 50.5 | 9910 |
| total amount | 96 | 29,283 |

The nonstandard use of -$s^j a$ is not very frequent in our data (the most frequent grammatical peculiarities are the omission of prepositions and gender disagreement). In our annotated corpus, we found 71 cases of nonstandard uses of -$s^j a$ in total:46 uses in Tungusic subcorpus and 25 uses in Samoyedic subcorpus. Only 6% out of all uses of -$s^j a$ are nonstandard in Tungusic subcorpus (733 uses). The data, available at the moment, are not enough for consistent quantitative analysis. So, in this paper, we present a preliminary qualitative study, in which we analyzed possible factors that could have influenced the nonstandard uses of -$s^j a$ attested in the corpus.

## 3. Results

Some of the attested nonstandard uses of -$s^j a$, both omissions and overuses, can be indeed explained by the influence of indigenous languages. However, other cases seem to contradict this hypothesis. We show that some other factors connected to acquisition difficulties can affect the use of -$s^j a$ as well. First, we discuss overuses, which are easier to explain (Section 3.1), and then omissions

---

[2] ELAN (https://tla.mpi.nl/tools/tla-tools/elan/) is one of the annotation tools developed at the Max Planck Institute for Psycholinguistics, see (Sloetjes and Wittenburg 2008).

(Section 3.2). In Section 3.3, we give some quantitative data on the rate of omissions vs. overuses and the distribution across different semantic types of -sʲa uses.

### 3.1. Overuses of -sʲa

Overuses of -sʲa can be classified into three groups: (a) structural borrowing from the indigenous language (PAT-borrowing in terms of (Sakel 2007)); (b) incomplete acquisition of standard Russian: the existence of a particular Russian verb similar to that in question or the overgeneralization of a particular semantic type of sʲa-uses.

#### 3.1.1. Structural Borrowing

Examples (3)–(4) illustrate structural borrowing, which leads to the overuse of -sʲa. (3) is a calque from the Nanai impersonal construction (4). The affix -sʲa can have the meaning presented in (3)–(4); however, the argument encoding differs from that of the Russian sʲa-verbs and repeats that of the Nanai impersonal forms: the direct object *takuju* 'such a thing.f' does not move to the subject position and takes the accusative case, in the same way as *čolombani* 'soup.ACC.3SG' in (4). So, -sʲa appears in (3) as an equivalent of the Nanai impersonal suffix *-wu*.

3. to      tam      potom    jesli    etot      vot     tak-uju         dela-jet-sʲa ...
   that    there    then     if       this.M    here    such-ACC.F      do-PRS.2SG-SJA
   'And then there one makes such a ... ' (L1 Nanai)

Cf. the Nanai impersonal construction in (4):

4. oakta          čolom-ba-ni       Xon'      puju-u-r'
   wormwood       soup-ACC-3SG      how       cook-IMPS-PRS
   'How does one cook wormwood soup'? (Nanai corpus)

Example (5) is more complicated. The Russian verb *snʲatʲ* 'take off' does not take the anticausative -sʲa in Russian monolinguals. The overuse of *snʲatʲ-sʲa* in (5) corresponds to the Nanai *ačo-p* 'come taken off' [take.off-DECAUS]. However, *snʲatʲ-sʲa* inherits not only the Nanai morphological pattern but also the lexical one. In (5), it has the meaning 'to come untied' and not 'to come taken off'. This is explained by the fact that its correlate *ačo—ačo-p* is polysemous:along with the meaning 'to take off—to come/be taken off', it has another meaning 'to untie—to come/be untied'[3].

5. i       mladšij          syn ...    kak     eto ...    snʲa-l-sʲa             ot      etogo
   and     youngest.SG.M    son        how     this.N     take.off-PST.SG.M-SJA   from    this.GEN
   'And the younger brother come untied from this (pole) ... ' (L1 Nanai)

#### 3.1.2. Incomplete Acquisition of Russian

One of the factors that can affect the use of -sʲa, besides the systems of the indigenous language, is the existence of Russian verbs that have a synonymous meaning but behave differently with respect to the -sʲa derivation.

In (1) repeated below as (6), a possible contamination with the Russian reflexive verb *tʲerjatʲ-sʲa* 'get lost' might have played a part in using *propadaj-sʲa* instead of *propadaj*.

6. davaj           ne         propadaj-sʲa
   let's           NEG        disappear.IMP-SJA
   'Don't disappear'. (L1 Nganasan)

---

[3] The lexical calquing might be even more important here, because the verb *otvazatʲ-sʲa* 'to come untied' [untie-REFL] does exist in monolinguals' Russian, in contrast to *snʲatʲ-sʲa*.

In a similar manner, in (7), there could have been contamination with the Russian verb *perepravi-l-sʲa* (cross-PST.M.SG-SJA).

7. potom, govorʲ-at, **pereply-l-sʲa** i ruk-oj,
   later say-PRS.3PL cross-PST.M. SG-SJA and hand-INS
   govorj-at, mah-nu-l
   say-PRS.3PL wave-SEM-PST.M.SG
   'They say then he swam across the river and waved his hand (to show that he should go as well)'.
   (L1 Nganasan)

In (8), a non-standard verb *obitatʲ-sʲa* is used instead of the Russian verb *obitatʲ* 'dwell'.

8. by-va-jut=to, vot, oni tam I
   be-IPFV-PRS.3PL=PTCL here 3PL there and
   **obita-jut-sʲa,** eto, kormʲ-at-sʲa
   dwell-PRS.3PL-SJA this.N feed-PRS.3PL-SJA
   'There are ... so, they dwell there, feed themselves'. (L1 Enets)

Enets stative verbs like 'dwell' normally do not bear reflexive suffixes, so this cannot be a calque. There is a synonymous Russian verb *voditʲ-sʲa* 'be found, live' which has -*sʲa*. However, one could propose a different explanation: the verb *kormjatsʲa* in the right context triggers the -*sʲa* suffix on the verb *obitatʲ*.

The verb *torgovalisʲ* in (9) is used in the object impersonal meaning ('to sell' > 'to sell different things').

9. nu ranʲshe zhe kitajtsy zdesʲ torgova-l-i-sʲ
   PTCL earlier PTCL chinese.PL here sale-PST-PL-REFL
   'Well, earlier, Chinese sold different things here'. (Nanai corpus)

This particular derived form is absent in standard Russian, despite the object impersonal meaning is one of the productive meanings of -*sʲa*. So, in Tungusic Russian, we are dealing with the overgeneralization of this meaning. It is not a calque from the indigenous language (Nanai), since in Nanai there is no affix with this meaning at all.

### 3.2. Omissions of -sʲa

It is more difficult to explain an unexpected absence of -*sʲa* than its overuse. On the one hand, some omissions can be explained by the absence of sʲa-type markers in the corresponding indigenous language. For example, the form *rodila* instead of *rodilasʲ* 'to be born' in Nanai Russian is supported by the Nanai verb *balǯe-* 'to be born' which is not connected to the verb 'to give birth', unlike its Russian correlate.

10. ja zhe derevne rodi-l-a
    1SG PTCL village.LOC be.born-PST-F
    'Actually, I was born in the village.' (L1 Nanai)

11. mī balǯe-xam-bi Muxu-du
    1SG be.born-PST-1SG Muhu-DAT
    'I was born in the village of Muxu.' (Nanai, field records)

Example (12) can have a similar explanation; the absence of the sʲa-type marker (the reflexive conjugation). See (12) with no -*sʲa* and no reflexive conjugation in the corresponding Nganasan verb from the parallel version of the Russian text (13).

12. a         vmesto    nego      opʲatʲ   eta      vot    eta     vot    povʲazka
    and       instead   he.GEN    again    this.F   here   this.F  here   bandage
    valʲa-jet-s̶ʲa̶
    roll-PRS.3SG-SJA
    'And instead of it again this bandage is lying'. (L1 Nganasan)

13. dʼaŋku                    taa-ni-ə                        dʼüðü-tə
    NEG.EX                    that.remote-LOC.PRON-ADJZ       hand-GEN.SG.2SG
    sʼügümü-ə-dʼəə-raa        takəə                           dʼübə-i-ti
    bandage-ADJZ-ANT-LIM      that.remote                     throw-DRV[STAT]-PRS
    nʼülʼiã-jtʼi-ti
    lie.down.straight-DRV-PRS
    'Nothing, only your finger bandage is lying there'. (Nganasan corpus (Brykina et al. 2016))

However, in these two examples, there might be alternative explanations. In standard Russian, the relations between sʲa-forms and forms without -sʲa are not always so regular, as in reflexive, reciprocal, anticausative, and passive uses. For instance, the relation between Russian verbs valʲatʲ 'to drag' and valʲatʲ-sʲa 'to lie' is not transparent. The omission of -sʲa in (12) can be explained by an under-acquisition of such irregular relations. Moreover, there is a synonymous Russian verb lezhatʲ 'lie'.

On the other hand, there are cases where the omission cannot be explained as a calque.

In (14), the verb ispugatʲ-sʲa is used without -sʲa, although the corresponding verb requires the reflexive marker in Enets (15).

14. ot                    tebe             ja       ispuga-l
    ABL                   2SG.LOC          1SG      frighten-PST.M
    I got afraid of you. (L1 Enets)

15. nɔzunʲʔ?                       lumu-e-zʔ
    1SG.ABL                        be.frightened.PFV-REFL-3PL.REFL
    [The reindeers] got afraid of me. (Enets corpus)

It seems that there is no equivalent Russian verb without -sʲa that could have affected this use. The semantic relation between ispugatʲ and ispugatʲ-sʲa is regular as well (anticausative). Presumably, this omission could be explained by a general tendency to omit it, which may have been inherited from the local Pidgin variety. Example (14) was taken from a text of the oldest speaker of Forest Enets (1910 year of birth). He probably knew Taimyr Pidgin Russian, or Govorka, which is now extinct (on Govorka see (Stern 2005)). In the basilect of this pidgin, -sʲa is indeed regularly omitted (Urmanchieva 2010, p. 199).

The same explanation can be proposed for (16) from Nganasan Russian. This example cannot be attributed to the Nganasan influence since in Nganasan, inchoative verbs have the reflexive conjugation (Tereschenko 1979, p. 195). Example (16) comes from a speaker of an older generation (1923), who is regarded as a mesolect speaker of Govorka[4].

16. purge            načina-l-s̶ʲa̶              sovsem
    blizzard         begin-PST.SG.M-SJA        entirely
    'A raging blizzard started'. (L1 Nganasan)

### 3.3. Quantitative Data

Table 2 shows that both in the Tungusic sample and in the Samoyedic one, the number of omissions is higher than the number of overuses.

---

[4] Urmanchieva (2010) and Stern (2012) worked with him while describing Govorka.

**Table 2.** Overuses vs. omissions of -sʲa.

|  | Overuse | Omission | % of Overuse |
|---|---|---|---|
| Tungusic | 17 | 29 | 37% |
| Samoyedic | 8 | 17 | 32% |
| total | 23 | 46 | 33% |

Table 3 shows the distribution of overuses and omissions across different meanings typical of -sʲa (on the data of Tungusic subcorpus[5]). A significantly higher rate of nonstandard uses compared to standard ones is attested for anticausative sʲa-verbs (such as lomatʲ—lomatʲ-sʲa 'break (intransitive)—break (transitive)')[6]. Deponent verbs and verbs with an irregular semantic relation to the base verb, which amounts to the majority of sʲa-verbs used in a nonstandard way, do not deviate significantly from that of other semantic classes of sʲa-verbs.

**Table 3.** Distribution across meanings of -sʲa (Tungusic subcorpus).

| Meaning | Nonstand | Stand | % Nonstand |
|---|---|---|---|
| deponent&irregular | 18 | 281 | 6% |
| decaus | 15 | 130 | 10% |
| refl+ | 6 | 168 | 3% |
| object_impers | 4 | 8 | 33%[7] |
| pass+ | 3 | 64 | 4% |
| recip | 0 | 16 | 0% |
| prefixal | 0 | 20 | 0% |

Table 4 shows the correlation between the meaning of -sʲa and the type of nonstandard use. As expected, only omissions are attested across deponent verbs and verbs with irregular semantic relations between the base verb and the derived form and all overuses belong to the productive meanings of -sʲa. Moreover, across productive meanings, the above-mentioned asymmetry between omissions and overuses is not attested.

**Table 4.** Different meanings of -sʲa: omission vs. overuse (Tungusic and Samoyedic)[8].

|  | Omission | Overuse |
|---|---|---|
| Deponent and irregular | 27 | 0 |
| productive meanings | 19 | 25 |

Table 5 demonstrates the distribution of overuses of -sʲa motivated by different factors.

**Table 5.** Types of overuses (Tungusic and Samoyedic).

|  | N (%) |
|---|---|
| structural borrowing | 4 (16%) |
| synonymous Russian verb | 8 (32%) |
| overgeneralization | 2 (8%) |
| non-evident | 11 (44%) |

---

[5] The number of nonstandard uses in Samoyedic subcorpus is too small for the quantitative analysis.
[6] Two-tailed exact Fisher's test, $p = 0.0339$.
[7] We do not take into account this semantic type, since it is too rare even across standard uses.
[8] Two-tailed exact Fisher's test, $p < 0.0001$.

Clear cases of structural borrowing are rarer than cases of incomplete acquisition (the interference with a synonymous verb without -sʲa and overgeneralization of productive meanings of -sʲa).

## 4. Discussion

Thus, we have analyzed the nonstandard uses of the reflexive suffix -sʲa in the Russian speech of bilingual speakers of indigenous languages of Siberia, namely Samoyedic and Tungusic languages. Such uses are quite infrequent in the text sample. Since there are many more uses of -sʲa that follow the rules of standard Russian, the uses observed in the data do not form a consistent system that differs from standard Russian. Moreover, sometimes we witness a variation: -sʲa can be omitted and used correctly within one paragraph or even within one sentence, as in (17).

17. kak         budto      vverh       **podnima-jet-sʲa.** <…>
    how         as.if       up          rise-NPST.3SG-SJA
    **podnima-jet-sʲa,**    kak         budto       rastʲ-ot
    rise-NPST.3SG-SJA       how         as.if        grow-NPST.3SG
    'As if he is rising. (And more … like this. He encircles it more. More, like this.) He is rising, as if he is growing'. (L1 Nganasan)

We do not observe notable differences between the Samoyedic and Tungusic data. However, this might be partly explained by the extremely small number of nonstandard -sʲa uses in the Samoyedic sample.

We divided all nonstandard uses of -sʲa into two groups: omissions (the unexpected absence of -sʲa) and overuses (the unexpected presence of -sʲa). Both in the Tungusic text sample and in the Samoyedic one, omissions were more frequent than overuses. This generally agrees with our expectations on the influence of the indigenous system. The prevalence of overuses indeed is not expected, unless the correlate of -sʲa in the source language was much more productive. This was not the case either in Tungusic or in Samoyedic.

However, if we exclude deponent verbs, for which omission is logically the only option, and irregular sʲa-derivates, for which overuses are not attested either, overuses, in contrast, become even more frequent than omissions.

Not all nonstandard uses of -sʲa are caused by structural borrowing. There are even more cases that can be interpreted rather as manifestations of incomplete acquisition. In particular, these are the cases of interference with particular synonymous Russian verbs without -sʲa and overgeneralization of productive meanings of -sʲa. Some nonstandard uses of -sʲa in the speech of older speakers may be inherited from the local pidgin.

The Tungusic data show a significant prevalence of anticausatives across nonstandard uses of -sʲa. This agrees with our expectations on the interference with the anticausative -p in Tungusic. At the same time, deponent verbs do not show any prevalence, as could be expected according to the hypothesis of under-acquisition of the Russian system.

To conclude, we cannot fully explain the picture observed either by direct calquing of the pattern of the indigenous language or by the incomplete acquisition of standard Russian. We are dealing rather with the interaction of both types of factors and probably also with some additional ones.

**Author Contributions:** Resources: Samoyedic Subcorpus, I.K. and P.P.; Tungusic Subcorpus, N.S.; Data curation: Nganasan and Tundra Enets data, I.K.; Nenets and Enets data, P.P.; Nanai and Ulch data, N.S.; Investigation, all co-authors; Writing—Original Draft Preparation, all co-authors.

**Funding:** This research was funded by RSF grant number 17-18-01649.

**Conflicts of Interest:** The authors declare no conflict of interest.

## References

Avrorin, Valentin A. 1961. *Grammatika nanajskogo jazyka [Nanai Grammar]*. Moscow: Nauka.

Brykina, Maria, Valentin Gusev, Sándor Szeverényi, and Beáta Wagner-Nagy. 2016. Nganasan Spoken Language Corpus (NSLC). Archived in Hamburger Zentrum für Sprachkorpora. Version 0.1. December 23. Available online: http://hdl.handle.net/11022/0000-0001-B36C-C (accessed on 15 June 2019).

Daniel, Michael, Nina Dobrushina, and Sergey Knyazev. 2010. Highlanders' Russian: Case Study in Bilingualism and Language Interference in Central Daghestan. *Slavica Helsingiensia* 40: 68–97.

Kasatkin, Leonid Leonidovich. 2005. *Russkaja dialektologija [Russian dialectology]*. Moscow: Akademija.

Kemmer, Suzanne. 1993. *The Middle Voice*. Amsterdam and Philadelphia: Benjamins.

Khanina, Olesya, and Andrey Shluinsky. 2019. Intransitive verbs in Enets: A contribution to the typology of split intransitivity. *Zeitschrift für Sprachwissenschaft* 38: 1–36. [CrossRef]

Letuchiy, Aleksandr B. 2016. Vozvratnostj [Reflexivity]. In *Materialy k korpusnoj grammatike russkogo jazyka*. Sankt-Petersburg: Nestor-Istorija, vol. I, pp. 268–340.

Nikolaeva, Irina. 2014. A grammar of Tundra Nenets. In *Mouton Grammar Library*. Edited by George Bossong, Bernard Comrie, Matthew Dryer and Patience Epps. Berlin and Boston: Walter de Gruyter GmbH, vol. 65.

Sakel, Jeanette. 2007. Types of loan: Matter and pattern. In *Grammatical Borrowing in Cross-Linguistic Perspective*. Edited by Yaron Matras and Jeanette Sakel. Berlin: Walter de Gruyter, vol. 38, pp. 15–30.

Shagal, Ksenia. 2016. Contact-induced grammatical phenomena in the Russian of Erzya Speakers. In *Mordvin Languages in the Field*. Edited by Ksenia Shagal and Heini Arjava. Helsinki: Uralica Helsingiensia, vol. 10, pp. 363–77.

Siegl, Florian. 2013. Materials on Forest Enets, an Indigenous Language of Northern Siberia. Ph.D. Dissertation, Société Finno-Ougrienne, Helsinki, Finland.

Sloetjes, Han, and Peter Wittenburg. 2008. Annotation by category—ELAN and ISO DCR. Paper presented at 6th International Conference on Language Resources and Evaluation (LREC 2008), Marrakech, Morocco, May 28–30.

Stern, Dieter. 2005. Taimyr Pidgin Russian (Govorka). *Russian Linguistics* 29: 289–318. [CrossRef]

Stern, Dieter. 2012. *Tajmyr-Pidgin-Russisch*. Kolonialer Sprachkontakt in Nordsibirien. Muenchen: Verlag Otto Sagner.

Stoynova, Natalia. 2016. Impersonaljnyje konstrukcii v nanajskom jazyke: Aktantnyje preobrazovanija, modaljnostj, habitualis [Impersonal in Nanai: Valency-changing, modality, genericity]. *Acta Linguistica Petropolitana* 12: 679–91.

Tereschenko, Natalia M. 1979. *Nganasanskij jazyk. [The Nganasan Language]*. Leningradskoje otd-nie: Nauka.

Urmanchieva, Anna Iu. 2010. Govorka: Primer strukturno smeshannogo iazyka [Govorka: An example of structurally mixed language]. In *Instrumentarium of Linguistics: Sociolinguistic Approaches to Non-Standard Russian*. Edited by Arto Mustajoki, Ekaterina Protassova and Nikolai Vakhtin. Helsinki: Slavica Helsingiensia, vol. 40, pp. 188–209.

© 2019 by the authors. Licensee MDPI, Basel, Switzerland. This article is an open access article distributed under the terms and conditions of the Creative Commons Attribution (CC BY) license (http://creativecommons.org/licenses/by/4.0/).

Article

# The 'Carbon Capture' Metaphor: An English-Arabic Terminological Case Study

**Amal Haddad Haddad *** and Silvia Montero-Martínez

Department of Translation and Interpreting, University of Granada, 18002 Granada, Spain; smontero@ugr.es
* Correspondence: amalhaddad@ugr.es

Received: 4 May 2019; Accepted: 23 September 2019; Published: 26 September 2019

**Abstract:** The study of metaphorization processes in scientific texts is essential in terminological studies and the conceptual representation of specialized knowledge. It is considered to be a prolific tool in the creation of neologisms. Many cognitive models tried to study metaphorisation processes by drawing on metaphor and metonymy based on linguistic evidence. However, recent studies have highlighted the necessity of carrying out empirical tests in order to provide refined results that go beyond the traditional theories of conceptual metaphor and metonymy. This paper analyzes the underlying metaphor in the 'carbon capture and sequestration' event in both English and Arabic. It also discusses the influence of English, the *lingua franca*, in the transfer of the neologism 'carbon capture and sequestration', via translation processes, and its role in the so-called domain loss in the target language. Results were obtained through a corpus-based contrastive terminological analysis, extracted from specialized texts in English and Arabic in the subdomain of climate change. Data analysis was approached from the perspective of Frame-Based Terminology and Conceptual Complexes.

**Keywords:** translation; corpus analysis; domain loss; frame-based terminology; conceptual complexes

## 1. Introduction

According to Lakoff's (1993) Conceptual Metaphor Theory (CMT), metaphor is considered as the mapping between two conceptual domains. At the linguistic level, these mappings reflect how our thoughts are structured metaphorically (Lakoff and Johnson 2003), and how metaphor is deeply engrained in the human cognitive system (Shuttleworth 2016), as it yields common crosslinguistic conceptualization patterns (Ureña Gómez-Moreno 2015, p. 258). Additionally, Ruiz de Mendoza (2017, p. 302) defined metaphor as a mapping of conceptual structure from a source to a target domain.

Interesting research on the use of metaphor in scientific discourse has been carried out by Ureña Gómez-Moreno (2012) in marine biology; Boquera Matarredona (2005) in civil engineering, Huang (2005) in medical texts related to AIDS, and Merakchi and Rogers (2013) in the Arabic scientific discourse. On the basis of CMT, Merakchi and Rogers (2013) confirmed that conceptual metaphors are used to add coherence to scientific discourse, as they "evoke the knowledge space of a particular source domain or sets of source domains" (Merakchi and Rogers 2013, p. 345). Bordet (2016) also highlighted the fact that conceptual construction of scientific neologisms varies across languages, but metaphors are frequently used. In the context of specialized translation, Merakchi and Rogers (2013) found that the translation of metaphor in scientific texts is crucial in the intercultural and communicative act. Translators frequently use them when they insert new and complex concepts in the target language. However, in an English-Arabic corpus based study in the domain of astronomy and astrophysics, Merakchi (2017) argued that metaphorical translation is controversial. Sometimes, the original texts try to facilitate the comprehension of science to laypersons by using shared author-reader experiences. Nevertheless, these experiences are not necessarily shared with the new target culture audience. In this case, unless translations are adapted, they may potentially lead to the misunderstanding of scientific concepts and endanger cross-linguistic communication (Merakchi 2017, p. 3). However, this is not an easy situation for translators when they deal with pairs of languages that have not developed specialized terminologies equally. For instance, Abdullah and Shuttleworth (2013), in their English-Malay case study, concluded that specialized translation becomes more difficult when it involves original texts that have new and innovative scientific and technology terms. They also observed that translating specialized metaphors did pose some challenges in terms of the translation strategies available in Malay, the target language (Abdullah and Shuttleworth 2013, p. 617). In this scenario, sometimes translation processes may lead to the standardization of the underlying conceptual constructions from the source specialized domains, and to domain loss or "epistemicide" in target languages and cultures (Bordet 2016). In other words, according to Hultgren (2013, p.166), this is the failing to develop adequate scientific terminology in a national language, especially at conceptual level.

One of the modern approaches that studies the conceptual constructions of specialized texts is the theory of Frame-Based Terminology (FBT) (Faber 2012). The FBT represents specialized knowledge by means of hierarchically organized terminological definitions, where each concept is delimited within a referential conceptual frame that delineates the entities, relations and actions within their specialized domains. All of this information is extracted with the help of terminological analysis tools (López-Rodríguez et al. 2010). Ureña Gómez-Moreno et al. (2013, p. 176) showed that the FBT is also appropriate to reveal the metaphorical relation between domains. Meaning is the result of a dynamic process, which can be explained by using frames (Ureña Gómez-Moreno et al. 2013, p. 178). Frames are built by abstracting away conceptual structure from multiple experiences (Ruiz de Mendoza 2017, p. 302). They are particularly useful to analyze the conceptualization of metaphor at a cognitive level, as the way we store frame elements (Fes) in our mind is schematic; consequently, when we are faced with instances of frames, we adapt them to our schematic notions (Ruiz de Mendoza 2017, p. 302). Ruiz de Mendoza (2017) further indicated that in order to study cognitive models such as metaphor, it is necessary to refine the linguistic analysis through the study of conceptual complexes, which are defined as "combinations of cognitive models whose existence can be detected from a careful examination of the meaning effects of some linguistic expressions" (Ruiz de Mendoza 2017, p. 298).

In this research, an approximation towards the processes of metaphorization in the subdomain of CLIMATE CHANGE was carried out, with a special focus on the conceptual metaphors and the effects in domain loss of translation processes from English into Arabic. This case study focused on the CARBON CAPTURE AND SEQUESTRATION (CCS) event, a knowledge structure created originally in English on a metaphorical basis, and introduced into the Arabic language via translation processes. It is a corpus-based case study which applies the principles of FBT in the extraction and codification of information from specialized texts (Faber 2015), and the notion of conceptual complexes. Reality is represented through cognitive frames which result from top-down and bottom-up processes. The aim was to categorize reality at a multidimensional level that facilitates the analysis of semantic and conceptual information from the corpus of study.

## 2. Materials and Methods

### 2.1. EcoLexicon and the Environmental Event

The multilingual terminological knowledge base Eco Lexicon (http://ecolexicon.ugr.es/visual/index_es.html) was developed by the research group Lexicon at the University of Granada. Based on the FBT, the specialized (sub-) domains of the environment are conceptually represented in the form of a visual thesaurus, in which each concept is located within a specialized frame that outlines its relation with other concepts. All related entities and processes in the domain of the environment are delimited within a general event-frame called the ENVIRONMENTAL EVENT (Figure 1). This macro-template is conceived as a "dynamic process initiated by a natural or human agent, which affects a patient and produces a result" (Ureña Gómez-Moreno et al. 2013, p. 177). All sub events taking place in the environment are specifications of this general macrostructure.

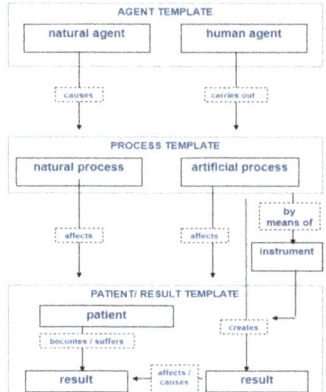

**Figure 1.** The ENVIRONMENTAL EVENT (http://ecolexicon.ugr.es/en/aboutecolexicon.htm).

For instance, the process of CLIMATE CHANGE responds to the dynamics found in Figure 1. A NATURAL AGENT (like the sun) or a HUMAN AGENT causes a NATURAL or ARTIFICIAL PROCESS of warming, such as the combustion of the fossil fuels which emit heat-trapping gases, which affect STATES and ENTITIES (climate, atmosphere of the Earth). These states and entities have the semantic role of PATIENT and, at the same time, provoke different PROCESSES/RESULTS in ENTITIES such as the sea, glaciers, etc. CLIMATE CHANGE is characterized by a series of attributes like long-term change (DURATION) and is fought by means of precautionary measures, such as the use of renewable energy sources. The specific representation of the CLIMATE CHANGE sub event is found in Figure 2, a conceptual structure that codifies knowledge at a basic level (Montero-Martínez 2008, p. 4).

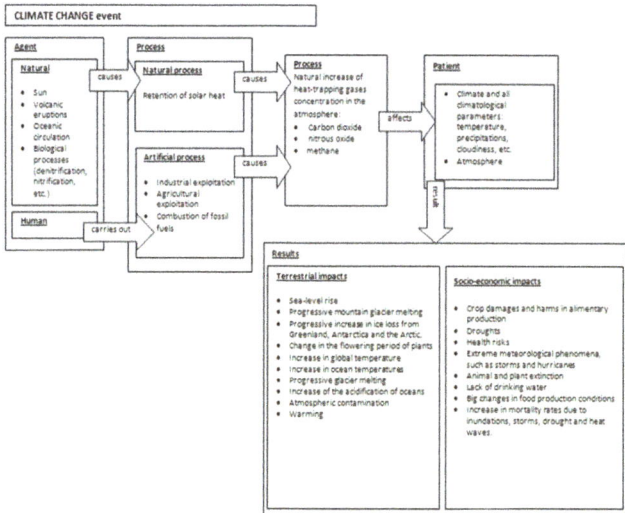

**Figure 2.** The CLIMATE CHANGE event.

For this study, a bottom-up process was complemented with a top-down perspective, where information was extracted from dictionaries and relevant texts in the concrete specialized subdomain. With respect to the bottom-up process, lexical constructions that evoke the concept CLIMATE CHANGE were identified, as they are considered access points towards knowledge related to this subdomain in the corpus of study.

## 2.2. Corpus Selection and Description

The selection criteria for the corpus of study coincides with the adequacy criteria established by Buendía Castro and Gómez-Moreno (2010), related to authority, content and design. Special emphasis was placed on the following parameters: (1) text authority, the identification of the author or the entity publishing a text is crucial as the internet contains many resources that are not always reliable; (2) topic, which in this case study must be related to the subject of climate change; (3) title of the text, which is indicative of the topic and helps in the searching criteria; (4) availability of full articles and texts, in order to adequately compile and cite the corpus; (5) impact factor, as it is especially important to choose journals with scientific quality. The corpora of the study contain specialized, semi-specialized, and informative texts. For this reason, parameters such as topic, availability of the complete text, and title were applicable in the selection of the entire corpus; however, the impact factor was taken into account in the case of specialized texts, and authority was especially important for informative texts. Following these criteria, three different corpora were compiled: (i) an English comparable corpus, (ii) an Arabic comparable corpus, (iii) a parallel English-Arabic corpus.

With respect to the English comparable corpus, it was compiled out of the Lexicon English corpus on the environment, available online in Sketch Engine. A selection of texts concerning climate change was used (with a total of 240,795 tokens) in order to obtain metaphorically based neologisms in this domain. Items in this corpus are obtained from academic articles, journals, books, and informative texts published in online newspapers or magazines. The informative texts were especially useful for their didactic function and simplified language, since they try to explain complicated scientific research to laypersons, sometimes through analogy and metaphor.

In relation to the Arabic comparable corpus (160,437 tokens), it was compiled with original texts in Arabic. However, this was not an easy task because of the scarcity of Arabic resources in comparison with the English ones, and the fact that it has not always been easy to evaluate the adequacy of the Arabic texts. For instance, in spite of being extracted from prestigious websites such as universities and national ministries, some of the texts in the Arabic corpus lack an exact bibliographic description, and vital elements such as type of text, name of the event in which it was presented, etc. For this reason, in general, it has not been possible to fulfill the criterion of impact factor in the case of texts originally written in Arabic. Additionally, in spite of the availability of the full texts, it was not possible to obtain a machine readable format for Sketch Engine, the corpus analysis tool. Consequently, the Arabic comparable corpus posed a challenge.

Finally, a parallel corpus was also created with original texts in English (29,430 tokens) and their translations into Arabic (36,326 tokens). It was adequately aligned by means of the tool Align documents, founding TRADOS Studio 2015. Texts were extracted from the journal *Nature* (http://www.nature.com/), together with their Arabic version; and from *Scientific American* (https://www.scientificamerican.com/), and their translation into Arabic available in *Al-Oloom Magazine* (http://www.oloommagazine.com/Home/Default.aspx). Both publications have an elevated *h index* according to SJR (Scimago Journal and Country Report) (http://www.scimagojr.com/index.php). A book on climate change edited by the UNESCO was also included, together with some articles from *Permaculture Research Institute*. Finally, relevant texts from the *Integrated Regional Information Networks* (IRIN) and their Arabic official translation are found in the corpus.

The complete list of references in the corpus can be found in the following link: https://www.dropbox.com/s/x8p8uobk1jaermr/Appendixes_Carbon%20Capture%20and%20Sequestration%20An%20English%20Arabic%20Terminological%20Case%20Study.pdf?dl=0.

## 2.3. Candidate Metaphorical Terms and the CARBON CAPTURE and SEQUESTRATION Event

In order to extract useful information related to metaphorization processes, the framework described in Montero-Martínez (2008) was implemented. It was based on the FBT and allows the precise identification and characterization of the lexical constructions which form part of an event. The process was divided into: (a) identification of constructions evoking the frame; (b) description of the frame lexical and conceptual profile; (c) specification of the frame relations and attributes; (d) representation of the frame definitional template. First, the corpus was analyzed in order to obtain candidate metaphorical terms and the Arabic equivalents. A word list, ordered by frequency, was generated with the help of Sketch Engine. Afterwards, it was manually analyzed to obtain a series of metaphorical candidate terms. One of the candidate terms is the lexeme 'capture' which appears in the corpus 52 times, as seen in Table 1.

Table 1. List of words and frequency.

|   | Word | Frequency |
|---|------|-----------|
| 1. | capture | 43 |
| 2. | captured | 9 |

The lexical unit 'capture' is defined in the *Cambridge Online Dictionary* (https://dictionary.cambridge.org/es/) as "to take someone as a prisoner, or to take something into your possession, especially by force". Therefore, it was selected as a metaphorical candidate to study whether, in fact, it entailed a metaphorization process or not. The contextual analysis showed that 'capture' frequently co-appears with the lexical units 'sequestration', 'storage', and 'carbon', resulting in the term 'carbon capture and sequestration' or 'carbon capture and storage' (CSS), as shown in Example (1.a), (1.b), (1.c) and (1.d) extracted from the English corpus. The fact that the argument carbon is not an animated or material object indicates that the predicate CAPTURE is used metaphorically in such examples. In other words, the argument selection carried out by the predicate in this specialized context differs from the selection described by the *Cambridge Dictionary* for the predicate CAPTURE in general language. Additionally, the fact that the lexeme "capture" frequently co-occurs in the corpus with 'sequestration' activates a semantic area within the realm of criminal acts and police action. Further evidence is also found in concordance (1.c.), where CSS is described as a type of "sequestration technique".

1. Examples (1.a), (1.b), (1.c) and (1.d.) show how the CCS appears in context as 'carbon capture and sequestration' or 'carbon capture and storage'.

    a. " ... is one step in the process of carbon capture and sequestration (CCS), and involves ... "
    b. " ... Carbon Capture and Sequestration (CCS) is a set of ... "
    c. " ... sequestration techniques such as carbon capture and storage (CCS) will be able to reduce the ... "
    d. " ... systems or bioenergy coupled with carbon capture and sequestration setups. This poses an ... "

The lexical constructions related to the term CCS represent the lexical formalization of the CARBON CAPTURE AND SEQUESTRATION event. These related units help in the identification of the conceptual profile of the frame, as they represent the concepts which are part of it. For example, some of the contexts retrieved from the corpus in relation to the lexical profile of the event are (2), (3), and (4). They show some key lexical constructions in italics which were further analyzed in order to understand the conceptual dynamics of the CCS event.

2. Carbon capture and sequestration (CCS) is a set of technologies that can greatly reduce carbon dioxide emissions from new and existing coal- and gas-fired power plants, industrial processes, and other stationary sources of carbon dioxide.
3. Carbon Capture and Storage (CCS). A suite of technologies exists that allows for $CO2$ from the combustion or gasification of coal and other fossil fuels to be captured rather than released to the atmosphere. Once captured, $CO_2$ from fossil fuel use can be injected into and permanently sequestered in underground geologic formations.

4. It is *a three-step* process that includes the capture of carbon dioxide from power plants or industrial sources; transport of the captured and compressed carbon dioxide (usually in pipelines); and underground injection and geologic sequestration, or permanent storage, of that carbon dioxide in rock formations that contain tiny openings or pores that trap and hold the carbon dioxide.

This information was also enriched with a top-down approach, where some units were extracted from specialized resources, such as dictionaries, encyclopedias, etc. For instance, The Intergovernmental Panel on Climate Change report of 2005 (Bert et al. 2005, p. 3) defines the terminological variant carbon capture and storage (CCS) as "a process consisting of the separation of $CO_2$ from industrial and energy-related sources, transport to a storage location and long-term isolation from the atmosphere. This report considers CCS as an option in the portfolio of mitigation actions for stabilization of atmospheric greenhouse gas concentrations" [sic].Thus, Figure 3 shows the conceptual representation of the CCS event, defined as the process (PROCESS) to capture (PROCESS) the carbon dioxide (PATIENT) produced by the human activity (AGENT) of combustion of fossil fuel (PROCESS);to transport (PROCESS) and, finally, to storage it (PROCESS) permanently (DURATION), in geological formations or in deep sea-beds (ENTITY), in order to prevent it from reaching the atmosphere (PATIENT), and, consequently, mitigate climate change (PROCESS).The event presents its own specificity in terms of the entities and processes that take part in CCS (for instance, transportation of $CO_2$ to a storage place); however, it can be seen that the scheme of the event also responds to the more general conceptual configuration found in Figures 1 and 2, the CLIMATE CHANGE and the ENVIRONMENTAL EVENT, correspondingly. This way, definitional templates are established and systematically applied in FBT to all concepts related to a common area of meaning.

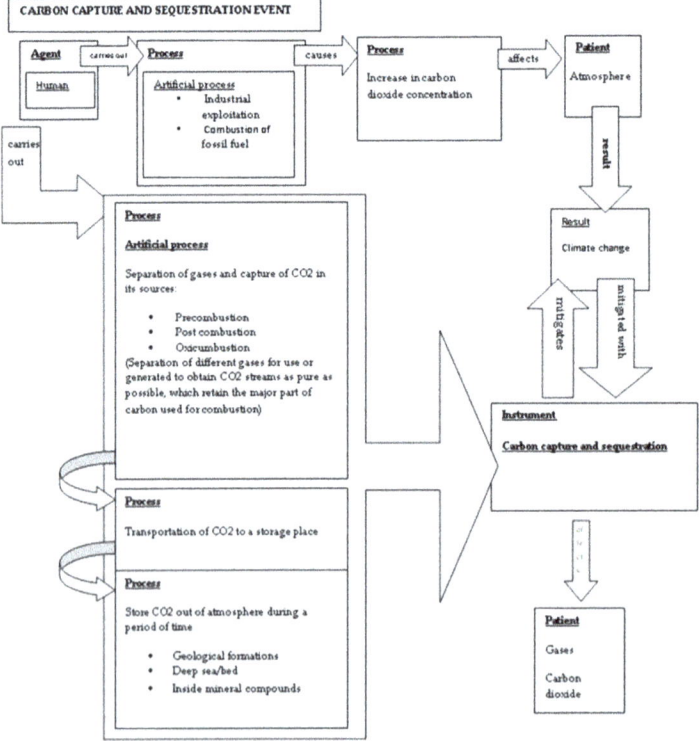

**Figure 3.** The CARBON CAPTURE AND SEQUESTRATION event.

## 3. Results and Discussion

*3.1. Metaphorical Projection of CARBON CAPTURE AND SEQUESTRATION in English*

The contextual analysis of the lexical units which formalize the concept CARBON CAPTURE AND SEQUESTRATION in the English corpus reflects how this process is conceptualized in discourse. For instance, examples (5) and (6) give the following information:

5. ( … ) we would employ a method that is receiving increasing attention: capturing carbon dioxide and storing, or sequestering, it underground rather than releasing it into the atmosphere. Nothing says that $CO_2$ must be emitted into the air (Socolow 2005a, p. 50).
6. Carbon Capture and Storage (CCS), a suite of technologies exists that allows for $CO_2$ from the combustion or gasification of coal and other fossil fuels to be captured rather than released to the atmosphere (Smith 2011, p. 28).

In this case, the CARBON CAPTURE AND SEQUESTRATION process is described as an action of police seizure and capture of a criminal, to judge them properly and decide whether they are guilty or not; and if declared guilty, imprison them for a determined period of time. This police action can be conceptualized as a frame, in which we find elements such as those in Table 2.

**Table 2.** Frame elements of POLICE SEIZURE frame.

| POLICE SEIZURE Frame |
| :---: |
| Capture (PROCESS) |
| Imprisonment (PROCESS) |
| Transportation (PROCESS) |
| Liberation (PROCESS) |
| Police (ENTITY) (AGENT) |
| Criminal (ENTITY) (PATIENT) |
| Judge (ENTITY) (AGENT) |
| Crime (PROCESS) |
| Duration (ATTRIBUTE: TIME) |
| Prison (ENTITY) (LOCATION) |
| Victim (ENTITY) (PATIENT) |
| Police Car (ENTITY) (INSTRUMENT) |

Some of the Frame Elements (FEs) that appear in Table 3 are used metaphorically in discourse to conceptualize the CARBON CAPTURE AND STORAGE phenomenon, resulting in a metaphorical frame, as can be seen in Table 3. The structure and logic of the CCS target frame determines the nature of the source (POLICE SEIZURE), which needs to have elements that correspond to the target in a significant way (Ruiz de Mendoza 2017, p. 302). For example, the mapping between the FEs in Table 3 shows that CO2 is conceptualized as a CRIMINAL agent who harms the Atmosphere/Earth-System (VICTIM) by provoking Global Warming/Climate-Change (CRIMES). Therefore, Carbon Capture (CAPTURE) and Transportation (TRANSPORT) are carried out by scientists (POLICE), taking CO2 (CRIMINAL) to deep sea-beds or underground (PRISON), by means of pipelines (POLICE CARS).

However, to refine the results of this analysis, it is important to go a step further and analyze how frame complexes are exploited metaphorically and metonymically. For instance, example 7 shows that two FEs of POLICE SEIZURE (i.e., PRISON and CRIMINAL) have been metaphorically used in the CCS frame. In the common frame of police seizure, we usually see the police chasing the criminal and putting them in jail where there are usually many security measures to prevent the prisoners from escaping. However, in example 7, there is an unusual development of the frame POLICE SEIZURE, that is, a different development from what is usual or expected. Here, the imprisonment of the criminal requires special measures to prevent him/her from escaping from prison (prevent it from migrating upward), and harm society. This scenario happens when the criminal tries to break out of jail using unusual escaping techniques. For this reason, when the criminal shows any signs of disobedience, special measures are taken to prevent them from escaping from prison. One of these measures is keeping the location of prison away from society (a mile or more beneath the surface), or isolating the criminal in special cells with enhanced security (porous rock; impermeable, non-porous layers of rock). Such description leads to think of a very dangerous prisoner (CO2) in case of escaping. Furthermore, at the same time, it entails a metonymic shift from these elements to the quality of DANGEROUSNESS of the CRIMINAL. More specifically, the allusion to special measures to prevent the criminal from escaping activates the quality of dangerousness. A case of target-in-source metonymy is found in which the whole stands for the part; the CRIMINAL (CO2) stands for the quality of its dangerousness.

**Table 3.** Mapping between the frames POLICE SEIZURE and CARBON CAPTURE AND SEQUESTRATION.

|  | FEs of POLICE SEIZURE | FEs of CARBON CAPTURE AND SEQUESTRATION |
|---|---|---|
| 1. | Capture (PROCESS) | Carbon Capture |
| 2. | Imprisonment (PROCESS) | Storage/Sequestration |
| 3. | Transportation (PROCESS) | Transportation |
| 4. | Liberation (PROCESS) | Release |
| 5. | Police (ENTITY) (AGENT) | Scientist |
| 6. | Criminal (ENTITY) (PATIENT) | Carbon-Dioxide |
| 7. | Crime (PROCESS) | Global Warming/Climate-Change |
| 8. | Duration (ATTRIBUTE: TIME) | Duration (Temporary/Permanent) |
| 9. | Prison (ENTITY) (LOCATION) | Underground/Sea-Bed |
| 10. | Victim(ENTITY) (PATIENT) | Atmosphere/Earth-System |
| 11. | Police Car (ENTITY) INSTRUMENT) | Pipelines |
| 12. | Criminal (AGENT) | CO2 |

7. Underground injection and geologic sequestration (also referred to as storage) of the CO2 into deep underground rock formations. These formations are often *a mile or more beneath the surface* and consist of *porous rock* that holds the *CO2*. Overlying these formations are *impermeable, non-porous layers of rock* that trap the *CO2* and *prevent it from migrating upward* (Socolow 2005a, p. 50).

*3.2. Metaphorical Projection of CARBON CAPTURE AND SEQUESTRATION in Arabic*

In order to analyze whether the CARBON CAPTURE AND SEQUESTRATION process is metaphorically projected in Arabic as well, the first step was to identify the terms used to make reference to this concept. The parallel corpus showed that carbon capture is equivalent to 'احتباس الكربون' [ihtiba:s al-karbwn][1] [carbon imprisonment][2] and 'تخزين الكربون' [takhzi:n al-karbwn] [carbon storage]. Meanwhile, the comparable corpus led to the identification of the terms 'احتجاز ثنائي أكسيد الكربون' [ihtija:z thuna:?i: ?uksi:d al-karbwn] [carbon dioxide imprisonment] and 'احتجاز الكربون' [ihtija:z al-karbwn] [carbon imprisonment], with a frequency of 58 for 'احتجاز ثنائي أكسيد الكربون' [ihtija:z thuna:?i: ?uksi:d al-karbwn] [imprisonment of carbon dioxide] and a frequency of twofor 'حجز الكربون' [hajz al-karbwn] [carbon imprisonment]. Examples such as (8) were identified in which the use of the term can be observed.

---

[1] Transliteration is provided in italics between square brackets. Transliteration symbols can be found in Appendix A.
[2] Translation into English between square brackets.

. ثمة استراتيجية يمكن ان تجمع بين حجز انبعاثا ت ثنائي اكسيد الكربون من محطات توليد الطاقة التي تعمل بالفحم وحقنها بعد ذلك في التكوينات الجيولوجية لخزنها لفترات طويلة. ويمكن ان تسهم هذه الاستراتيجية بشكل ملموس في الحد من زيادة تركيز ثنائي اكسيد الكربون في الغلاف الجوي. تعد التقانات المنخفضة الكلفة التي تستهدف الحصول على ثنائي اكسيد الكربون في محطات الطاقة وزيادة الخبرة في حقن ثنائي اكسيد الكربون لتجنب تسربها لسطح الارض من العوامل الاساسية في نجاح المشاريع الكبرى لحجز ثنائي اكسيد الكربون وخزنه.

(Socolow 2005b)

8. [thammata istra:ti:jya yumkin an tajmac bayn inbica:tha:t thuna:ʔi: ʔuksi:d al karbwn min maḥata:t tawli:d atta:qa allati: taʿmal bilfaḥm waḥaqniha: baʿd dha:likfi: attakwi:na:t al-jiywlwjyya likhazniha: fatara:t ṭawi:la. Wayumkin an tus'him ha:dhih al-istra:tyjyya bishakl malmu:s fi: alḥadd min zya:dat thuna:ʔi: ʔuksi:d al karbwn fi: al-ghila:f al-jawwy. Tuʿadd al-taqa:na:t al-munkhafiḍat al-kulfaallati: tastahdif al-ḥuṣu:l ʿala: thuna:ʔi: ʔuksi:d al karbwn fi: maḥatta:t al-ṭa:qa wa zya:dat al-khibra fi: ḥaqn thuna:ʔi: ʔuksi:d al karbwn litajannub tasarrubihi li:sat'ḥ al-ard min al-ʿawa:mil al-asa:syya fi: naja:ḥ al-masha:riːʿ al-kubra: liḥajz thuna:ʔi: ʔuksi:d al karbwn wakhaznih] [There is a strategy that consists of the imprisonment of carbon dioxide emissions from coal power plants and its injection afterwards in geological formations to store it fora long period of time. This strategy may noticeably help in the reduction of the concentration of carbon dioxide in the atmosphere. It is a low cost technology which aims at obtaining carbon dioxide from energy generation stations. It also aims at increasing the expertise in carbon dioxide injection to avoid infiltrations. These two objectives are considered the main elements for the success of big projects to imprison and storage carbon dioxide].

In fragment 8, it can be observed that CCS is also described in terms of an anthropomorphic activity, which has the act of police seizure and capture of a criminal as a source domain (i.e., 'imprisonments of carbon dioxide emissions', 'to imprison carbon dioxide and storage it'). Examples in Table 4 show some of the similarities found in the lexical constructions of CCS in English and Arabic in relation to the FEs of POLICE SEIZURE listed in Tables 2 and 3. For instance, in example 1, the FEs Capture, Criminal and Imprisonment are evoked by expressions such as 'احتجاز ثنائي اكسيد الكربون وتخزينه' [iḥtija:z thuna:ʔi: ʔuksi:d al-karbwn watakhzi:nih] [capture and sequestration of carbon dioxide], and 'اسر ثنائي اكسيد الكربون وفصله' [asr thuna:ʔi: ʔuksi:d al-karbwn wafaṣluh] [imprisonment of carbon dioxide and its separation]. Additionally, in example 3, expressions such as 'امتصاص الغاز الكربوني وحجزه في تلك الصخور' [imtiṣa:ṣ al-ga:z al-karbwny waḥajzih fi: tilka al-ṣukhu:r] [the absorption of the carbonic gas and its imprisonment in those rocks] activate FEs such as Imprisonment, Capture, Criminal, and Prison; while example 4 shows expressions such as 'تنحية الكربون' [tanḥiyat al-karbwn] [the isolation of carbon] and 'عزل الكربون' [ʿazl al-karbwn] [the insulation of carbon], evoking FEs such as Imprisonment and Criminal, etc.

Table 4. Metaphoriclexical projection of CARBON CAPTURE AND SEQUESTRATION in English and Arabic.

| | Lexical Constructions in English and Arabic | Fes *Police Seizure* |
|---|---|---|
| 1. | 'capture and sequestration of carbon dioxide'"<br>'احتجاز ثاني أكسيد الكربون وتخزينه'؛'أسر ثنائي أكسيد الكربون وفصله'<br>[asrthuna:?i: ?uksi:d al-karbwnwafasluh]; [ihtija:zthuna:?i: ?uksi:d al-karbwnwatakhzi:nih]<br>[imprisonment of carbon dioxide and its separation; imprisonment of carbon dioxide and its storage] | Capture—Criminal—Imprisonment |
| 2. | 'the sequestration of greenhouse gases such ascarbondioxide'<br>'احتباس غازات الدفيئة ولاسيما ثاني أكسيد الكربون'<br>[ihtiba:s gha:za:t al-dafy?a wala:siyama: thuna:?i: ?uksi:d al-karbwn]<br>[the confinement of global greenhouse gases, above all, carbon dioxide] | Criminal—Imprisonment |
| 3. | 'storing captured carbon dioxide underground'<br>'امتصاص الغاز الكربوني وحجزه في تلك الصخور'<br>[imtisa:s al-ga:z al-karbwny wahajzih fi: tilka al-sukhu:r]<br>[the absorption of the carbonic gas and its imprisonment in those rocks] | Imprisonment—Capture—Criminal-Prison |
| 4. | 'carbon sequestration'<br>'تنحية الكربون'؛'عزل الكربون'<br>[tanhiyat al-karbwn]; [ʕazl al-karbwn]<br>[the isolation of carbon]; [the insulation of carbon] | Imprisonment—Criminal |

In sum, the implementation of the methodology described in Montero-Martínez (2008) helped in the creation of the CARBON CAPTURE AND SEQUESTRATION event, defining it as a technique or method of climate change mitigation, which consists of capturing the emitted carbon dioxide and storing it underground, instead of leaving it in the atmosphere. Corpus and manual analysis allowed the identification of the metaphorical term 'Carbon capture and sequestration' and its Arabic equivalent 'احتجازالكربون'" [ihtija:z al-karbwn] [imprisonment of Carbon]. Such methodology implies that a mapping between the conceptual categories (entities, processes, and attributes) in the CCS frame and the FEs found in POLICE SEIZURE has been established. Consequently, the principles of frame-based analysis were applied in order to identify the frame elements, and establish the correspondence between them. The results of the analysis suggest that the English term 'carbon capture and sequestration' was created on a metaphorical basis, and that the Arabic term 'احتجازالكربون'" [ihtija:z al-karbwn] [imprisonment of carbon] was created as a result of the transfer from English into Arabic via translation processes.

Frequency searches with Google operators "site: .edu", filtering documents in websites of universities and research institutions, and exact matches for the English terms 'carbon capture and sequestration' (freq. 16700) and 'carbon capture and storage' (freq. 37,100) were carried out. In Arabic, the same operators retrieved only a frequency of five for each of the variants studied, 'احتجازثنائي أكسيد الكربون' [ihtija:z thuna:?i: ?uksi:d al-karbwn] [imprisonment of carbon dioxide] and 'احتجازالكربون' [ihtija:z al-karbwn] [imprisonment of carbon]. However, queries for only exact matches of these Arabic terms gave frequencies of 4300 and 6540, respectively. The enormous difference between the frequencies obtained in Arabic, with and without site filter.edu, is due to several factors. The first is that university and research institutions in Arab countries have hardly any presence in the domain .edu on the Internet. The second is that there is a lack of indexation of documents written in Arabic language, something already noted in the description of the comparable corpus in Arabic. Therefore, to see the presence of these metaphorical terms, it was necessary to make less demanding searches with regards to the sites hosting the reference documents. In short, it can be concluded that both the original English terms and their Arabic translations have a significant presence in specialized and semi-specialized discourse, judging by the frequency figures obtained.

## 4. Conclusions

In this study, the principles and methodology of the FBT have been applied in order to analyze metaphorization processes in the subdomain of CLIMATE CHANGE, in both English and Arabic. The results of the analysis suggest that metaphorization is a useful method in the creation of new terms in the field of climate change (Haddad and Montero-Martínez 2019). Very frequently, terms and concepts are borrowed from English in order to create terminological neologisms in many languages, Arabic amongst them. In this case study, the frame-based analysis demonstrates that the term 'carbon capture and sequestration' is originally constructed on a metaphorical basis. As a matter of fact, the creation of the term 'احتجاز الكربون' [iḥtija:z al-karbwn] [imprisonment of carbon] in Arabic results from the transmission of the metaphorical frame originally used in English. The analysis showed similarities in the lexical formalizations of the concept CARBON CAPTURE AND SEQUESTRATION in both English and Arabic, and the metaphorical projection of the frame POLICE SEIZURE was found in both languages. Additionally, the analysis of conceptual complexes showed how frame complexes were exploited metaphorically and metonymically.

The direct influence of English in the conceptualization of this phenomenon led to the standardization in Arabic of the conceptual constructions found in the English metaphorical source domain. Some authors have argued that this results from the failing to create new terms and concepts in a national language (Hultgren 2013), something that impoverishes conceptual systems and prevents the growth of scientific languages at cultural and conceptual levels (Bordet 2016). When domain loss in the target language and culture occurs (Bordet 2016), some give a negative assessment of the solutions applied in the process of transferring knowledge from one language to another, either by the translators or by the experts themselves. Nevertheless, Montero-Martínez et al. (2001, p. 692) argued that, in the case of scientific and technical translation, the use of loans in the transfer of terms may also act as a fertilizer of communication techniques in other languages and, in many cases, it is more adequate than the creation of artificial and new terminology in the native language. In the current stage of development of the scientific Arabic language, this is probably the case. Experts in all fields of knowledge, especially in science and technology, learn about new concepts and terminology in specialized journals and conferences, where English is most of the times the language of communication. Thus, in order to facilitate the common understanding of scientific concepts, they frequently tend to use common cross-linguistic conceptualization patterns found in metaphorical and metonymic terms (Ureña Gómez-Moreno 2015), a fact that was also observed in the comparable Arabic corpus with original texts written by experts. In the case of the parallel corpus, translators also used the same metaphorical patterns found in the original English texts. Many times the translator's choice was determined by the resources used for terminological documentation, which very frequently included the specialized papers, conference proceedings and reports published by the experts in the field. As seen in the frequency searches carried out with Google operators to refine document quality, the terms carbon capture and sequestration, carbon capture and storage, and the Arabic loans 'احتباس الكربون' [iḥtiba:s al-karbwn] [carbon imprisonment] and 'تخزين الكربون' [takhzi:n al-karbwn] [carbon storage] are considerably used in discourse. Therefore, it seems that the use of conceptualization patterns and conceptual metaphors shared by English and Arabic helps climate change experts in the Arabic world to communicate and illustrate specialized concepts (Haddad and Montero-Martínez 2019) to diverse audiences.

Consequently, this case study showed that the analysis carried out within the framework of FBT and the notion of conceptual complexes is an adequate approach to the study of metaphor-based neologisms in scientific discourse. On the one hand, it allowed identifying the conceptual structure underlying the carbon capture and sequestration event, as well as the identification of the lexical profile of the frame and the establishment of the definitional template for the concepts formalizing the CCS event. All this information is essential to further process the lexical profile of CCS, identified in the study. To describe the terms in Eco Lexicon, where the subdomains of the environment are conceptually represented in the form of a visual thesaurus, each concept is located within a specialized frame that outlines its relation with other concepts. On the other hand, the observation that the climate change discourse in Arabic borrows from the conceptual patterns found in English seems to confirm that languages lagging behind in the production of scientific texts, which is the case of Arabic, also use this strategy instead of creating pure neologisms, that is, terms not based on previous patterns coming from a source language. However, these preliminary results obtained from this case study need to be tested with a larger quantitative and qualitative study in order to determine if pure neologisms are coexisting with "borrowed" ones. This would have implications in the field of translation training in the Arabic language.

**Author Contributions:** For research articles with several authors, a short paragraph specifying their individual contributions must be provided. The following statements should be used "conceptualization, A.H. and S.M.; methodology, A.H. and S.M.; software, A.H. and S.M.; validation, A.H. and S.M.; formal analysis, A.H. and S.M.; investigation, A.H. and S.M.; resources, A.H. and S.M.; data curation, A.H. and S.M..; writing—original draft preparation, A.H. and S.M.; writing—review and editing, A.H. and S.M.; visualization, A.H. and S.M.; supervision, S.M.; project administration, A.H. and S.M.; funding acquisition, A.H. and S.M.", please turn to the CRediT taxonomy for the term explanation. Authorship must be limited to those who have contributed substantially to the work reported.

**Funding:** This research was funded by the project FFI2017-89127-P, Translation oriented Terminology Tools for Environmental Texts (TOTEM), funded by the Spanish Ministry of Economy and Competitiveness.

**Conflicts of Interest:** The authors declare no conflict of interest.

## Appendix A

Table A1 provides the transliteration symbols for Arabic vowels and consonants.

**Table A1.** Arabic transliteration symbols.

| Arabic Alphabet | Symbol |
|---|---|
| ء | ʔ |
| ث | th |
| ج | j |
| ح | ḥ |
| خ | kh |
| ذ | dh |
| ز | z |
| ش | sh |
| ص | ṣ |
| ض | ḍ |
| ط | ṭ |
| ظ | TH |
| ع | ʿ |
| غ | gh |
| ق | q |
| وَ | w |
| يَ | y |
| (فتحة) | a |
| (ضمة) | u |
| (كسرة) | i |
| مد طويل ا/ى | a: |
| ضمة طويلة و | u: |
| كسرة طويلة ي | i: |
| Diphthongs | aw |
| (أصوات علة مركبة) | ay |

## References

Abdullah, Sharmini, and Mark Shuttleworth. 2013. Metaphors in the translation of English technical texts into Malay: A preliminary study. *Journal of Asian Scientific Research* 3: 608–29.

Bert, Metz, Davidson Ogunlade, Heleen de Coninck, Manuela Loos, and Leo Meyer, eds. 2005. *Carbon Dioxide Capture and Storage*. Cambridge: Cambridge University Press, Available online: https://www.ipcc.ch/report/carbon-dioxide-capture-and-storage/ (accessed on 22 February 2018).

Boquera Matarredona, María. 2005. Las Metáforas en Textos de Ingeniería Civil: Estudio Contrastivo Español-Inglés. Ph.D. Thesis, Universitat de Valencia, Valencia, Spain, October 5.

Bordet, Geneviève. 2016. Counteracting domain loss and epistemicide in specialized discourse: A case study on the translation of Anglophone metaphors to French. *Publications* 4: 18. [CrossRef]

Buendía Castro, Miriam, and Jose Manuel Ureña Gómez-Moreno. 2010. ¿Cómo diseñar un corpus de calidad? Parámetros de evaluación. *Sendebar* 21: 165–80.

Faber, Pamela. 2012. *A Cognitive Linguistics View of Terminology and Specialized Language*. Berlin (Boston): De Gruyter Mouton.

Faber, Pamela. 2015. 'Frames as a framework for Terminology'. In *Handbook of Terminology*. Edited by Hendrik J. Kockaert and Frieda Steurs. Amsterdam and Philadelphia: John Benjamins, pp. 14–33.

Haddad, Amal, and Silvia Montero-Martínez. 2019. 'Radiative Forcing' Metaphor: An English-Arabic Terminological and Cultural Case Study. *International Journal of Arabic-English Studies* 19: 139–58.

Huang, Carolina. 2005. A Metáfora no Texto Científico de Medicina: Um Estudo Terminológico da Linguagem Sobre AIDS. Master's thesis, Universida de Federal do Rio Grande do Sul, Porto Alegre, Brazil.

Hultgren, Anna Kristina. 2013. Lexical borrowing from English into Danish in the Sciences: An empirical investigation of 'domain loss'. *International Journal of Applied Linguistics* 23: 166–82. [CrossRef]

Lakoff, George. 1993. A contemporary theory of metaphor. In *Metaphor and Thought*. Edited by Ortony Andrew. Cambridge: Cambridge University Press, pp. 202–51.

Lakoff, George, and Mark Johnson. 2003. *Metaphors We Live By*. Chicago and London: The University of Chicago Press.

López-Rodríguez, Clara Inés, Pamela Faber, Pilar León Araúz, Juan Antonio Prieto Velasco, and Maribel Tercedor. 2010. La terminología basada en marcos y su aplicación a las ciencias ambientales: Los Proyectos MARCOCOSTA y ECOSISTEMA. *Arena Romanistica* 7: 52–74.

Merakchi, Khadidja. 2017. The Translation of Metaphors in Popular Science from English into Arabic in the domain of Astronomy and Astrophysics. Ph.D. Thesis, University of Surrey, Guildford, UK, August 31.

Merakchi, Khadidja, and Margaret Rogers. 2013. The translation of culturally bound metaphors in the genre of popular science articles: A corpus-based case study from scientific American translated into Arabic. *Intercultural Pragmatics* 10: 341–72. [CrossRef]

Montero-Martínez, Silvia. 2008. Tidying up tides: Modelling coastal processes in terminology management. Paper Presented at XVIII FIT 2008 World Congress of Shanghai, Shangahai, China, August 4–7.

Montero-Martínez, Silvia, A. Fuertes-Olivera Pedro, and García de Quesada Mercedes. 2001. The translator as 'Language Planner': Syntactic calquing in an English-Spanish technical translation of chemical engineering. *Meta: Journaldes Traducteurs/Meta: Translators' Journal* 46: 687–98. [CrossRef]

Ruiz de Mendoza, Francisco José. 2017. Conceptual complexes in cognitive modeling. *Revista Española de Linguistica Aplicada* 30: 297–322. [CrossRef]

Shuttleworth, Mark. 2016. *Studying Scientific Metaphor in Translation: An Inquiry into Cross-Lingual Translation Practices*. New York and London: Routledge.

Smith, Sandy. 2011. *Climate Change 101: Understanding and Responding to Global Climate Change Overview Science and Impacts Adaptation Technological Solutions Business Solutions International Action*. Arlington: PEW Center on Global Climate Change: Available online: https://es.calameo.com/read/00057071332f28f1d59a1 (accessed on 22 February 2018).

Socolow, Robert. 2005a. Can We Bury Global Warming? Pumping carbon dioxide underground to avoid warming the atmosphere is feasible, but only if several key challenges can be met. *Scientific American* 293: 49–55. Available online: https://www.scientificamerican.com/ (accessed on 22 February 2018).

Socolow, Robert. 2005b. ضخ ثنائي أكسيد الكربون في باطن الأرض، غير أن ذلك يتطلب منا مواجهة تحديات جساما ghila:f al-jawwi: yumkin dakh thuna?i: ?uksi:d هل يمكننا دفن الاحترار العالمي؟ لتجنب احترار الغلاف الجوي يمكن al-karbwn fi: batin al-ard ghayr an dha:lik yatatallab minna mwajahat tahadya:t jisa:m]. *Majallat Al-Oloom21*. Available online: http://www.oloommagazine.com/Articles/Archieve.aspx (accessed on 22 February 2018).

Ureña Gómez-Moreno, Jose Manuel. 2012. Conceptual types of terminological metaphors in marine biology. An English-Spanish contrastive analysis from an experientialist perspective. In *Metaphor in Use: Context, Culture, and Communication*. Edited by Fiona MacArthur, José Luis Oncins-Martínez, Manuel Sánchez García and Ana Marí Piquer Píriz. Amsterdam: John Benjamins Publishing, pp. 239–60.

Ureña Gómez-Moreno, Jose Manuel. 2015. Refining the understanding of novel metaphor in specialised language discourse. *Terminology* 22: 1–29.

Ureña Gómez-Moreno, Jose Manuel, Faber Pamela, and Buendía Castro Miriam. 2013. Frame blending in specialized language: Harmfulalgalbloom. *Terminology* 19: 175–201.

© 2019 by the authors. Licensee MDPI, Basel, Switzerland. This article is an open access article distributed under the terms and conditions of the Creative Commons Attribution (CC BY) license (http://creativecommons.org/licenses/by/4.0/).

Article
# Metaphor and Metonymy in Food Idioms

**Isabel Negro**

Department of English Studies, School of Economics, Universidad Complutense de Madrid,
28223 Pozuelo de Alarcón, Spain; inegro@ccee.ucm.es

Received: 15 May 2019; Accepted: 23 June 2019; Published: 27 June 2019

**Abstract:** In recent decades, the development of the Conceptual Metaphor Theory, put forward by Lakoff and other scholars. In this light, metaphor and metonymy have been found to provide a semantic motivation for a considerable number of idiomatic expressions. Within this framework, the present contribution explores the cognitive motivation of food idioms in English (e.g., 'be a cup of tea,' 'bread and butter,' 'walking on eggshells') and Spanish (e.g., *darse pisto, tener mala uva, cortar el bacalao*). The analysis reveals that idiomatic meaning often relies on metaphoric amalgams and metonymic chains, or on the interaction between metaphor and metonymy.

**Keywords:** food; idiom; metaphor; metonymy

## 1. Introduction

In recent decades, metaphor and metonymy have been investigated within the cognitive linguistics framework. Metaphor and metonymy are conceptual mechanisms that contribute to providing structure to the human conceptual system. The development of the Conceptual Metaphor Theory, put forward by Lakoff and other scholars (e.g., Lakoff and Johnson 1980; Lakoff 1987, 2006; Lakoff and Turner 1989; Kövecses 2002; cf. Ruiz de Mendoza and Pérez 2011 for assessment on the later versions) has led to research along different lines. One such line is the cognitive basis of idioms (Dobrovol'skij and Piirainen 2005; Langlotz 2006; Boers and Lindstromberg 2008). In this light, a number of studies have shown the role of metaphor and metonymy in building the meaning of numerous idiomatic expressions. Within this framework, the present article discusses the metaphorical/metonymic basis of a set of food idioms in English and Spanish.

## 2. Theoretical Framework

From a cognitive linguistics perspective, metaphor and metonymy occupy a central role in our conceptual structure.

The Conceptual Metaphor Theory is based on the following principles (Lakoff 2006):

- Metaphor is primarily a cognitive mechanism.
- Metaphor involves understanding a domain of experience (the target domain) in terms of a more concrete domain (the source domain).
- A metaphor is to be regarded as a mapping (e.g., a fixed set of conceptual correspondences) between a source domain and a target domain, where one or more features of the source are projected upon the target. As Lakoff (2006, p. 192) remarks, a metaphor is "an ontological mapping across conceptual domains," so that "the essence of meaning is understanding and experiencing one kind of thing in terms of another" (Lakoff and Johnson 1980, p. 5).
- Any linguistic metaphor, or metaphoric expression, is an instantiation of a conceptual metaphor.

While a metaphor is a mapping (i.e., a set of correspondences) between two different conceptual domains, a metonymy is a domain-internal mapping. Ruiz de Mendoza and Otal (2002, p. 58) suggest two types of metonymy based on the domain-internal nature of metonymic mappings:

(a) Source-in-target metonymies are those in which the source domain is a subdomain of the target domain, e.g., SIGN FOR STATE ('to raise one's eyebrows'). They involve domain expansion, which consists of broadening the amount of conceptual material associated with a domain.
(b) Target-in-source metonymies are those in which the target is a subdomain of the source, for example PART-FOR-PART metonymies. They involve domain reduction and the consequent highlighting of part of a domain.

Following Ruiz de Mendoza and Galera (2014), metaphors may occur within metaphoric amalgams, and metonymies can be integrated within metonymic chains. There are two types of metaphoric amalgam: (i) A single-source metaphoric amalgam consists of integrating one of the metaphors in a complex into the conceptual configuration of the other; (ii) A double-source metaphoric amalgam results from mapping two different source domains onto the same target domain. Metonymic chains consist of combining two or more metonymies in such a way that the target domain of the first constitutes the source domain of the following one.

Metaphor and metonymy often interplay. Some authors (e.g., Radden 2000; Barcelona 2000; Ruiz de Mendoza and Díez 2002; Ruiz de Mendoza and Otal 2002) have discussed the conceptual interaction between metaphor and metonymy. In this contribution, we follow Ruiz de Mendoza and Otal (2002) that, whenever metaphor and metonymy interact, it is the latter that is subsidiary to the former. This claim results from the nature of the two mappings. While a metaphor involves two conceptual domains, a metonymy involves just one. Therefore, the two domains of metaphor cannot operate within the single domain of a metonymy. Ruiz de Mendoza and Otal (2002) propose several patterns of interaction between metaphor and metonymy:

1. Metonymic expansion of the metaphoric source or one of its correspondences, as in "to turn one's back on somebody." The action of turning one's back in the metaphoric source domain is metonymically expanded onto a situation in which a person turns his back in order to ignore somebody.
2. Metonymic reduction of the metaphoric source or one of its correspondences, as in "to have big ears." The ears metonymically stand for good hearing (ORGAN FOR SENSE).
3. This element of the source domain is then projected upon a target domain in which a person eavesdrops.
4. Metonymic expansion of a metaphoric target or one of its correspondences, as in "to clear one's throat." There is a metaphoric correspondence between clearing one's throat and coughing. The result of this metaphoric mapping is then expanded by means of a metonymy, cough being understood as a sign to attract somebody's attention.
5. Metonymic reduction of the metaphoric target or one of its correspondences, as in "to open one's eyes to something." The person who opens his eyes describes metaphorically the person who becomes aware of something important. This metaphor relies on a metonymy, inasmuch as the open eyes represent the reality seen through a person's eyes.

## 3. Methodology

We selected a sample of 50 metaphorically- or metonymically-based food idioms (25 in English and 25 in Spanish) from two dictionaries: *Diccionario de dichos y frases hechas* (Buitrago 2012) and *Oxford Dictionary of English Idioms* (Siefrig 2004).

## 4. Discussion

The source domain of food is used in both English and Spanish to represent people, as shown in the idiomatic expressions 'top banana' (most important person in a group/organization), 'bad egg' (bad/dishonest/unreliable person), 'tough cookie' (determined person), 'smart cookie' (intelligent person), 'a big cheese' (very important person), 'the cream/*la flor y nata*, *un pedazo de pan* 'a piece of bread' (very kind person), *un bombón* (beautiful woman), and *un coco* (ugly person).

Food also provides the source for the conceptualization of money, as exemplified by the English idiom 'peanuts' (a very small amount of money).

The meaning of some idioms is based on a single-source metaphoric amalgam. It is the case of 'lemon' (silly person), 'peach' (lovely person), *un mendrugo/un berzas* (unintelligent person), and *un bombón*. The main metaphor operating in the interpretation of these expressions is PEOPLE ARE FOODS, but it needs to be conceptually enriched in order to explain why a silly person is said to be a lemon, a lovely person is said to be a peach, an attractive woman is said to be a chocolate (*bombón*), and an unintelligent person is said to be a crust of bread (*mendrugo*) or a cabbage (*berza*). This meaning effect is achieved through the application of a metaphor that maps a property of these food items onto a specific personality feature. Thus, sourness and little value are mapped onto lack of intelligence ('a lemon', *mendrugo/berzas*), and sweetness onto charm ('a peach') or attractiveness (*un bombón*). These metaphors combine into single-source metaphoric amalgams with the more general metaphor PEOPLE ARE FOODS. Figure 1 provides an illustration of this process.

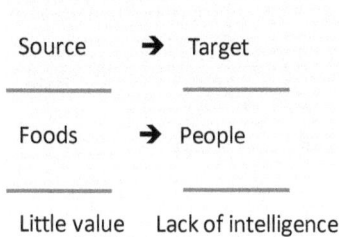

**Figure 1.** Metaphoric amalgam underlying the interpretation of *ser un mendrugo/un berzas*.

Metonymy underlies a few idioms such as 'full of beans' (full of energy') and *tener mala leche* 'sour milk' (to be bad-tempered). The first expression calls for an OBJECT FOR ITS PROPERTIES source-in-target metonymy, since beans make an excellent source of protein and energy. The second idiom activates a CAUSE FOR EFFECT metonymy, based on the belief that the milk supplied by the mother affected the baby's character. Other idioms are based on a metonymic complex. It is the case of 'to bring home the bacon' (earn the household income), *ganarse el pan* 'bread'/*los garbanzos* 'chickpeas'/*el cocido*[1]/*las lentejas* 'lentils'/*las habichuelas* 'beans' ('earn a living'), and 'bread and butter' (job/activity that provides you with a steady income). In the initial metonymy, the food items are made to stand for food by virtue of a GENUS FOR SPECIES target-in-source metonymy. The second metonymic process makes food stand for the money necessary to obtain it. This metonymic operation highlights the subdomain that is relevant for interpretation, in this case, MONEY. In the idiom 'bread and butter' (job/activity that provides you with a steady income), a third domain reduction process makes money stand for the activity done to earn it (PURPOSE OF THE ACTION FOR ACTION). Figure 2 schematizes this combination of metonymies.

---

[1] *Cocido* is a dish made with chickpeas, meat and vegetables.

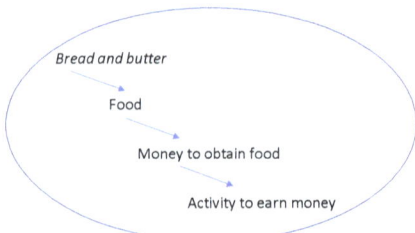

**Figure 2.** Metonymic complex underlying the interpretation of *bread and butter*.

In much the same way, a double metonymy underlies the idiom *hacer buenas migas*, which evokes the migrating shepherds' habit of meeting up to cook and then eat this dish[2]. Cooking this dish metonymically represents the good relationship between the shepherds who prepared it together. Such a good relationship then stands for good relationships between people in general.

The interpretation of a set of idioms in our sample relies on four types of interaction between metaphor and metonymy: (1) Metonymic expansion of the metaphoric source; (2) metonymic reduction of the metaphoric source; (3) metonymic reduction of the metaphoric target; and (4) metonymic expansion of the metaphoric source and metonymic reduction of the metaphoric target.

(1) Metonymic expansion of the metaphoric source

Let us consider the idiom *cortar el bacalao*. In the source domain, we have a fishmonger cutting cod. The action stands for the fishmonger's ability to cut cod—a fish that breaks easily into pieces—by virtue of a source-in-target metonymy. This ability is then mapped onto authority, which gives rise to the meaning 'direct, control.' The resulting pattern is one of metonymic expansion of the metaphoric source domain, as shown in Figure 3.

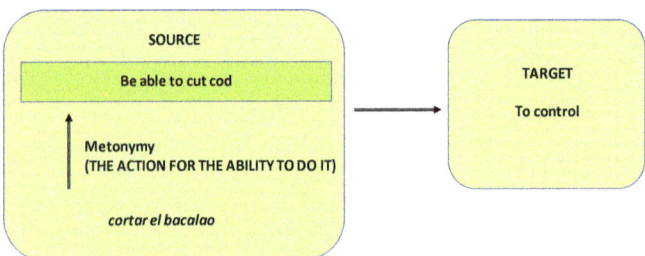

**Figure 3.** Metonymic expansion of the metaphoric source underlying the interpretation of *cortar el bacalao*.

The idiom 'spill the beans' (reveal a secret) evokes the ancient Greek method of placing black or white beans in a jar to cast votes (a white bean indicated a positive vote and a black bean was negative). If someone spilled the jar of beans, the election results would be known earlier. We highlight the result of spilling the beans by virtue of the ACTION FOR RESULT source-in-target metonymy. This metaphorical process is schematized in Figure 4.

---

[2] The dish consists of breadcrumbs fried with garlic and paprika.

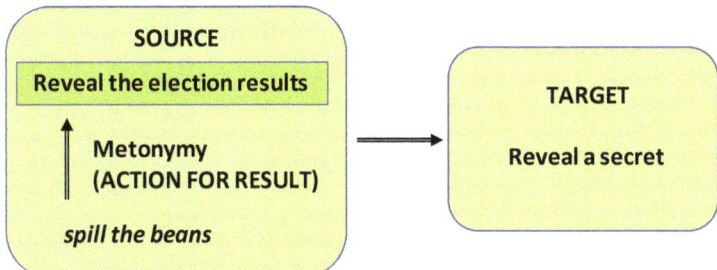

**Figure 4.** Metonymic expansion of the metaphoric source underlying the interpretation of 'spill the beans'.

The idiomatic expression *descubrir el pastel* calls for a WHOLE-FOR-PART source-in-target metonymy. *Pastel* refers to a meat pie eaten in the 16th and 17th centuries. Pastry cooks used to make it with more pastry than mince, so that people had to find where the meat was. The pie is made to stand for the meat inside it through an operation of metonymic expansion. Then finding the meat hidden in the pastry is mapped onto hidden information in order to yield the idiomatic meaning.

(2) Metonymic reduction of the metaphoric source

The idioms *mandar a freír espárragos*, 'to have your cake and eat it' and 'walking on eggshells' are all based on the SPECIFIC FOR GENERIC target-in-source metonymy. In the expression *mandar a freír espárragos* frying asparagus, which is a useless task, since it is easier to boil it, stands for any useless task though an operation of metonymic reduction. Making someone do something useless is then understood as keeping them away for as long as possible.

To have your cake and eat it at the same time is impossible. This situation metonymically stands for any situation in which somebody attempts to obtain two incompatible things. Trying to have two incompatible things is then understood as wanting more than one deserves or can handle.

The same SPECIFIC FOR GENERIC metonymy gives rise to the meaning of the idiom 'walking on eggshells.' The action metonymically stands for any action requiring caution. Hence the metaphorical meaning 'to act sensitively to avoid offending somebody.'

The idioms *estar a la sopa boba, darse pisto* and 'meat and potatoes' reflect another target-in-source metonymy, namely THE GENUS FOR THE SPECIES. In *estar a la sopa boba*, the word *sopa* evokes the broth given to the homeless outside convents in the 16th century. The soup is made to stand for food. The metonymy allows for the interpretation of being fed by someone as living at their expense. In the idiom *darse pisto*, *pisto* (fried vegetable hash) used to be a dish made up of different kinds of minced meat that well-off people ate. Again, the dish metonymically stands for food, particularly the food that only some people could afford. Eating fine foods and dishes is then metaphorically understood as showing off. In much the same way, 'meat and potatoes' stand for basic food. Basic food in the metaphorical source domain is then made to correspond with the basic needs of life, or of something in the target domain.

The expression *atar los perros con longanizas* is based on the metonymy THE SIGN OF WEALTH FOR WEALTH. Sausages being used as a leash indicate a person's wealth, hence the idiomatic meaning 'to live in opulence.'

A further target-in-source metonymy integrated into a metaphor is exemplified in the idiom 'to have one finger in every pie,' where the finger metonymically represents the action of eating from many pies (GESTURE FOR ACTION). The metonymy allows the action of eating to be interpreted as doing many different things.

A similar interactional pattern underlies the interpretation of the idiom *tener mala uva*, although the metaphorical mapping integrates a metonymic chain rather than a single metonymy. The grapes in the metaphoric source domain undergo a process of metonymic reduction that serves to highlight those aspects that are relevant to the metaphoric mapping. Such a process involves four consecutive domain reduction operations (see Figure 5). The first operation highlights wine by virtue of a PART-FOR-WHOLE metonymy. The second operation gives access to drinking through an OBJECT FOR ACTION metonymy. In the third operation, wine drinking is made to stand for its effects, namely aggressive behavior. Aggressiveness as a result of wine drinking is then set in metaphoric correspondence with bad temper.

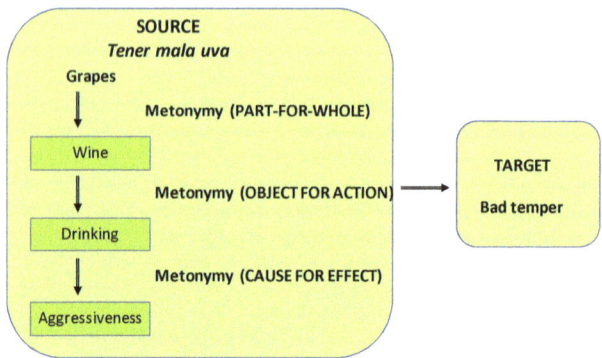

**Figure 5.** Metonymic chain underlying the interpretation of *tener mala uva*.

Another metonymic chain involving metonymic reduction underlies the expression 'it's not my cup of tea.' First, the cup of tea stands for the action of tea drinking (OBJECT FOR ACTION). By virtue of a further target-in-source metonymy, tea drinking is then made to stand for any pleasant activity (SPECIFIC FOR GENERIC). This metonymic process allows for the use of the idiom to refer to something that the speaker enjoys doing.

(3) Metonymic reduction of the metaphoric target

The idioms *comerse el coco* ('to think over and over'), *tener huevos* ('be courageous'), and *estar hasta los huevos* ('be fed up with something') profile the metaphor BODY PARTS ARE FOODS. This metaphor licenses the shift from a coconut to a person's head, and from eggs to a man's testicles. The expression *comerse el coco* reflects the metonymy BODY PART FOR ITS TYPICAL FUNCTIONS (Barcelona 2000, p. 265), or, as per Ruiz de Mendoza and Galera (2014, p. 113), the high-level metonymy INSTRUMENT FOR FUNCTION. This target-in-source metonymy highlights the instrumental role of the head/brain in thinking. Figure 6 provides an illustration of this process.

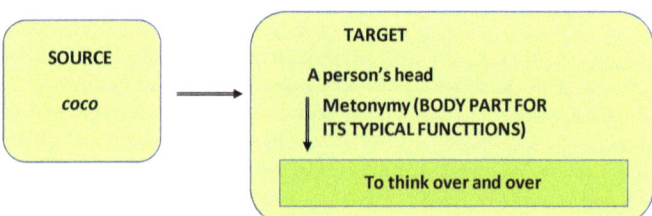

**Figure 6.** Metonymic reduction of the metaphoric target underlying the interpretation of *comerse el coco*.

In the idioms *tener huevos* and *estar hasta los huevos*, the BODY PARTS ARE FOODS metaphor subsumes the metonymy BODY PART FOR ITS TYPICAL FUNCTIONS AND FOR THE ATTRIBUTES CONNECTED WITH THEM (Barcelona 2000, p. 265), as illustrated in Figure 7. The testicles are the seat of courage (*tener huevos*) or anger (*estar hasta los huevos*).

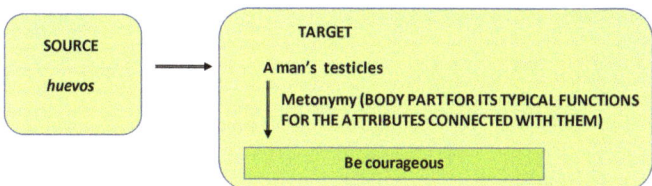

**Figure 7.** Metonymic reduction of the metaphoric target underlying the interpretation of *tener huevos*.

(4) Metonymic expansion of the metaphoric source and metonymic reduction of the metaphoric target

The meaning of the Spanish idiom *poner cara de vinagre*—'to be angry/bad-tempered'—is based on a metonymic process. In the metaphoric source domain we find vinegar. The target domain depicts someone who is angry or bad-tempered. Vinegar, which is made to stand for sourness (one of its properties) through metonymic expansion, maps onto anger/bad temper in the metaphoric domain. This mapping is activated through a SIGN OF EMOTION FOR EMOTION target-in-source metonymy, whereby a person's angry expression stands for the feeling of anger. See Figure 8 for the schematization of this interactional pattern.

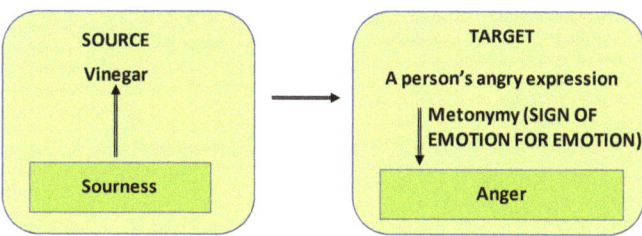

**Figure 8.** Metonymic reduction of the metaphoric target underlying the interpretation of *estar hasta los huevos*.

## 5. Conclusions

The present article has sought to give evidence of the metaphorical/metonymic basis of idioms across languages. The study of a sample of food idioms in English and Spanish has revealed (1) the role of metaphor and metonymy in construing idiomatic meaning, and (2) the interaction between metaphor and metonymy. The study has also shown that metaphor and metonymy may combine in different ways, giving rise to metaphoric amalgams and metonymic chains.

The scope of the paper being limited, further research needs to explore this topic on the basis of a large corpus.

**Funding:** This research received no external funding.

**Conflicts of Interest:** The author declares no conflict of interest.

## References

Barcelona, Antonio. 2000. *Metaphor and Metonymy at the Crossroads*. Berlin and New York: Mouton de Gruyter.
Boers, Frank, and Seth Lindstromberg, eds. 2008. *Cognitive Linguistic Approaches to Teaching Vocabulary and Phraseology*. Berlin: Mouton de Gruyter.
Buitrago, Alberto. 2012. *Diccionario de dichos y frases hechas*. Madrid: Espasa Libros.
Dobrovol'skij, Dmitrij, and Elisabeth Piirainen. 2005. *Figurative Language: Cross-Cultural and Cross-Linguistic Perspectives*. Amsterdam: Elsevier.
Kövecses, Zoltan. 2002. *Metaphor: A Practical Introduction*. Oxford: Oxford University Press.

Lakoff, George. 1987. *Women, Fire and Dangerous Things: What Categories Reveal about the Mind*. Chicago: University of Chicago Press.

Lakoff, George. 2006. The contemporary theory of metaphor. In *Cognitive Linguistics: Basic Readings*. Edited by Dirk Geeraerts. Berlin and New York: Mouton de Gruyter, pp. 186–238.

Lakoff, George, and Mark Johnson. 1980. *Metaphors We Live By*. Chicago: Chicago University Press.

Lakoff, George, and Mark Turner. 1989. *More Than Cool Reason: A Field Guide to Poetic Metaphor*. Chicago: University of Chicago Press.

Langlotz, Andreas. 2006. *Idiomatic Creativity: A Cognitive-Linguistic Model of Idiom-Representation and Idiom-Variation in English*. Amsterdam/Philadelphia: John Benjamins Publishing, vol. 17.

Radden, Günter. 2000. How metonymic are metaphors? In *Metaphor and Metonymy at the Crossroads*. Edited by Antonio Barcelona. Berlin and New York: Mouton de Gruyter, pp. 93–108.

Ruiz de Mendoza, Francisco José, and Olga Díez. 2002. Patterns of conceptual interaction. In *Metaphor and Metonymy in Comparison and Contrast*. Edited by Rene Dirven and Ralph Pörings. Berlin and New York: Mouton de Gruyter, pp. 489–532.

Ruiz de Mendoza, Francisco José, and Alicia Galera. 2014. *Cognitive Modeling. A Linguistic Perspective*. Amsterdam and Philadelphia: John Benjamins.

Ruiz de Mendoza, Francisco José, and José Luis Otal. 2002. *Metonymy, Grammar and Communication*. Granada: Comares.

Ruiz de Mendoza, Francisco José, and Lorena Pérez. 2011. The Contemporary Theory of Metaphor: Myths, Developments and Challenges. *Metaphor and Symbol* 26: 161–85. [CrossRef]

Siefrig, Judit. 2004. *Oxford Dictionary of Idioms*. Oxford: Oxford University Press.

© 2019 by the author. Licensee MDPI, Basel, Switzerland. This article is an open access article distributed under the terms and conditions of the Creative Commons Attribution (CC BY) license (http://creativecommons.org/licenses/by/4.0/).

*Article*

# Spanish Grammatical Gender Interference in Papiamentu

**Jorge R. Valdés Kroff [1],\*, Frederieke Rooijakkers [2] and M. Carmen Parafita Couto [2,\*]**

[1] Spanish and Portuguese Studies, University of Florida, Gainesville, FL 32611, USA
[2] Centre for Linguistics, Leiden University, 2311 EZ Leiden, The Netherlands; frederiekerooijakkers@hotmail.nl
\* Correspondence: jvaldeskroff@ufl.edu (J.R.V.K.); m.parafita.couto@hum.leidenuniv.nl (M.C.P.C.); Tel.: +1-352-273-3744 (J.R.V.K.); +31-71-527-2644 (M.C.P.C.)

Received: 16 May 2019; Accepted: 11 October 2019; Published: 16 October 2019

**Abstract:** The aim of this study is to determine whether Spanish-like gender agreement causes interference in speakers of Papiamentu (a Western Romance-lexified creole language) who also speak Spanish. Papiamentu and Spanish are highly cognate languages in terms of their lexicons. However, Papiamentu lacks grammatical gender assignment and agreement, leading to cognate words with major morpho-syntactic differences. A total of 41 participants with different linguistic profiles (Papiamentu-dominant, Dutch-dominant, Spanish-dominant, and Spanish heritage speaker-Papiamentu bilinguals) listened to 82 Papiamentu sentences, of which 40 contained a Spanish-like gender-agreeing element on the Determiner, Adjective, or Determiner + Adjective and with half of the experimental items marked with overtly masculine (i.e., -*o*) or feminine (i.e., -*a*) gender morphology. Participants performed a forced-choice acceptability task and were asked to repeat each sentence. Results showed that Spanish-dominant speakers experienced the greatest interference of Spanish gender features in Papiamentu. This suggests that in cases where speakers must suppress gender in their second language (L2), this is not easy to do. This is especially the case in highly cognate languages that differ in whether they realize gender features.

**Keywords:** grammatical gender; interference; cognates; Papiamentu; Spanish

---

## 1. Introduction

Grammatical differences between languages often result in difficulties in second language (L2) acquisition and bilingual strategies in language contact (e.g., Hopp 2013; Muysken 2013). This cross-linguistic interference is likely to occur in the case of highly cognate languages due to increased lexical and semantic overlap. The current study examines what happens when speakers of a morphologically rich language (Spanish) also speak a highly cognate language that lacks a morphological feature (Papiamentu). We examine this issue through gender agreement due to it being a well-studied morpho-syntactic element in first language (L1) and L2 acquisition (Montrul 2004). Its difficulty for L2 speakers who speak languages that lack gender agreement is also well-documented (e.g., Eddington 2002; Grüter et al. 2012; Montrul et al. 2008).

Papiamentu is an Iberian-lexifier creole language spoken on the islands of Aruba, Bonaire, and Curaçao (former Dutch Antilles) and in the Netherlands. The total number of Papiamentu speakers is approximately 200,000. Papiamentu speakers in Curaçao are highly multilingual, often speaking Papiamentu, Dutch, English, and Spanish to varying degrees. Despite the variety of languages present on the islands, Papiamentu is the first language of more than 80% of the population on the Caribbean islands (Kester 2011).

## 1.1. The Nominal Domain in Spanish and Papiamentu

Grammatically speaking, Spanish nouns are either masculine or feminine. Although the gender distribution between masculine and feminine nouns is roughly half, masculine is characterized as the default or unmarked gender (Harris 1991). Most Spanish nouns and adjectives mark grammatical gender in canonical endings such as -o for masculine and -a for feminine. Spanish determiners and adjectives agree with the noun in gender and number, with most adjectives following the noun. Unlike Spanish, Papiamentu has no gender distinction but the relative position of Papiamentu adjectives with respect to the noun is like Spanish. Adjectives in Papiamentu are invariant typically ending in -o or -u. Examples (1) and (2) illustrate the lexical and word order similarities between Spanish (a) and Papiamentu (b).

1. a. La$_{fem}$ mesa$_{fem}$ redonda$_{fem}$
   b. E$_\emptyset$ mesa$_\emptyset$ rondó$_\emptyset$
   The table round
   'The round table'
2. a. El$_{masc}$ pato$_{masc}$ blanco$_{masc}$
   b. E$_\emptyset$ patu$_\emptyset$ blanku$_\emptyset$
   The duck white
   'The white duck'

## 1.2. Gender Interference in Palenquero-Spanish Speakers

Lipski (2015) investigated whether Spanish-Palenquero bilinguals accept and/or reproduce Spanish gender agreement in Palenquero. Palenquero is a Spanish-based Afro-Colombian creole language spoken in San Basilio de Palenque, Colombia. Palenquero and Spanish share largely cognate lexicons while Palenquero morpho-syntax is what Lipski describes as a subset of Spanish (i.e., it lacks grammatical gender).

To determine whether Spanish-like feminine gender agreement could be observed in Palenquero, Lipski (2015) first used a picture-describing task. He tests 10 first language (L1) Palenquero speakers, 10 Palenquero heritage speakers, 10 L2 Palenquero speakers, and 4 Palenquero language instruction teachers. The results confirm his hypotheses that Spanish gender agreement cannot be fully suppressed by L2 Palenquero speakers, who introduce some Spanish-like feminine gender agreement in Palenquero determiners and adjectives modifying nouns whose Spanish cognates are grammatically feminine. In contrast, L1 speakers and the metalinguistically sensitive Palenquero language teachers exhibit little Spanish-like feminine agreement. Nonetheless, the high activation level of Spanish prompted by the large number of cognates results in some carryover of gender agreement. Heritage speakers show greater inter-speaker variability.

Lipski additionally utilizes an acceptability task in which participants listen to stimuli and state whether the utterance is "good" Palenquero or not. Afterwards, they repeat each sentence exactly as they have heard it, regardless of their own intuitions on the acceptability of the sentence. Here, 12 L1 Palenquero speakers, 12 heritage Palenquero speakers, 15 L2 Palenquero speakers, and 6 Palenquero language teachers are tested. Results show that L1 speakers and teachers pattern together in accepting about half of the feminine gender-agreement stimuli. Heritage and L2 speakers, on the other hand, display an acceptance level of around 75%. As Lipski predicted, L1 speakers change many feminine endings in -a to the well-formed Palenquero gender-invariant -o while L2 speakers rarely do, thus demonstrating Spanish interference due to acceptance of Spanish-like gender agreement. Palenquero language teachers behave like L1 speakers when modifiers are immediately adjacent to the head noun but more like heritage speakers for predicate adjectives. Lipski suggests that even though the teachers are metalinguistically aware, Palenquero is not their dominant language.

In a more recent study, Lipski (2017) examines the tradeoff between the on-line construction of modifier-noun gender agreement and the automatization of agreement. In this study, he focuses on L1 Spanish speakers who are acquiring L2 Palenquero. When switching from the gender-agreeing L1 to the gender-less L2, the persistence or absence of gender agreement in cognate items is an indirect measure of the cost differential between producing morpho-syntactic agreement and suppressing the carryover of obligatory agreement to the L2. To test this, Lipski conducts a number recall + repetition experiment and a speeded translation task. The results reveal the strong influence of L1 Spanish gender agreement on L2 Palenquero. Furthermore, heritage Palenquero speakers' retention of gender agreement falls between L1 and L2 speakers.

Taken together, the results of Lipski's (2015, 2017) studies suggest that "less" is not always preferred to "more". Lipski posits that the appearance of Spanish-like gender agreement in the L2 and heritage Palenquero speakers may be due to the failure to inhibit cognate Spanish items and the corresponding syntactic projections responsible for gender agreement.

*1.3. Current Study: Spanish Grammatical Gender Interference in Papiamentu*

The current study extends Lipski (2015, 2017) to Papiamentu-Spanish multilinguals[1]. We test if dominant Papiamentu speakers—speakers born into Papiamentu-speaking families and raised on the islands who are also exposed to Spanish—accept and/or reproduce Spanish-like gender agreement in Papiamentu. Following Lipski, we hypothesize that dominant Papiamentu speakers will reject Spanish gender agreement in Papiamentu sentences. In contrast, Spanish heritage speakers, who have been raised and schooled in a Papiamentu-majority environment but whose home language is Spanish, and Spanish-dominant L2 speakers of Papiamentu who immigrated to the islands after puberty, are predicted to accept more sentences that contain Spanish-like gender agreement.

We additionally include a group of dominant Dutch speakers whose families immigrated from the Netherlands but who are brought up on the islands (and who are also exposed to Spanish) to test whether the presence of grammatical gender in the L1 more generally may lead to gender agreement interference. Like Spanish, Dutch has a two-way gender system which distinguishes between common gender (nouns that are preceded by the Dutch article *de*) and neuter gender (nouns that are preceded by the Dutch article *het*). These two gender categories are distributed unequally as the common gender comprises around 75% of all Dutch nouns (Pablos et al. 2019). The Dutch gender system is more opaque, and the distinction between common and neuter gender in Dutch is neutralized in the plural form (preceded by the Dutch article *de*).

Despite the experimental design and linguistic similarities between the two language pairs, our study is different from Lipski's (2015) study in several ways. First, most participants in Lipski's experiments were dominant Spanish speakers acquiring L2 Palenquero in a sociopolitical context in which Spanish is the prestige, government-sanctioned language and in which formal education is conducted. In our Papiamentu-Spanish study, Spanish remains primarily a minority language with environmental presence on the media and through tourism and is supplemented with formal education in public schools from eighth grade in Curaçao, partly due to close geographic proximity to Venezuela. Thus, this study allows us to examine the directionality of cross-linguistic effects of morpho-syntactic transfer in cognate languages and to compare the role of environmental factors.

## 2. Materials and Methods

*2.1. Participants*

Forty-one participants were tested in Curaçao during the period of June–August 2018. The participants were divided into four different categories, illustrated in (3):

---

[1] We refer to our participants as multilinguals because the residents on the island are regularly exposed to Dutch, English, Papiamentu, and Spanish to varying degrees, with the dominant or preferred language often intersecting with racial identity (Kester 2011). For further group characteristics and an extended discussion on Dutch grammatical gender, we refer the reader to the text and Table S1 in the Supplementary Materials.

3. a. Dutch Dominant (n = 7)
   b. Papiamentu Dominant (n = 22)
   c. Spanish Dominant (n = 6)
   d. Heritage Spanish (HS) Papiamentu (n = 6)

This group division was determined by the responses of a linguistic background questionnaire based on (1) self-reported Spanish and Papiamentu proficiency, (2) the age of acquisition of Spanish and Papiamentu, (3) the language spoken at home and the language spoken at school, and (4) the country of birth (see Table S1 in Supplementary Materials). Participants in the Dutch-dominant group were born in Curaçao, learned Papiamentu at a young age, and speak Dutch at home as the dominant language. Additionally, most participants in this group lived in the Netherlands when the experiment took place and thus are primarily exposed to Dutch. The Papiamentu-dominant group consists of L1 Papiamentu speakers that learned Papiamentu at a young age and grew up in households where Papiamentu was the dominant language. Most of the participants in this group are multilingual and learned Spanish in primary school. Two participants in this group were exposed to Spanish under the age of two. For the Spanish-dominant group, participants were born in a Spanish-speaking country, speak Spanish at home, and were exposed to Papiamentu as adults. Finally, the Spanish HS-Papiamentu group includes participants who were either born in a Spanish-speaking country or in Curaçao and learned Papiamentu in primary school. Their home language was reported to be Spanish. All participants of this group moved to Curaçao at a young age and still live in Curaçao today.

*2.2. Materials*

Eighty-two Papiamentu sentences were created, of which 38[2] contained a Spanish-like gender-agreeing element either on the determiner (n = 8), the adjective (n = 12), or both (n = 18). Out of these 38 manipulated sentences, 18 contained combinations of adjectives and/or determiners whose Spanish cognates are feminine (e.g., adjectives and/or determiners ending in –*a*). The other twenty sentences contained Spanish-like masculine gender-agreement (e.g., adjectives or plural determiners ending in –*o(s)*). The remaining 42 filler sentences were Papiamentu sentences with no gender manipulations (i.e., "correct" Papiamentu sentences). Two native Papiamentu speakers from Curaçao verified if the manipulated stimuli were correct Papiamentu sentences, apart from the experimentally manipulated target determiners and/or adjectives. All sentences were recorded by a Papiamentu-Spanish male speaker. After the recordings, the items were shortened with PRAAT software (version 5.3.16; Boersma and Weenink 2012). The entire list of 82 stimuli was randomized in Excel using the (=RAND) function, and four different lists were created. All stimuli were loaded on a laptop, and headphones with a built-in microphone were used to record responses. Two examples of stimuli that were used in the experiment, containing a masculine and feminine Spanish gender-agreeing element, are provided below in (5):

5. a. **Spanish-like feminine gender agreement**[3]:
      Example stimulus:      La$_{fem}$ pluma blanka$_{fem}$ ta suave
      Papiamentu Equivalent: E     pluma blanku     ta suave
                             det   feather white    TAM soft
      'The white feather is soft'

   b. **Spanish-like masculine gender agreement:**
      Example stimulus:      E paranan chikito$_{masc}$ ta kanta bunito[4]
      Papiamentu Equivalent: E paranan chikitu          ta kanta bunita
                             det bird-PL small          TAM sing beautiful
      'The small birds are singing beautifully'

---

[2] The original dataset had 40 experimental stimuli, but we subsequently discovered incorrect coding on 2 sentences and removed these from analyses.

As shown in (5), the manipulated adjectives and determiners occurred in different positions in the sentence (i.e., post-nominal and predicate adjectives were included). Tables 1 and 2 provide a more detailed overview of the distribution of the gendered adjectives and determiners, respectively.

Table 1. Examples of experimentally-manipulated adjectives.

| Adjective Endings | Feminine -*a* (-*o* in PAP [1]) | Feminine -*a* (-*u* in PAP) | Masculine -*o* (-*a* in PAP) | Masculine -*o* (-*u* in PAP) |
|---|---|---|---|---|
| Example stimulus | rondá | chikita | delegó | blanko |
| Papiamentu | rondó | chikitu | delegá | blanku |
| Spanish equivalent | redondo/a | pequeño/a | delgado/a | blanco/a |
| English translation | 'round' | 'small' | 'thin' | 'white' |

[1] PAP = Papiamentu.

Table 2. Examples of experimentally-manipulated determiners.

| Determiners | Masculine Singular *el* [1] (*e* in PAP) | Feminine Singular *la/una* (*e/un* in PAP) | Masculine Plural *los* (*e* in PAP) | Feminine Plural *las* (*e* in PAP) |
|---|---|---|---|---|
| Example stimulus | **el** aros | **una** kara | **los** piskánan | **las** islanan |
| Papiamentu | e aros | un kara | e piskánan | e islanan |
| Spanish equivalent | el arroz | una cara | los peces/pescados | las islas |
| English translation | 'the rice' | 'a face' | 'the fish (plural)' | 'the islands' |

[1] Spanish indefinite determiner *un* was not used because of its cognate status with Papiamentu.

### 2.3. Procedure

The experiment followed the Ethics Code for linguistic research in the faculty of Humanities at Leiden University, which approved its implementation. Participants were instructed that they would listen to 82 Papiamentu sentences over noise-cancelling headphones. Each sentence was immediately followed by a short "beep" sound. Upon hearing the beep, all participants were asked to indicate if the sentence was correct Papiamentu[5] by responding with "yes" or "no" within two seconds (i.e., acceptability judgment task) and to repeat the Papiamentu sentence exactly as they heard it (i.e., sentence repetition task). All answers outside of this time window were not used for the analysis, and the instructions were given in English or Dutch (i.e., languages in which the second author could provide instructions). All 41 participants completed the task without any objection and all answers were digitally recorded. After completing both tasks, all participants completed a language history questionnaire and signed a consent form giving permission to use all recorded data. Participants had the option to complete all forms in Spanish or Papiamentu (languages in which all participants were literate).

## 3. Results

We report on the results for accuracy for the acceptability judgment task: for experimental trials, the expected response is 'no'. First, we analyzed the unchanged Papiamentu filler items in which the expected response is 'yes' to ensure that participants were not randomly selecting answers. One participant from the Papiamentu-dominant group was removed from this analysis and all subsequent analyses for having scored only about half correct (45%) on filler trials. For the remaining 40 participants,

---

[3] For glosses, det = determiner, TAM = tense-aspect-mood particle, and PL = plural.
[4] A reviewer rightly points out that *bonito* is an adverb derived from an adjective and would not show gender agreement in Spanish. This is the only experimental sentence with such characteristics. For a list of experimental sentences, see Appendix A.
[5] For this experiment, 'correct' Papiamentu means that the participants would consider the Papiamentu sentence to be a grammatically well-formed sentence when speaking to another Papiamentu speaker.

the Dutch-dominant group correctly identified 93% (range: 76–100%); the Papiamentu-dominant group correctly identified 90% (range: 73–100%); the Spanish-dominant group correctly identified 89% (range: 80–95%); and the Heritage Spanish-Papiamentu group correctly identified 88% (range: 88–100%) of filler items. Thus, all remaining participants show high accuracy on identifying correct Papiamentu sentences.

For the main analysis, we conducted a 3 × 2 × 4 repeated-measures ANOVA in R (v. 3.5.1) in which the dependent variable is the proportion of correctly identifying experimental items as not well-formed, with the within-subjects factors Condition (Adjective, Determiner, Determiner + Adjective) and Gender (Masculine, Feminine) and the between-subjects factor Group (Dutch-dominant, Papiamentu-dominant, Spanish-dominant, Heritage Spanish-Papiamentu). The dataset consisted of 1558 tokens out of a possible 1640 tokens. The omnibus model revealed a main effect for Condition ($F[2,72] = 10.17$, $p < 0.001$), a main effect for Gender ($F[1,36] = 20.37$, $p < 0.001$), and a main effect for Group ($F[3, 36] = 29.29$, $p < 0.001$). The model also confirmed an interaction between Group and Condition ($F[6,72] = 5.79$, $p < 0.001$) and a 3-way Condition × Gender × Group interaction ($F[6,72] = 5.44$, $p < 0.001$). Due to the 3-way interaction, we conducted separate 3 × 2 repeated-measures ANOVAs per group.

### 3.1. Dutch-Dominant Group

For the Dutch-dominant group (n = 7), the statistical model revealed a main effect for Condition ($F[2,12] = 5.4$, $p = 0.021$) and a main effect for Gender ($F[1,6] = 12.43$, $p = 0.012$). There was no significant interaction between the two variables. As illustrated in Figure 1, this group was least accurate with the determiner condition and least accurate on masculine-marked trials.

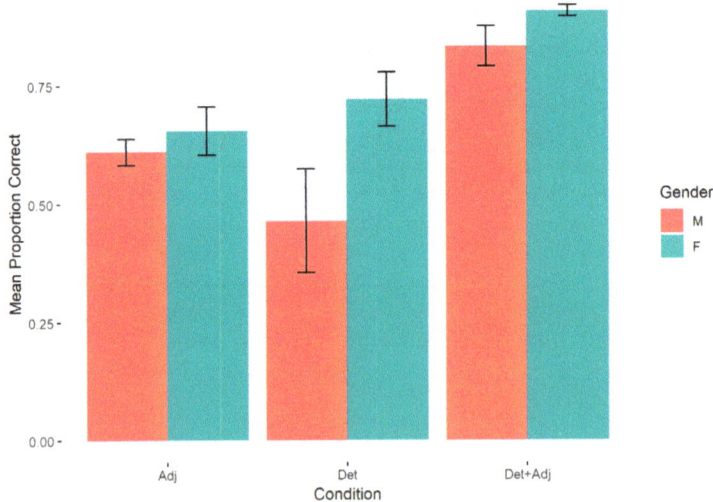

**Figure 1.** Mean proportion accuracy for the Dutch-dominant group. Error bars represent +/− 1 Standard Error of the Mean. Condition is plotted on the horizontal axis. Adj = adjective, Det = determiner, Det + Adj = determiner + adjective, M = masculine, F = feminine.

### 3.2. L1 Papiamentu-Dominant Group

For the Papiamentu-dominant group (n = 21), the statistical model revealed a main effect for Condition ($F[2,40] = 11.83$, $p < 0.001$), a main effect for Gender ($F[1, 20] = 19.14$, $p < 0.001$), and a significant interaction between Condition and Gender ($F[2,40] = 3.86$, $p = 0.029$). Due to the interaction, we conducted pairwise comparisons corrected for multiple comparisons using Tukey's test. In comparisons that test differences between gender within the same condition (e.g., feminine-marked vs. masculine-marked determiners, adjectives, or determiners + adjectives), the difference between feminine- and masculine-marked adjectives was significant (difference = 0.18, t = 4.639, $p < 0.001$), indicating that this group was more accurate on correctly rejecting trials in which the adjective was overtly marked with Spanish-like feminine agreement. Among contrasts of the same gender type but across conditions, the difference between masculine-marked determiners and adjectives was significant (difference = 0.16, t = 4.128, $p = 0.001$) as well as the difference between masculine-marked Determiner + Adjective trials and masculine-marked adjectives (difference = 0.174, t = 4.478, $p = 0.001$). In both cases, the rejection of Spanish-like masculine-marked adjectives was less accurate than the other conditions. All other contrasts were not significant (ps > 0.19). The results are plotted in Figure 2.

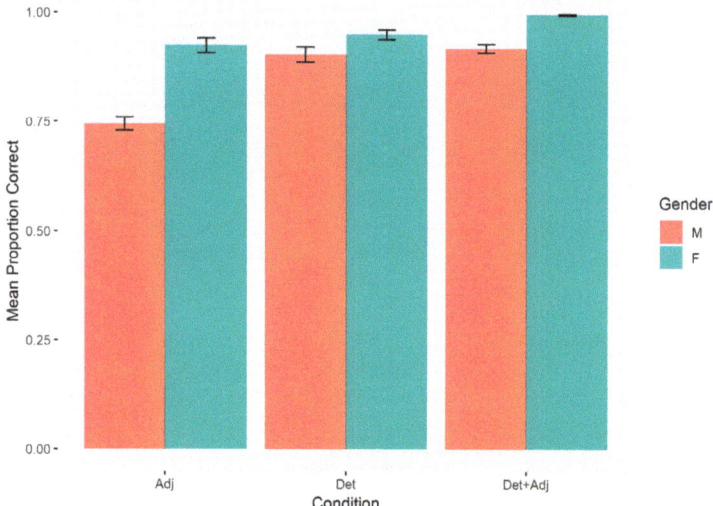

**Figure 2.** Mean proportion accuracy for the Papiamentu-dominant group. Error bars represent +/− 1 Standard Error of the Mean. Condition is plotted on the horizontal axis. Adj = adjective, Det = determiner, Det + Adj = determiner + adjective, M = masculine, F = feminine.

### 3.3. Spanish-Dominant Group

For the Spanish-dominant group (n = 6), the model revealed a main effect for Condition (F[2,10] = 4.147, $p = 0.049$) and a significant interaction between Condition and Gender (F[2,10] = 18.296, $p < 0.001$). No main effect was detected for Gender. We again conducted pairwise comparisons using Tukey's test. Only the contrast between masculine-marked determiners and adjectives was significant (difference = −0.494, t = −3.25, $p = 0.031$). This contrast indicates that the Spanish-dominant group was less accurate in rejecting Spanish-like masculine-marked features when manipulated on the determiner and more accurate with masculine-marked adjectives. All other contrasts were not significant (ps > 0.35). Results are plotted in Figure 3.

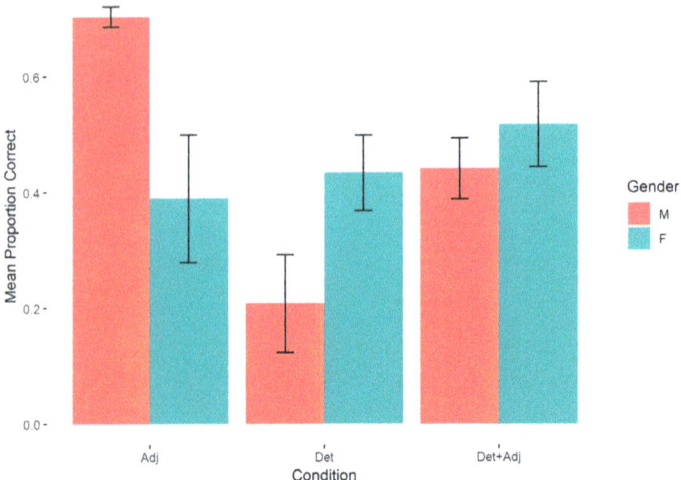

**Figure 3.** Mean proportion accuracy for the Spanish-dominant group. Error bars represent +/− 1 Standard Error of the Mean. Condition is plotted on the horizontal axis. Adj = adjective, Det = determiner, Det + Adj = determiner + adjective, M = masculine, F = feminine.

### 3.4. Heritage Spanish-Papiamentu Group

For the Spanish heritage speaker group (n = 6), the statistical model only found a marginal effect for Gender ($F[1,5] = 5.044$, $p = 0.075$) and no main effect for Condition or interaction between Condition and Gender. The marginal effect is reflected on the overall lower accuracy on masculine-marked trials as depicted in Figure 4.

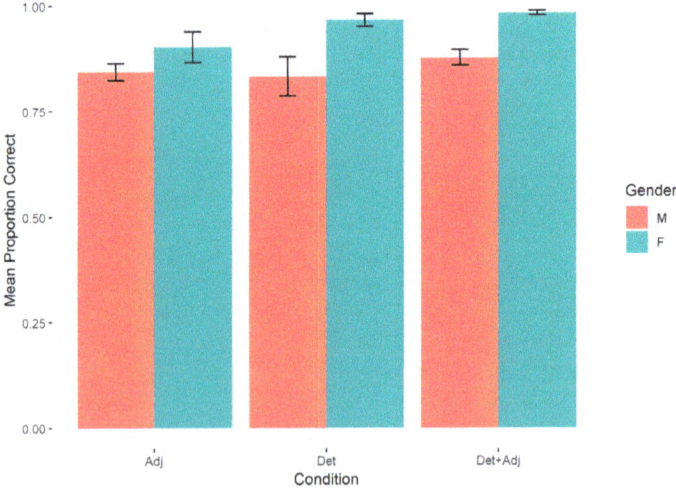

**Figure 4.** Mean proportion accuracy for the Spanish Heritage Spanish (HS)-Papiamentu group. Error bars represent +/− 1 Standard Error of the Mean. Condition is plotted on the horizontal axis. Adj = adjective, Det = determiner, Det + Adj = determiner + adjective, M = masculine, F = feminine.

## 4. Discussion

Most L2 acquisition studies that focus on how grammatical gender is acquired by speakers of a non-gendered language have shown that acquisition of gender assignment and agreement is difficult. Similar to Lipski (2015), we have shown that this difficulty is bidirectional. That is, in cases where the L2 speaker must suppress gender, gender interference can happen. This is especially the case in highly cognate languages that differ in whether they encode grammatical gender. Spanish-dominant speakers experienced the greatest interference of Spanish gender features in Papiamentu. However, the Dutch-dominant group also scored lower in rejecting Spanish gender features as compared to Papiamentu-dominant and Spanish HS-Papiamentu groups, possibly indicating that the presence of gender in Dutch also played a role (Sabourin and Stowe 2008). At the same time, Spanish HSs were better than Spanish-dominant speakers at suppressing gender interference. This suggests that going from a dominant language with gender to a language without gender is harder than suppressing gender from a less-dominant language.

Regarding interference according to word type (determiners and adjectives), the general tendency is to experience more interference with Determiners as compared to Adjectives (Dutch-dominant, Spanish-dominant, Heritage Spanish-Papiamentu). Speculatively, this difference may be due to the salience of determiners vs. adjectives as adjectives are also lexical (i.e., semantic) elements. From a syntactic point of view, determiners typically introduce the phrases in which they appear and have a fixed position. Abney (1987) posited in his "DP hypothesis" that the head of a nominal phrase is a determiner, D, rather than a noun (N). Under this account, determiners do not occupy the Specifier position of the NP. Instead, the determiner is the head of the DP. Attributive adjectives, on the other hand, have a more flexible order and are dependent on the noun, usually being treated as adjuncts.

As for interference related to gender (masculine vs. feminine), the results generally point towards greater interference on words marked with a Spanish masculine feature (-o) compared to Spanish feminine (-a), the exception being feminine-marked adjectives in the Spanish group. This was not surprising given the status of feminine as marked gender in Spanish and masculine as default (Harris 1991). In other words, the surfacing of feminine-marked morphemes is likely to be more salient and, subsequently, more easily rejected by our participants.

Moving away from the phenomenon under investigation, we see an interesting parallel with the current results and our own prior research on code-switching between gendered and non-gendered languages and the use of the analogical criterion vs. the default gender strategy. Across different language pairs and bilingual communities, the analogical criterion strategy (i.e., transfer of gender assignment to non-gendered language) seems to be absent from speakers who are not Spanish L1 speakers (cf. (Bellamy et al. 2018) for Purepecha-Spanish bilinguals), while L1 Spanish speakers seem more likely to follow the analogical criterion (see (Liceras et al. 2008) for Spanish-English or (Munarriz et al. 2019) for Basque-Spanish). At the same time, certain bilingual communities may also settle on specific code-switching patterns. For example, Valdés Kroff (2016) observed that Spanish-English bilinguals in Miami tend to use masculine as default, and Królikowska et al. (2019) compared the gender assignment patterns of four Spanish-English bilingual populations and observed that the more the bilinguals engaged in code-switching, the greater the tendency to assign the default masculine gender to mixed nominal constructions. Thus, the observed differences in gender assignment strategies across communities and language pairs may be due to a combination of proficiency and environmental factors, which we believe are factors that also play a greater role in the current study and should more explicitly be addressed in future studies.

We especially acknowledge that proficiency in Papiamentu may have played a role in our current results. It is perhaps not surprising that those groups who arguably have the highest proficiency in Papiamentu (Papiamentu-dominant and Heritage Spanish-Papiamentu) are least likely to experience gender interference, although we predicted greater interference for the latter group. Nevertheless, The Dutch-dominant group experienced greater interference despite their arguably weaker proficiency in Spanish. One speculative account for this finding is due to the presence of grammatical gender in Dutch, even though the system is quite different (see Supplementary Materials). However, both Spanish and Dutch have binary gender systems, and both have default genders (masculine in Spanish, common in Dutch). Finally, one limitation of the current study are the small sample sizes for three of our groups. We are currently collecting data from a population of Papiamentu speakers in the Netherlands (where Spanish is not common) to test whether Spanish gender interference would be reduced. However, this may in turn augment possible Dutch gender interference.

What is noteworthy is that we observe a similar entrenchment effect of L1 Spanish gender across (i) code-switching studies in different bilingual populations, (ii) Lipski's (2015, 2017) studies on Palenquero-Spanish, and (iii) our current study on Papiamentu-Spanish. The state of the research to date calls for further studies to be able to determine both the theoretical and empirical implications of our findings.

**Supplementary Materials:** The following are available online at http://www.mdpi.com/2226-471X/4/4/78/s1, Dutch Grammatical Gender, Table S1: Participant group characteristics from the Language History Questionnaire.

**Author Contributions:** Conceptualization, J.R.V.K., F.R. and M.C.P.C.; Methodology, J.R.V.K., F.R. and M.C.P.C.; Software, J.R.V.K., F.R. and M.C.P.C.; Validation, J.R.V.K., F.R. and M.C.P.C.; Formal Analysis, J.R.V.K.; Investigation, F.R.; Resources, F.R. and M.C.P.C.; Data Curation, F.R.; Writing-Original Draft Preparation, J.R.V.K., F.R. and M.C.P.C.; Writing-Review & Editing, J.R.V.K., F.R. and M.C.P.C.; Visualization, J.R.V.K.; Supervision, M.C.P.C.; Project Administration, J.R.V.K., F.R. and M.C.P.C.; Funding Acquisition, N/A.

**Conflicts of Interest:** The authors declare no conflict of interest.

## Appendix A

**Table A1.** Experimental materials used in the study.

| Stimuli | Condition | Translation | Gender |
|---|---|---|---|
| Mi amigunan tin un banjo *koró* [1]. | Adj | My friends have a red bathroom. | M |
| E kamisa tin hopi boton *koró*. | Adj | The shirt has many red buttons. | M |
| E mucha a disidí ku nos mester traha *una* pisina *rondá* di e buraku. | Det + Adj | The child decided that we had to make a round swimming pool out of the well. | F |
| *El* kurason a kuminsá bati masha lihé. | Det | The heart started beating faster. | M |
| *El* ehérsito semper tabata *armó*. | Det + Adj | The army was always armed. | M |
| *Las* islanan ta *chikita*. | Det + Adj | The islands are small. | F |
| *Las* bentananan habrí ta bunita. | Det | The open windows are beautiful. | F |
| *Las* bòternan ta será ku un tapa temporal. | Det | The bottles are closed with a temporary cork. | F |
| Mi primu semper ta bebe biña *koró*. | Adj | My cousin always drinks red wine. | M |
| Kada djadumingu nos ta bai na misa *blanka*. | Adj | Every Sunday we go to the white church. | F |
| E stranheronan ta bebe serbesnan bon *fria*. | Adj | The foreigners are drinking nice cold beers. | F |
| *Las* palombanan *preta* ta kome pan. | Det + Adj | The black pigeons are eating bread. | F |
| Einan mester a bende *los* piskánan. | Det | They sold the fish. | M |
| E mucha hòmber ta bisti un sombré *chikito*. | Adj | The boy is wearing a small hat. | M |
| *Las* baiskelnan tin *una* kadena korá. | Det | The bicycles have a red chain. | F |
| *Los* brasanan di e señora ta *blanko*. | Det + Adj | The arms of the woman are white. | M |
| *La* pluma *blanka* ta suave. | Det + Adj | The white feather is soft. | M |
| *Los* kangreunan ta kome e piedra. | Det | The crabs are eating the stone. | M |
| E eksibishon tin *una* pintura *preta*. | Det + Adj | The exhibition has a black painting. | F |
| Mi ta stima *el* aros *blanko*. | Det + Adj | I love the white rice. | M |
| *Los* paranan *chikito* ta kanta *bunito*. | Det + Adj | The small birds are singing beautifully. | M |
| Mi amigu tin *una* kara *rondá*. | Det + Adj | My friend has a round face. | F |
| *Los* pannan *preto* no ta dushi. | Det + Adj | The black loaves are not delicious. | M |
| Mi bisiña tin un kabai *preto*. | Adj | My neighbor has a black horse. | M |
| E hembra ta yuda brui *los* webunan. | Det | The female helps breading the eggs. | M |
| Den *la* kaha *korá*, e hòmber a haña algun potrèt. | Det + Adj | The man found a picture in the red box. | F |
| *Una* bela *blanka* a paga durante e seremonia. | Det + Adj | The white candle went out during the ceremony. | F |
| Mi tin un mapa *koró* di mundu. | Adj | I have a red world map. | M |
| *Las* uñanan di mi bisiña ta *preta*. | Det + Adj | The nails of my neighbor are black. | F |

**Table A1.** *Cont.*

| Stimuli | Condition | Translation | Gender |
|---|---|---|---|
| Mi a kumpra *una* mesa *rondá*. | Det + Adj | I bought a round table. | F |
| *Los* sapatunan tin furu *preto*. | Det + Adj | The shoes have black lining. | M |
| Nos ta respetá *las* banderanan komo un símbolo nashonal. | Det | We respect the flags as a national symbol. | F |
| *Las* kamisanan *blanka* ta grandi. | Det + Adj | The white shirts are large. | F |
| Kòrsou tin hopi playa *turístika*. | Adj | Curaçao has many touristic beaches. | F |
| Mi ruman tin un kurpa *delegó*. | Adj | My brother has a skinny body. | M |
| *Los* avionnan ta *chikito*. | Det + Adj | The airplanes are small. | M |
| Mi ofisina ta un edifisio *koró*. | Adj | My office is a red building. | M |
| Ayera mi a kumpra kuminda *spañá*. | Adj | Yesterday I bought Spanish food. | F |

[1] Items in italics were experimentally manipulated to exhibit Spanish-like gender agreement. Det = Determiner, Adj = Adjective, M = masculine, F = Feminine.

## References

Abney, Steven Paul. 1987. The English Noun Phrase in Its Sentential Aspect. Ph.D. thesis, MIT, Cambridge, MA, USA.

Bellamy, Kate, M. Carmen Parafita Couto, and Hans Stadthagen-González. 2018. Investigating Gender Assignment Strategies in Mixed Purepecha–Spanish Nominal Constructions. *Languages* 3: 28. [CrossRef]

Boersma, Paul, and David Weenink. 2012. Praat: Doing Phonetics by Computer [Computer Program]. Version 5.3.16. Available online: http://www.praat.org/ (accessed on 18 September 2019).

Eddington, David. 2002. Spanish gender assignment in an analogical framework. *Journal of Quantitative Linguistics* 9: 49–75. [CrossRef]

Grüter, Theres, Casey Lew-Williams, and Anne Fernald. 2012. Grammatical gender in L2: A production or real-time processing problem? *Second Language Research* 28: 191–215. [CrossRef] [PubMed]

Harris, James W. 1991. The Exponence of Gender in Spanish. *Linguistic Inquiry* 22: 27–62.

Hopp, Holger. 2013. Grammatical gender in adult L2 acquisition: Relations between lexical and syntactic variability. *Second Language Research* 29: 33–56. [CrossRef]

Kester, Ellen-Petra. 2011. Language use, language attitudes and identity among Curaçaoan high school students. In *Continuity, Divergence and Convergence in Language, Culture and Society on the ABC-Islands*. Edited by Nicholas Faraclas, Ronald Severing, Christa Weijer and Elisabeth Echteld. Willemstad: Fundashon di Planifikashon di Idioma, pp. 25–38.

Królikowska, Marta Anna, Emma Bierings, Anne L. Beatty-Martínez, Christian Navarro-Torres, Paola E. Dussias, and M. Carmen Parafita Couto. 2019. Gender-assignment strategies within the bilingual determiner phrase: four Spanish-English communities examined. Paper presented at the 3rd Conference on Bilingualism in the Hispanic and Lusophone World (BHL), Leiden, The Netherlands, January 9–11.

Liceras, Juana M., Raquel Fernández Fuertes, Susana Perales, Rocío Pérez-Tattam, and Kenton Todd Spradlin. 2008. Gender and gender agreement in bilingual native and non-native grammars: A view from child and adult functional-lexical mixings. *Lingua* 118: 827–51. [CrossRef]

Lipski, John. 2015. From 'more' to 'less': Spanish, Palenquero (Afro-Colombian creole) and gender agreement. *Language, Cognition and Neuroscience* 30: 1144–55. [CrossRef]

Lipski, John. 2017. Does gender agreement carry a production cost? Spanish gender vs. Palenquero. In *Romance Languages and Linguistic Theory 12: Selected papers from the 45th Linguistic Symposium on Romance Languages (LSRL)*. Edited by Ruth E.V. Lopes, Juanito Ornelas de Avelar and Sonia M. L. Cyrino. Campinas: John Benjamins Publishing Company, pp. 127–40.

Montrul, Silvina. 2004. *The Acquisition of Spanish: Morphosyntactic Development in Monolingual and Bilingual L1 Acquisition*. Amsterdam: John Benjamins.

Montrul, Silvina, Rebecca Foote, and Silvia Perpiñán. 2008. Gender agreement in adult second language learners and Spanish heritage speakers: The effects of age and context in acquisition. *Language Learning* 58: 503–53. [CrossRef]

Munarriz, Amaia, Varun de Castro Arrazola, M. Carmen Parafita Couto, and María José Ezeizabarrena. 2019. Gender in the production of Spanish-Basque mixed nominal constructions. Paper presented at the 3rd Conference on Bilingualism in the Hispanic and Lusophone World (BHL), Leiden, The Netherlands, January 9–11.

Muysken, Pieter. 2013. Language contact outcomes as the result of bilingual optimization strategies. *Bilingualism: Language and Cognition* 16: 709–30. [CrossRef]

Pablos, Leticia, M. Carmen Parafita Couto, Bastien Boutonnet, Amy de Jong, Marlou Perquin, Annelies de Haan, and Niels O. Schiller. 2019. Adjecitve-noun order in Papiamento-Dutch code-switching. *Linguistic Approaches to Bilingualism* 9: 710–735. [CrossRef]

Sabourin, Laura, and Laurie A. Stowe. 2008. Second language processing: When are first and second language processed similarly? *Second Language Research* 24: 397–430. [CrossRef]

Valdés Kroff, Jorge. 2016. Mixed NPs in Spanish–English bilingual speech: Using a corpus-based approach to inform models of sentence processing. In *Spanish–English Code-Switching in the Caribbean and the US*. Edited by Rosa E. Guzzardo Tamargo, Catherine M. Mazak and M. Carmen Parafita Couto. Amsterdam: John Benjamins, pp. 281–300.

© 2019 by the authors. Licensee MDPI, Basel, Switzerland. This article is an open access article distributed under the terms and conditions of the Creative Commons Attribution (CC BY) license (http://creativecommons.org/licenses/by/4.0/).

Article

# The Linguistic Landscape of the Valencian Community: A Comparative Analysis of Bilingual and Multilingual Signs in Three Different Areas

Lucía Bellés-Calvera

Department of History, Geography and Art, Universitat Jaume I, 12071 Castelló de la Plana, Spain; lucia.belles@uji.es

Received: 10 May 2019; Accepted: 12 June 2019; Published: 16 June 2019

**Abstract:** During the last decades, the promotion of multilingualism has been key when designing linguistic policies in Europe. Previous research studies have focused on how languages are employed in fields such as education, media, and urban sites, among others. Bearing all this in mind, the aim of this paper is to analyse the linguistic landscapes of three municipalities located in a bilingual region in Spain, that of the Valencian Community. Thus, issues such as language contact, language dominance, and the languages used by a number of institutions on private and public signs were examined. As for the method, over 140 pictures of language signs were taken in order to examine language contact, language dominance, and the influence of official and foreign languages on private and public signs. The results suggest that the presence of languages may vary depending on the population living in these settings, the citizens' mother tongue, and the policy regarding the minority language. The findings also indicate that the power of the two co-official languages is reinforced by public signs, whereas rich linguistic diversity is shown in private signs. All in all, it can be stated that the linguistic policy in the Valencian Community is not homogeneous throughout the region.

**Keywords:** linguistic landscape; minority language; bilingualism; multilingualism; language contact

## 1. Introduction

In recent years, official institutions have regulated linguistic policies dealing with the protection of minority languages (European Parliament 2017) and the introduction of foreign languages within a given territory, particularly in Europe (European Commission 2015). In this sense, bilingual and multilingual phenomena may occur in the linguistic landscape of an area.

This concept has been regarded as the "language of public road signs, advertising billboards, street names, place names, commercial shop signs, and public signs on government buildings which is combined to form the linguistic landscape of a given territory, region, or urban agglomeration" (Landry and Bourhis 1997, p. 25). These signs may be categorised into top-down or bottom-up depending on their nature. Top-down signs are those which have official status since they are issued by the government, whereas bottom-up signs are nonofficial signs regulated by private organisations or individuals.

Previous research studies have acknowledged bilingual and multilingual practices in urban sites (Cenoz and Gorter 2006; Gorter 2006; Huebner 2006; Ben-Rafael et al. 2006; Shohamy et al. 2010). Gorter (2006) compared the linguistic landscape of two commercial streets set in Basque Country and The Netherlands, giving special emphasis to the use of the minority language. The case study about multilingualism in some Israeli cities was based on the use of Hebrew, Arabic, and English on public and private signs, also known as top-down and bottom-up signs, respectively (Ben-Rafael et al. 2006). Another major contribution by Huebner (2006) explored language mixing in Bangkok.

This paper focuses on language contact, language dominance, and the languages used on the private and public signs of three municipalities located in the Valencian Community: Benasal, Almazora, and Valencia.

Benasal, a small village set in the Castellón province, is a traditional Valencian-speaking area where most individuals have Valencian as their mother tongue. Its economy is mainly based on rural tourism and pig farming as well as on cheese and meat production.

Almazora is a town located in the southeast of the Castellón province. Even though Valencian has been the predominant language of the area, the linguistic repertoire of the city has increased due to several factors. These include waves of immigration in past decades as well as the promotion of Almazora as a tourist destination.

Valencia, which is the capital city of the Valencian Community and the third largest city in Spain, has roughly 1.6 million inhabitants. Unlike Benasal and Almazora, in Valencia most individuals have Spanish as their mother tongue. As it is one of the most popular tourist destinations in Spain, a wide range of nationalities and languages can be found in the area.

That being said, the languages of this study are not limited to the national and regional languages, but other foreign languages are also considered. Thus, the languages included in this study are Valencian—a dialectal variety of Catalan—as a minority language, Spanish as the official language of the state, English as the language of international communication, and other languages.

The objective of this study is twofold. On the one hand, the linguistic landscape of rural and urban settings is examined to determine the number of languages displayed as well as how the power and status of minority, national, and international languages are portrayed in these urban and rural settings. On the other hand, the study of these linguistic landscapes is aimed at examining how the coexistence of several languages may have an influence on language use.

The current paper departs from the following hypotheses:

(a) The linguistic landscape of Benasal portrays the preference of the Valencian language in monolingual and bilingual signs set up by local and regional authorities. The opposite occurs in the private sector, where Spanish is the language of communication.

(b) The linguistic landscape of Almazora is more likely to have bilingual and multilingual patterns in official and nonofficial signs, where Valencian is the dominant language. As to bottom-up signs, bilingual or multilingual instances are not likely to be identified given that Spanish is the preferred language.

(c) The linguistic landscape of Valencia is likely to have Spanish as the dominant language in monolingual, bilingual, and multilingual signs issued by official institutions. Similarly, most bilingual and monolingual signs are in Spanish, followed by English due to its prestige as an international language. On the contrary, Valencian-only signs may not appear on private enterprises.

The relevance of this research has to do with the implementation of language policies in urban and rural settings. The findings indicate that citizens' and tourists' origins may not only differ, but they also shape official and nonofficial language policies.

## 2. Method

*2.1. Materials*

As for the method, a corpus was developed for this study. The linguistic landscape of three municipalities was examined to address existing issues in urban and rural areas related to language contact, language dominance, and the distribution of official and foreign languages on private and public signs. To achieve this goal, a total of 185 pictures was collected. Some bottom-up signs were analysed as a combination of monolingual, bilingual, and multilingual signs since they belonged to the same business.

## 2.2. Procedure

A coding scheme (based on Shohamy et al. 2010) was developed for this study. The variables included to codify the different pictures have to do with the number of languages, language and power relations, and the public or private origin of the signs.

Drawing on Ben-Rafael et al. (2006) classification the data were categorised in top-down and bottom-up signs (see Table 1). Top-down signs are official signs regulated by public institutions, whether national, regional, or local. These items were sub-classified as religious, educational, cultural, medical, or governmental. On the contrary, bottom-up signs are issued by private institutions; professionals can choose their brand language. The sub-categories analysed in the bottom-up signs were shops, bars, restaurants and cafés, academies, and billboards.

**Table 1.** Coding scheme.

| Category | Type of Item | Language |
|---|---|---|
| Top-down | Religious: churches, chapels | Monolingual, bilingual and multilingual |
| | Cultural: tourist and historical areas | |
| | Medical: outpatient clinic | |
| | Governmental: street names, traffic signs, schools | |
| Bottom-up | Shops: food, clothing | Monolingual bilingual and multilingual |
| | Bars, restaurants, and cafés | |
| | Academies | |
| | Billboards | |

## 3. Results

The results of the study concerning the languages displayed on signs, language dominance, and language contact are now considered.

### 3.1. Linguistic Repertoire

#### 3.1.1. Top-Down Signs

Concerning Benasal, nearly 72% of top-down signs are monolingual, either in Valencian or in Spanish. They are unequally spread over the village. As can be observed in cultural and religious buildings, the frequency of Valencian (44%) in monolingual signs is higher than that of Spanish (28%) (Figure 1).

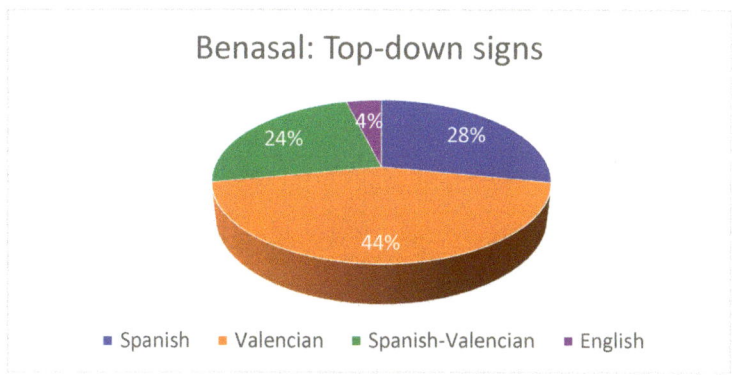

**Figure 1.** Benasal: Top-down signs.

Clear examples in Valencian include religious and historical buildings such as chapels (e.g., Capella de la Puríssima) and castles (e.g., *Castell de la Mola* 'Mola's castle'), respectively (Figures 2 and 3). On the contrary, monolingual signs in Spanish involve its well-known spa (Figure 4) and other historical signs (Figure 5). In some cases, tourists and locals are provided with a detailed explanation of the sites.

**Figure 2.** Benasal: Valencian-only sign on a castle.

**Figure 3.** Benasal: Valencian-only sign on a chapel.

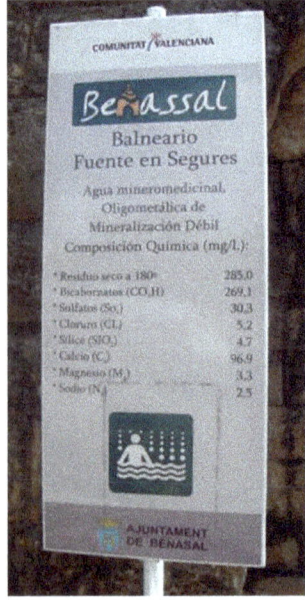

**Figure 4.** Benasal: Spanish-only sign on a spa.

**Figure 5.** Benasal: Spanish-only historical sign.

The different linguistic policies that have been implemented since the 20th century have had an impact on the linguistic landscape of Benasal. When it comes to governmental signs, monolingual and bilingual street names were identified (Figures 6–8).

**Figure 6.** Benasal: Spanish-only street name.

**Figure 7.** Benasal: Bilingual street name.

**Figure 8.** Benasal: Valencian-only street name.

As can be seen above, the number of languages in bilingual signs (24%) is limited to Spanish and Valencian. Thus, the dominant language may vary depending on the time these governmental signs were issued. Evidence can be found in street names, plastic recycling containers (Figure 9), as well as in the Spanish postal service sign (i.e., *Correos* 'post office service') (Figure 10).

Figure 9. Benasal: Bilingual sign on a plastic recycling container.

Figure 10. Benasal: Bilingual sign on a post office document.

For most of the 20th century, the first linguistic policies promoted the use of Spanish (Figure 2). Towards the end of the 20th century the regional government regulated the languages included in bilingual signs. Figure 3 shows the power of Spanish over Valencian as it is the first language appearing on the top of the sign, whereas the opposite occurs in Figures 5 and 6. These latter seem to be more recent signs, as Valencian is the first language used in an attempt to preserve the village's local identity. At the beginning of the 21st century, there was a trend to foster the use of Valencian as the main language within that linguistic community. Despite this heterogeneous use of languages, it can be inferred that comprehension is not hindered.

Multilingual signs containing Spanish, Valencian, and English could not be found. So far, the English language is used once, as can be seen in the Tourist Info sign below (Figure 11). The main reasons for this have to do with a generational gap and tourists' origins. The proportion of elderly living in this village who did not have the opportunity to learn a foreign language is higher than the proportion of young people. In addition, tourism is primarily national and regional.

Figure 11. Benasal: English-only sign.

Focusing on Almazora, the vast majority of top-down signs are monolingual (92%) (Figure 12). Cultural, medical, and governmental monolingual signs show the overwhelming use of the Valencian language in this town (67%). Public spaces including the central market, a local infant school, a hermitage path, and a museum, among others, are all signed in Valencian.

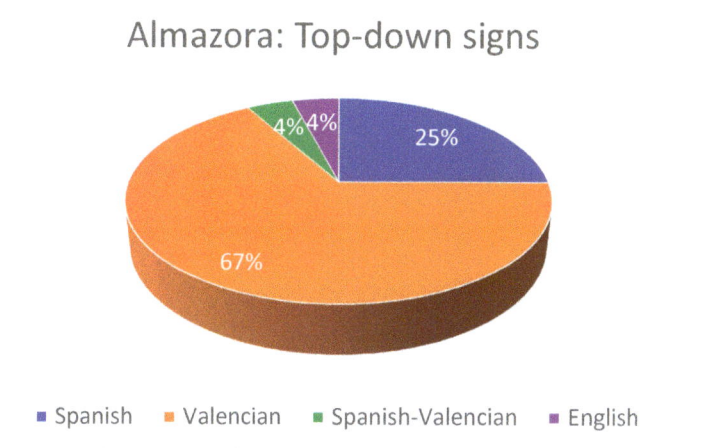

**Figure 12.** Almazora: Top-down signs.

The regional legislation of the Valencian Community states that Valencian-speaking areas should implement linguistic policies that boost exposure to the minority language. This initiative is key to making Valencian (67%) more visible than Spanish (25%). Such monolingual signs include traffic and medical signs that can be observed as a combination of signs. Clear examples involve an outpatient clinic where monolingual signs in Spanish and Valencian can be observed. More specifically, the language employed in the official name of this medical building is Valencian (Figure 13) rather than Spanish. However, Spanish is used to provide patients with general information of the healthcare fields offered in this area (Figure 14). In this sense, similar signs that aim at generating bilingual experiences are spread throughout the town.

**Figure 13.** Almazora: Valencian-only sign on an outpatient clinic.

**Figure 14.** Almazora: Spanish-only sign on an outpatient clinic.

Contrary to all expectations, the distribution of bilingual and multilingual signs is barely noticeable. As in Benasal, bilingual signs (4%) correspond to street names regulated by the town council, where Valencian is the dominant language (Figures 15 and 16). Even though there are no official signs where Spanish or Valencian are combined with other foreign languages, English is displayed in the monolingual Tourist Info sign.

**Figure 15.** Almazora: Bilingual street name.

**Figure 16.** Almazora: Bilingual street name.

Even though the population of the city by and large has Spanish as its mother tongue, policies have been developed to include the minority language. In the centre of Valencia, approximately 55% of the signs are monolingual (Figure 17). There seems to be a balance in the use of Spanish-only (22%) and Valencian-only (33%) items. Although both languages are co-official, Valencian is still the preferred language to preserve the identity of the city.

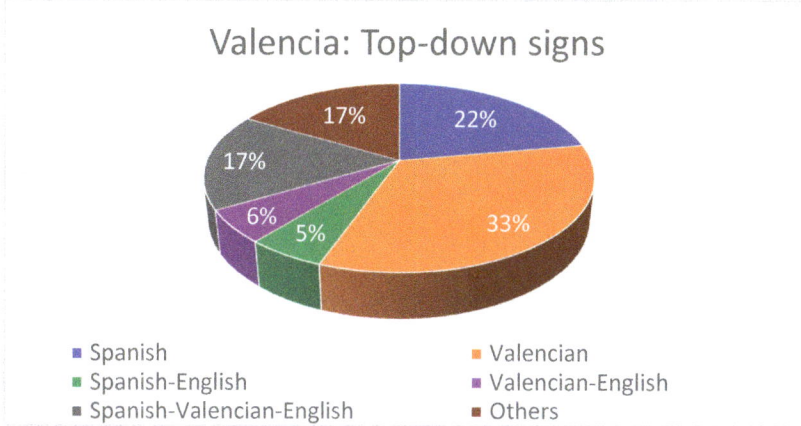

**Figure 17.** Valencia: Top-down signs.

Both languages can be found in historical, religious, and governmental signs. For instance, Valencian is the language displayed in the archaeological centre (Figure 18). By contrast, Spanish can be seen in the traders' market, which was declared a UNESCO World Heritage Site (Figure 19).

**Figure 18.** Valencia: Valencian-only sign on an archeological centre.

**Figure 19.** Valencia: Spanish-only sign on a traders' market.

The distribution of bilingual signs in Valencia (11%) is higher than in Almazora. As the centre of Valencia is an eminent tourist area, languages other than Spanish and Valencian are used, particularly English. Hence, it is possible to find bilingual signs combining Spanish and English, and Valencian and English. The sign in Figure 20 is predominantly for national and international tourists. The font size and colour are the same for both languages; however, Spanish seems to be the more powerful language as it is on the top.

**Figure 20.** Valencia: Spanish-English sign on a car park.

Figure 21 shows a governmental sign in Valencian and English. As can be observed, this is a combination of two signs. The sign on the top has to do with the name of the organisation, but the focus of this picture is on the sign below, where English is the first language appearing. It seems to be addressed to locals and international individuals who work with these languages on a regular basis, especially because it is a regional institution.

**Figure 21.** Valencia: Bilingual sign on an official institution.

Multilingualism (30%) in Valencia involves the use of Spanish, Valencian, and English (24%). The power relations established suggest that Spanish is the dominant language as it is the first language employed to address locals and tourists (Figure 22). The inclusion of the minority language involves the use of italics and a light colour, which makes it difficult to read. However, even though English is the third language, it can be read without difficulty.

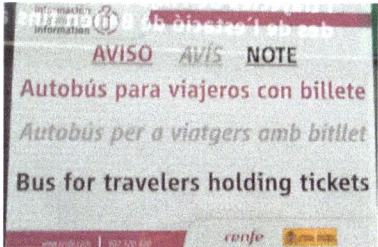

**Figure 22.** Valencia: Trilingual sign on a bus station.

Linguistic diversity is also determined by the presence of other international languages in multilingual signs (6%). Figure 23 below shows a wide range of languages including Spanish, Valencian, English, French, Italian, and German. The inclusion of these languages may be related to the main nationalities of the tourists who visit Valencia. The first three languages have the same font size, whereas the font size of the rest of the languages seems to be smaller.

**Figure 23.** Valencia: Multilingual sign on a traders' market.

3.1.2. Bottom-Up

Regarding bottom-up signs, clear differences can be found in terms of bilingual and multilingual patterns. In Benasal, a total of 67% of bottom-up signs are monolingual whilst the remaining 33% are bilingual signs (Figure 24).

## Benasal: Bottom-up signs

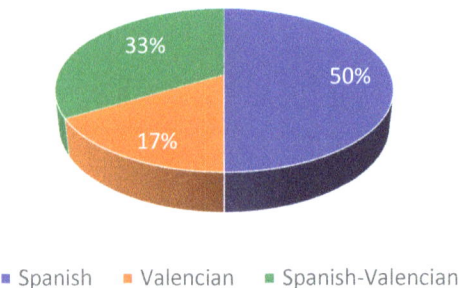

**Figure 24.** Benasal: Bottom-up signs.

Nonofficial signs in Benasal are characterised by the predominance of Spanish-only items (50%). The presence of Spanish in the private sector does not only have to do with the establishment of international companies but also with the opening of businesses that took place during the second half of the 20th century. This is the case of bakeries and bank offices whose brand name is in Spanish (Figures 25 and 26). Interestingly, the role of the Valencian language in the private sector is not as frequent as expected (17%).

**Figure 25.** Benasal: Spanish-only sign on a confectionery and candy store.

**Figure 26.** Benasal: Valencian-only sign on a bakery.

Bilingual signs are addressed to potential customers. Hence, local businesses try to develop appropriate communication strategies by addressing individuals in Spanish and Valencian. In Figures 27 and 28 there is no doubt that Valencian is the most relevant language, as it highlighted in bold, whereas its translation in Spanish may appear in italics and different colours.

Figure 27. Benasal: Bilingual sign on a butchery.

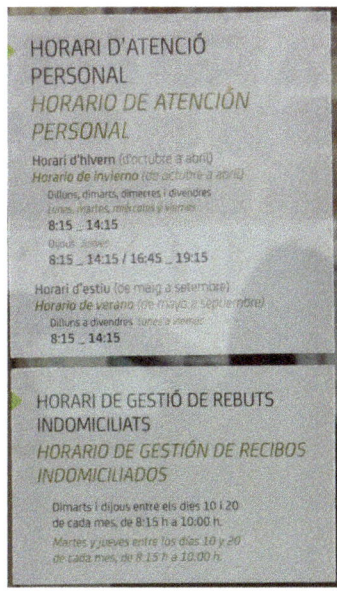

Figure 28. Benasal: Bilingual sign on a bank office.

Unlike in Benasal, there is no considerable differences in the use of Valencian-only (27%) and Spanish-only (23%) signs in Almazora (Figure 29). Valencian patterns are found in a variety of areas, such as architecture, podiatry, butchery, haberdashery, bakeries, and language academies, among others. Similarly, Spanish items can be identified in dentists, cafés, hairdressers, and butcheries.

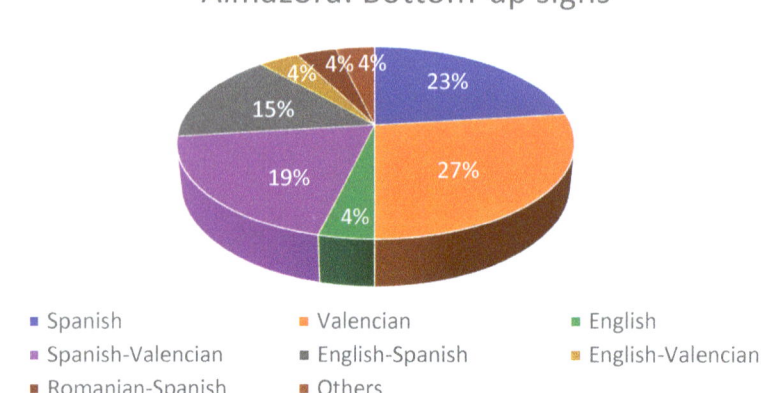

**Figure 29.** Almazora: Bottom-up signs.

The recurrent pattern in bilingual signs (42%) has to do with the two co-official languages of the region. Some shop names are in Valencian, but Spanish is the selected language to communicate additional information. Evidence can be found in health food (Figure 30) and stationery shops (Figure 31).

**Figure 30.** Almazora: Bilingual sign on a health food shop.

**Figure 31.** Almazora: Bilingual sign on a stationery shop.

Notwithstanding, bilingual signs in English-Valencian (4%), English-Spanish (15%), and Romanian-Spanish (4%) can be observed. English is the dominant language in the items below as English is the language of instruction in these language academies. In Figure 32, Valencian patterns seem to be smaller, whereas in Figure 33 Spanish is highlighted with a different colour and font size.

**Figure 32.** Almazora: English-Valencian sign on a language academy.

**Figure 33.** Almazora: English-Spanish sign on a language academy.

Figure 34 is a Romanian-Spanish sign. The flag and the shop name are Romanian rather than Spanish, which is used to attract the Romanian community living in Almazora as well as local customers. Other international languages such as Italian appear as the only language on certain signs (Figure 35).

**Figure 34.** Almazora: Romanian-Spanish sign on a butchery.

**Figure 35.** Almazora: Italian sign on a restaurant.

When it comes to Valencia, 65% of nonofficial signs are monolingual. The linguistic landscape of the city seems to be dominated by Spanish (26%), closely followed by Valencian (23%) and English (16%) (Figure 36).

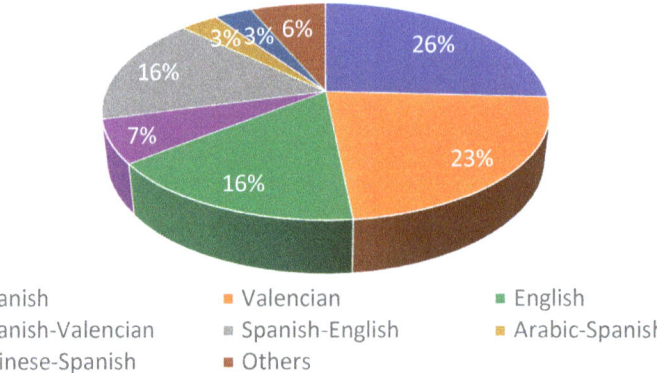

Figure 36. Valencia: Bottom-up signs.

The bilingual landscape (29%) in Valencia is determined by private initiatives, since they are concerned with strategic marketing decisions dealing with companies' international orientation. Taking this into account, the most predominant languages in bottom-up signs include Spanish, Valencian, and English. Figure 37 is a Spanish-English sign. As can be observed, the properties of the font-size employed in this bilingual item reveal that Spanish is the dominant language. Actually, the name of the bookshop, which is in English, is smaller.

Figure 37. Valencia: Spanish-English sign on a bookshop.

Efforts to promote the minority language have also been made by regional supermarkets, where products are signed in both co-official languages. No differences in terms of font properties are recognised, so it can be stated that Spanish and Valencian have the same status (Figure 38).

Figure 38. Valencia: Bilingual sign in a supermarket.

Other languages used in nonofficial signs are Arabic, Italian, and Chinese. A clear example is that of the Arabic butchery (Figure 39). The presence of both Arabic and Spanish indicates that the patrons of this business are local and Arabic communities. Nonetheless, the use of Arabic is limited to translate the Spanish name, with the latter also being used to describe the kind of products they offer.

**Figure 39.** Valencia: Arabic-Spanish sign on a butchery.

*3.2. Language Contact*

The co-existence of a number of languages in the same area may lead to language contact or mixing in terms of syntax and lexicon. This process can be observed in the three municipalities under study.

In Benasal, language contact occurs between Spanish and Valencian. Surprisingly, this phenomenon is observed in top-down signs, which are expected to be precise within the rules of the languages used. Thus, even though there exist signs that appear to be completely written in Spanish, some lexical items are introduced in Valencian. Despite having a Spanish version, the Valencian name is used in Figure 40. Another example is found in the laundry sign, where the century is described in the minority language (Figure 41).

**Figure 40.** Benasal: Language contact on a museum sign.

**Figure 41.** Benasal: Language contact on a laundry sign.

In Almazora, a different combination of languages can be recognised in bottom-up signs. For instance, the lexical borrowing 'stop' used in a driving school sign has been adapted to Spanish spelling (Figure 42). This is a strategy to catch potential users who would not pronounce the starting liquid "s", but would change the phonology of the term by adding an "e" sound.

**Figure 42.** Almazora: Language contact on a driving school sign.

The impact of bilingualism in the linguistic landscape can also be seen in Valencia. At a syntactic level, it can be seen how English rules are followed given that the Spanish adjective is placed before the noun (Figure 43).

**Figure 43.** Valencia: Language contact on a food shop sign.

## 4. Discussion and Conclusions

Focusing on the number of languages displayed on signs, several languages can be identified: Valencian as the minority language, Spanish as the national language, and other foreign languages. English is the most prestigious international language in Almazora and Valencia, which tends to appear alongside Spanish. In this sense, the use of English in top-down signs may have a communicative function with tourists, while its use in commercial signs evidences their international orientation, success, or sophistication (Piller 2003). Languages other than English, such as Arabic, Romanian, or Italian, which are only placed by private initiative, are less frequent and are limited to urban contexts. Thus, it can be inferred that if Arabic is used, it is likely to be a bottom-up sign set in areas where those linguistic communities live.

As to power and language relations, the findings show that the power of the two co-official languages is reinforced by public signs, whereas rich linguistic diversity is shown in private signs. All municipalities have Valencian as the most prominent language in top-down signs, followed by Spanish as the second language. In third place, the presence of English is barely noticeable in Benasal and Almazora in contrast to Valencia, where it plays a significant role in tourism. The order of languages differs when it comes to bottom-up signs. Spanish is strongly present in Benasal and Valencia as the first language, followed by Valencian and English, whereas Valencian is much more salient in Almazora, followed by Spanish and English. The prevailing pattern in Benasal and Almazora concerning bilingual items is Valencian-Spanish. Valencian is thus the dominant language in these small urban and rural settings. Unlike Benasal and Almazora, bilingual patterns show that Spanish is the recurrent language in both official and nonofficial signs.

Language mixing occurs in areas where multiple languages coexist. Borrowing and adaptation from one language to another are found at lexical and syntactical levels. The fact that such a phenomenon is observed in official signs may reflect the need for local authorities to preserve their identity. In bottom-up signs, the incorporation of these traits is designed to attract potential clients by stressing their international and sophisticated status (Piller 2003).

All things considered, even though the weaker or stronger presence of Valencian in private and public institutions depends on whether Spanish or Valencian is the most predominant language in a certain area (Statute of Autonomy of the Region of Valencia), it seems that the linguistic policy is not implemented homogeneously. The languages displayed on signs have an impact on society's perception and attitudes towards them. Further research on the linguistic landscape of the Valencian Community is needed to determine the efficiency of its regional language policy.

**Funding:** This research received no external funding.

**Conflicts of Interest:** The author declares no conflict of interest.

## References

Ben-Rafael, Eliezer, Elana Shohamy, Muhammad Hasan Amara, and Nira Trumper-Hecht. 2006. Linguistic landscape as symbolic construction of the public space: The case of Israel. *International Journal of Multilingualism* 3: 7–30. [CrossRef]

Cenoz, Jasone, and Durk Gorter. 2006. Linguistic landscape and minority languages. *International Journal of Multilingualism* 3: 67–80. [CrossRef]

European Commission. 2015. Language Teaching and Learning in Multilingual Classrooms. *Education and Training*. Available online: http://ec.europa.eu/dgs/education_culture/repository/languages/library/studies/multilingual-classroom_en.pdf (accessed on 6 May 2019).

European Parliament. 2017. *Research for CULT Committee—Minority Languages and Education: Best Practices and Pitfalls*. Available online: http://www.europarl.europa.eu/RegData/etudes/STUD/2017/585915/IPOL_STU(2017)585915_EN.pdf (accessed on 6 May 2019).

Gorter, Durk, ed. 2006. *Linguistic Landscape: A New Approach to Multilingualism*. Bristol: Multilingual Matters.

Huebner, Thom. 2006. Bangkok's linguistic landscapes: Environmental print, codemixing and language change. *International Journal of Multilingualism* 3: 31–51. [CrossRef]

Landry, Rodrigue, and Richard Y. Bourhis. 1997. Linguistic landscape and ethnolinguistic vitality: An empirical study. *Journal of Language and Social Psychology* 16: 23–49. [CrossRef]

Piller, Ingrid. 2003. 10. Advertising as a site of language contact. *Annual Review of Applied Linguistics* 23: 170–83. [CrossRef]

Shohamy, Elana Goldberg, Eliezer Ben-Rafael, and Monica Barni, eds. 2010. *Linguistic Landscape in the City*. Bristol: Multilingual Matters.

© 2019 by the author. Licensee MDPI, Basel, Switzerland. This article is an open access article distributed under the terms and conditions of the Creative Commons Attribution (CC BY) license (http://creativecommons.org/licenses/by/4.0/).

*Article*

# The Role of Language Policy Documents in the Internationalisation of Multilingual Higher Education: An Exploratory Corpus-Based Study

Rosana Villares

Department of English and German Studies, University of Zaragoza, 50009 Zaragoza, Spain; rosanavillares92@gmail.com

Received: 13 May 2019; Accepted: 11 July 2019; Published: 15 July 2019

**Abstract:** Using corpus methods, this study explores the role of Language Policy (LP) documents in the internationalisation process of Spanish universities. It aims at understanding how non-Anglophone universities integrate English and local languages in the functions of education, research, and administration. Content analysis was used for the identification of key themes, and discourse analysis examined how those themes were textually expressed. Consistent with previous literature, this study shows that relevant strategic areas of LP deal with training, regulation, accreditation, and support measures. Results also highlight the role played by institutions in LP and the presence of language hierarchies between English and local languages. The discussion of these findings leads to further inquiry of mismatches between top-down institutional expectations and bottom-up realities regarding the design and implementation of institutional policies.

**Keywords:** language policy; higher education; internationalisation; discourse analysis; language diversity; language attitudes; English linguistic imperialism; Spanish universities

## 1. Introduction

Over the last decades, internationalisation, regarded as an indicator of excellence and quality, has become one of the main strategic objectives of universities worldwide (EHEA 2015; Maringe and Foskett 2010). Following European recommendations (European Commission 2010, 2013), the national strategy for the internationalisation of Spanish universities 2015–2020 (MECD 2014) is based on four main pillars: The consolidation of a strong national university system, the increase of the international attractiveness of the university system, the creation of international competitive universities, and the promotion of cooperation with other regions of the world (MECD 2014). The actions proposed to achieve these objectives tend to focus on mobility, international collaboration, and the development of language-related initiatives, such as the implementation of English-medium instruction (EMI) that foster the international and multilingual profile of universities (Wächter and Maiworm 2014).

Ferguson (2010) or Hultgren (2014), among others, have noted that there is a direct correlation between internationalisation and the use of English, which is considered to be the academic lingua franca for international communication. This hegemonic position of English is also supported by the concept of language hierarchy that classifies languages according to a series of given values and functions. Within this hierarchy, English holds the position of a 'hypercentral' language, thus becoming a global lingua franca (de Swaan 2001). This situation is encountered in many contexts, yet the Spanish sociolinguistic landscape presents some special characteristics. On the one hand, Spanish as the national official language holds the status of an international language with Spanish-speaking Latin American countries that works as an attractive factor for those interested in the Spanish culture and language (MECD 2014; SEPIE 2017). On the other hand, regional co-official languages are promoted in universities located in bilingual regions. Thus, the introduction of a powerful foreign language brings certain challenges that are generally addressed in Language Policy documents (LP), tools whose purpose is the regulation of languages in specific contexts and domains (Spolsky 2012). Currently, it is possible to track multiple studies on students and academics' language practices and beliefs towards English and multilingualism in universities (e.g., Fortanet-Gómez 2012; Hultgren 2014; Pérez-Llantada 2018; Soler-Carbonell and Karaoglu 2015), but, to the best of my knowledge, there seems to be a lack of critical studies on the role held by policy documents regulating language(s) use in the Spanish national context.

This paper aims to explore how non-Anglophone universities integrate English and the local languages in their LP documents to become more internationalised and to match bottom-up practices. For this task, the following research questions will be addressed:

RQ1 Do LP documents share similar language concerns to those stated in the national LP (CRUE 2017)?
RQ2 What is the role played by institutional agents in the implementation of LP?
RQ3 How is the relationship between English and the local languages discursively expressed?

## 2. Methodology

The corpus compiled for this study included 37 institutional LP documents created between 2001 and 2018 from 29 Spanish universities. Depending on the origin of the LP, the documents were written in Spanish or in the co-official language of the region—Catalan, Valencian, or Galician. Several analytical approaches were used to analyse the documents following Bocanegra-Valle (2017). Content analysis and inductive coding were carried out using the qualitative software Atlas.ti v8 to identify key themes and strategic areas in the LP documents. Discourse analytical techniques were used to examine the way institutional actors presented themselves, their roles and responsibilities in the creation of LP, and the discursive strategies the authors of these documents used to align with their readers' opinions. Lastly, a comparative analysis was carried out to describe the English language in contrast to the local languages.

## 3. Results

### 3.1. Strategic Actions

Similar to the recommendations included in the Spanish national LP created for higher education (CRUE 2017), the corpus findings pointed out to the following strategic areas as recurrent concerns in LP: Language training, language regulation, language accreditation, and support measures. It was found that the majority of the strategies were related to the dimension of training and aimed at increasing university members' language competence by means of language courses and innovative methodologies—the latter addressed to the teaching staff so they could acquire teaching techniques that adapt contents and communicative styles when teaching in a foreign language. Other initiatives referred to the possibility to participate in extra-curricular activities that promoted language learning outside the classroom. International trends, such as those stated by Wächter and Maiworm (2014), were also present in the form of modules taught in a foreign language or co-official language in undergraduate and graduate degrees.

From the content analysis, it became evident that there was a common agreement on the need to regulate language use, especially in those areas where more than one language could compete for the same functions. LP was described as the most suitable tool to organise and regulate language choice and language use, a tool also fostered by European institutions to promote multilingualism and internationalisation (European Commission 2012). References to language regulation highlighted the recurrent concept of 'linguistic security', which referred to both the LP's general objective of communicating the language initiatives taking place at the university, as well as the specific objective of informing university members about language use in particular settings. For example, in the case of

EMI courses and bilingual teaching programs, information regarding the vehicular language used in the classroom should be available to students before the enrolment period.

The third dimension dealt with the accreditation of language competence (CRUE 2017; European Commission 2012). The corpus results established a direct relationship between accreditation, language competence, and language requirements. The required language level changed depending on the initiative's purpose and target group. For example, undergraduate students were expected to acquire at least a B1 level for graduation, teaching staff who wanted to participate in EMI courses a B2-C1 level, students who wished to learn by means of bilingual degrees needed at least a B2 level for enrolment, and administrative staff working in areas related to international relations or seeking a job promotion needed a B2 level of English and/or the co-official language of the region.

The last area concerned support measures. In the documents, these measures were considered essential in the implementation of university LP. The findings explicitly recognised the efforts of communicating in a second language made by the university staff (CRUE 2017; Pérez-Llantada 2018, p. 38). Support measures included both incentives—financial, job promotion, added value for participation in mobility programmes and courses—and the creation of language service units that offered online language resources, translation and proofreading services for academic writing, or the creation of teaching materials in a language different than the mother tongue.

*3.2. Institutional Agency*

3.2.1. Accountability towards Languages

It was observed that depending on each university's context, the LP objectives varied and favoured certain languages over others. For instance, there was a dichotomy between the goal to become international through the use of English and foreign languages and universities' interest in protecting local languages, which translated into the desire to give them a more predominant use in the university context. The following extracts suggest a protectionist view of languages associated with co-official languages, which creates a space for the local community in a globalised world.

1.  Será o que entre todos e todas queiramos que sexa, exactamente igual que o futuro da lingua galega na nosa universidade (Universidade da Coruña 2006, Plano de normalización lingüística).

    It will be whatever we, all of us, want it to be, exactly the same as the future of Galician in our university.

2.  La UPV/EHU siempre ha mostrado una actitud claramente favorable al euskera, postura que este nuevo plan pretende mantener, en la línea del esfuerzo que la universidad lleva años realizando por lograr una universidad bilingüe (Universidad del País Vaso 2013, II Plan Director del Euskera de la UPV/EHU).

    The university has always shown a clear positive attitude towards Basque, an attitude this new plan is expected to maintain, similar to the effort the university has been carrying out to become a bilingual university.

Generally, the university presents itself as the actor responsible for fostering the use of a specific language. In Example (1), the co-official language (Galician) is presented with inclusive possessive pronouns (*nosa*, 'our') and noun phrases (*entre todos e todas*, 'all of us (men and women)') to turn an institutional objective into the reader's objective through a sense of proximity and community. In the case of Example (2), a more explicit discourse is found in relation to the use of the co-official language (Basque). The university's voice is clearly identified in the document with the use of adverbs and attitude markers that state the importance of language objectives (*actitud claramente favorable*, 'a clearly positive attitude'; *postura ... pretende mantener*, 'attitude [it is] expected to maintain; *esfuerzo ... lograr una universidad bilingüe*, 'effort ... to become a bilingual university') and the current efforts undertaken by the university to normalise the use of such language in the local context.

3. El entorno global en el que los futuros graduados deberán desarrollar sus carreras profesionales exige la familiarización con contenidos con carácter internacional y el dominio del inglés, actual lingua franca (Universidad de Navarra 2017, Bilingüismo en la universidad).

    The global context in which future graduates must develop their professional careers demands the familiarisation with international contents and proficiency in English, the current lingua franca.

Example (3), on the other hand, illustrates how the institution must adapt to the external pressures of a globalised society, which means English should be introduced in the university context as a consequence of social demands and needs (*actual lingua franca*, 'current lingua franca') (Ferguson 2010; Hultgren 2014). This situation is reflected in the use of obligation verbs (*exige*, 'demands') and modal verbs (*deberán*, 'must') that identify universities as the entities responsible for providing the necessary tools to learn English, the taken-for-granted lingua franca of international communication.

### 3.2.2. Prestige and Excellence

The institution's role in LP was closely related to the desire to project an international prestigious image of the university. Prestige and excellence are two aspects that tend to be linked to internationalisation, and a way to achieve them is through the introduction of English and other languages in the university context (EHEA 2015; MECD 2014; SEPIE 2017).

4. La dilatada historia de la UGR, su reconocimiento como una universidad europea de prestigio y sus perspectivas de futuro exigen un enfoque constructivo hacia las lenguas y el plurilingüismo que las considere un importante recurso (Universidad de Granada 2017, Política lingüística).

    The extensive history of the university, its recognition as a prestigious European university, and its long-term plans demand a constructive approach towards languages and plurilingualism that considers them an important resource.

In Example (4), the institution bases its argumentation on positive features to support the strategic objective of internationalisation (*dilatada historia*, 'extensive history'; *reconocimiento ... universidad europea de prestigio*, 'recognition as a prestigious European university'). In doing so, it also acknowledges the importance of languages in the process (*exigen un enfoque ... hacia las lenguas y el plurilingualismo*, 'demand an approach ... towards languages and plurilingualism'), which relates to Section 3.1 and the view of LP as a necessary tool for higher education institutions. The institution uses an authoritarian voice that creates a direct connection between prestige and languages.

5. Por tanto, la Universidad CEU San Pablo, consciente de que la apuesta por la calidad y la internacionalización exige dar pasos cada vez más firmes en la exigencia de competencias transversales a todos sus grados, establece el siguiente Reglamento que obliga a que todos sus estudiantes, [ ... ], acrediten un nivel mínimo de conocimientos y de competencias en lengua inglesa (CEU Universidad San Pablo 2017, Acreditación de nivel de inglés para la obtención de los títulos de grado)

    The university CEU San Pablo is aware of the fact that quality and internationalisation demand sound steps to move forward, which requires the presence of transversal competences in all the degrees. Therefore, it establishes the following Regulation that makes it compulsory for all students [ ... ] to certify a minimum level of English competence and knowledge.

Similarly, Example (5) explicitly links the discourses of internationalisation and quality to English, which indicates that the three of them are tools that boost the excellence standards of the university (*la calidad y la internacionalización exige ... competencias en lengua inglesa*, 'quality and internationalisation that demand ... English competence and knowledge'). The establishment of language requirements also highlights one of the main areas of concern of LP in Spain, which is the accreditation of university stakeholders' language competence, as seen above in Section 3.1 and CRUE (2017).

At the textual level, the exertion of top-down authority is often established by the use of obligation verbs (*exige, exigencia,* 'demands', 'makes compulsory') as well as the external social situation (*perspectivas de futuro,* 'long-term plans'; *por lo tanto ... consciente de que la apuesta,* 'therefore, [the university] is aware of ... ').

3.2.3. Institutional Authoritarian Voice

A more thorough examination of the institution's voice shows the use of different discursive strategies to fulfil its demands for language skills. Authority is conveyed not only through the use of modal verbs and attitude markers, but also through the use of argumentation based on social practices, global demands, or aligning its objectives to external circumstances like supranational policies, national and regional regulation, or research studies. Institutional actions are consequently justified by the government's policies and experts' opinions.

An example of the latter strategy is seen in Example (6), which gives a sense of well-founded argumentation (*de común acuerdo,* 'of common agreement'; *como queda reflejado,* 'as it is said by'). This strategy was frequently found when languages were discussed in general, without explicitly addressing a specific language, giving more predominance to the expert's voice and reducing the institution's voice to a neutral stance.

6. Respecto al reto particular de la cualificación lingüística del profesorado es de común acuerdo, tal y como queda reflejado en la literatura científica, que el nivel mínimo exigible es un nivel C1 (Universidad de Salamanca 2016, Plan para la Internacionalización Lingüística).

   Regarding the specific challenge of the teaching staff's language training, it is of common agreement that, as it is said by the literature, the minimum level that can be required is C1.

7. Eso, ni qué decir tiene, exige que el personal que atiende al público conozca tanto el euskera como el castellano (ibid. (2)).

   That, without hesitation, demands that the staff who offer public-oriented services know both Basque and Spanish.

However, a different approach was used when references to a specific language appeared, especially in the case of co-official languages. For instance, in Example (7), the institution used a subjective position through the use of attitude markers (*eso ni que decir tiene exige,* 'that, without hesitation, demands ... ') that shows implications regarding language expectations—e.g., importance and obligation. This change of attitude could be linked to what was observed in Section 3.2.1, when the institution adopted an inclusive and protective stance towards local languages—e.g., Basque and Spanish in the case of Example (7).

*3.3. Languages in LP*

3.3.1. Language Functions

Lastly, a comparative analysis was carried out to describe the English language in contrast to the local languages. One of the objectives of LP is to identify and establish the functions of the different languages that co-exist in a specific context when a situation demands regulation of use. According to the documents analysed, languages perform several functions. The introduction of English in the local context has created two scenarios, either replacement or duplication of uses (Hultgren 2014). For example, Examples (8), (9), and (10) explicitly state the different statuses and functions that languages can hold in the university ('own language', 'official languages', 'lingua franca', 'working language'), whether granted by law—e.g., Catalan, Spanish—or by daily use in certain domains—English, other languages/foreign languages. Challenges appear though, in the case of languages whose presence has become expected in certain spheres, like English, but its implications are not clearly discussed (Pérez-Llantada 2018; Soler-Carbonell and Karaoglu 2015).

8. La transparencia y la efectividad de los derechos y los deberes lingüísticos que se derivan del estatus de las lenguas: del catalán como lengua propia, del catalán y del castellano como lenguas oficiales, del inglés como lengua franca de la comunidad académica internacional, y también de otras lenguas en contextos específicos (Universitat Autònoma de Barcelona 2016, Plan de lenguas).

    The transparency and effectiveness of language rights and duties result from the status of languages: Catalan as the own language, Catalan and Spanish as official languages, English as the lingua franca of the international academic community, and other languages in specific contexts too.

9. Reconoce el papel de la lengua inglesa como lingua franca académica internacional, lo que se refleja en la necesidad de regular de forma específica su estatus en nuestra institución (ibid. (4)).

    It recognises the role of English as the international academic lingua franca, which is reflected in the need to regulate its status in a specific way within our institution.

10. Anglès com a llengua de treball o d'ús corrent a la Universitat Pompeu Fabra té una sèrie de conseqüències pràctiques i jurídiques (Universitat Pompeu Fabra 2007, Pla d'acció pel multilingüisme).

    English as the common use or working language at the University Pompeu Fabra has a series of practical and legal consequences.

Several languages can be used when they fulfil a similar function, as seen in Example (11): English is used for international communication in the domain of research dissemination, while Catalan and Spanish are used for specific research purposes, which may be influenced by the research topic and target audience.

11. En les activitats de recerca i difusió, la UOC vol potenciar l'ús de la llengua anglesa com a principal vehicle d'intercanvi científic internacional, mantenint l'ús del català i l'espanyol per a la difusió de la recerca en contextos més específics (Universitat Oberta de Catalunya 2015, Princips generals de política lingüística).

    In the activities of research and dissemination, the university wants to promote the use of English as the main vehicle of international scientific exchange, keeping the use of Catalan and Spanish for the dissemination of research in more specific contexts.

It can then be deduced that in this scenario, the functions of languages might be shaped by the geographical location of the target audience. Example (11) illustrates how the institutional protective view of local languages reflects concern towards the maintenance of local languages, especially in domains where English has become the predominant language choice. In general, universities (Examples (9), (10)) are aware of the need for regulation of the presence of English (*en la necesidad de regular de forma explícita*, 'need for explicit regulation'; *conseqüències pràctiques i jurídiques*, 'practical and legal consequences'), as seen in Section 3.1, but this also brings to the fore implications for policymakers, e.g., the extent to which it can be institutionalised and become an official working language of the university; or the language requirements that will be asked for depending on different purposes or stakeholders' needs.

3.3.2. Language Hierarchies

I ended the previous section with Example (11) that insinuated a certain level of resistance to the linguistic hegemony of English. This section specifically focuses on the way in which language attitudes are translated into the LP documents at a textual level, which on some occasions may favour English, and in others the local languages. This is generally expressed at the textual level with the use of attitude markers, adverbs, enumeration, coordination, disjunction, and so on.

12. A investigación realízase principalmente en castelán ou en inglés (ibid. (1)).

Research should be done mainly in Spanish or English.

13. Enseñanza en las dos lenguas oficiales y la posibilidad de impartir en una lengua no oficial, preferentemente el inglés (Universitat d'Alacant 2013, Plan de política lingüística).

    Teaching in the two official languages, and the possibility to teach in a non-official language, preferably English.

14. Hacer que el valenciano sea, de verdad, lengua de atención a los usuarios y de relación profesional [ ... ], y, en determinados puestos de trabajo, el inglés u otras lenguas no oficiales (ibid. (13)).

    Making Valencian, really, the language used for communication with users and for professional relations [ ... ] and, in specific job positions, English or other non-official languages.

An analysis of these examples shows a balanced position of Spanish and English in the research field (Example (12)): 'In Spanish or in English'); in other cases (Examples (13) and (14)), local languages hold a privileged position as they are described as the preferred language choice (*enseñanza en las dos lenguas oficiales*, 'teaching in the two official languages'; *hacer que el valenciaso sea, de verdad, lengua* ... , 'make Valencian the real language of ... '). Despite relegating English to a second position in these two examples, it is still more valued than other foreign languages, which is marked with the use of adverbs (*preferentemente*, 'preferably') and the position in the disjunctive phrase 'English or other non-official languages' because its name is specified in contrast to the general noun phrase of 'non-official languages'. Therefore, it still maintains a privileged status, which shows language beliefs towards the practicality and benefits of English in comparison to other languages.

## 4. Discussion and Concluding Remarks

In this paper, I have examined how LP documents from Spanish universities convey language beliefs and regulate language practices. Regarding RQ1, the corpus findings indicated, as expected, that universities follow a similar line to the one established by the national LP framework (CRUE 2017), particularly in terms of training, regulation, accreditation, and support. From these areas, language training gains special attention in the form of, firstly, training staff and students so that they can communicate in at least two languages—mother tongue and another language—and secondly, the creation of language resources and real opportunities for (multilingual) language use.

Answers to RQ2 suggest that universities generally show positive attitudes towards languages. These beliefs and attitudes tend to shape LP objectives and rationales according to the institution's geographical and sociolinguistic context. Additionally, a desire is observed to promote language diversity (European Commission 2012; Fortanet-Gómez 2012), especially in the case of co-official languages and the introduction of English in the university domains of teaching and research. In doing so, while universities adopt a protectionist role regarding co-official language promotion, the introduction of English is regarded as a duty or responsibility. Thus, this supports the view that LP, as a regulatory tool, is essential when tensions might arise from the introduction of a new language in the local context.

As far as RQ3 is concerned, English is explicitly linked to the discourse of internationalisation and excellence, which justifies the introduction of English in a non-Anglophone context (Ferguson 2010; Hultgren 2014; Wächter and Maiworm 2014). Despite the general agreement that English is a necessary element of modern higher education, its presence is rather seen as a consequence of external circumstances whereas the references to co-official languages seem to come from an internal motivation of universities. This may explain the variation of discursive strategies found in relation to languages (Bocanegra-Valle 2017). While co-official languages present engaging and persuasive strategies, and Spanish is mentioned with a neutral stance, English is more likely to be found in relation to obligation, reflected in the use of modal verbs and intertextuality—external sources of argumentation.

To conclude, this paper is hoped to add new insights on the relevance of critical understanding of institutional documents to the field of LP and internationalisation in the Spanish context; these hold important implications for establishing the role languages should play in the modernisation of universities and academia, either involving the form of the monolingual advancement of English, or, what seems to be in line with current trends, the promotion of language diversity.

**Funding:** This research was supported by the Spanish Ministry of Economy and Competitiveness and the European Social Fund (project code: FFI2015-68638-R) and by the Regional Government of Aragón (project code: H16_17R).

**Conflicts of Interest:** The author declares no conflict of interest.

## References

Bocanegra-Valle, Ana. 2017. Promotional Discourse at Internationalised Universities: A Critical Discourse Analysis Approach. Paper presented at 35th International Conference of the Spanish Society of Applied Linguistics, Jaén, Spain, May 4–6. Available online: https://genresandlanguages.org/wp-content/uploads/2018/03/2017.05.05_BocanegraValle_Promotional-discourse.pdf (accessed on 13 May 2019).

CRUE. 2017. Documento Marco de Política Lingüística para la Internacionalización del Sistema Universitario Español. Available online: https://www.crue.org/Documentos%20compartidos/Sectoriales/Internacionalización%20y%20Coorperación/Marco_Final_Documento%20de%20Política%20Linguistica%20reducido.pdf (accessed on 13 May 2019).

de Swaan, A. 2001. *Words of the World: The Global Language System*. Cambridge: Polity Press and Blackwell.

EHEA (European Higher Education Area). 2015. *The European Higher Education Area*. Edited by Adrian Curaj, Liviu Matei, Remus Pricopie, Jamil Salmi and Peter Scott. Cham: Springer International Publishing. [CrossRef]

European Commission. 2010. Council Conclusions of 11 May 2010 on the Internationalisation of Higher Education. Available online: https://eur-lex.europa.eu/LexUriServ/LexUriServ.do?uri=OJ:C:2010:135:0012:0014:EN:PDF (accessed on 13 May 2019).

European Commission. 2012. Language Competences for Employability, Mobility and Growth. Available online: https://eur-lex.europa.eu/legal-content/EN/TXT/PDF/?uri=CELEX:52012SC0372&from=NL (accessed on 13 May 2019).

European Commission. 2013. European Higher Education in the World. Available online: http://ec.europa.eu/transparency/regdoc/rep/1/2013/EN/1-2013-499-EN-F1-1.Pdf (accessed on 13 May 2019).

Ferguson, Gibson. 2010. English in Language Policy and Management. In *The Cambridge Handbook of Language Policy*. Edited by Bernard Spolsky. Cambridge: Cambridge University Press, pp. 475–98.

Fortanet-Gómez, Inmaculada. 2012. Academics' Beliefs about Language Use and Proficiency in Spanish Multilingual Higher Education. *AILA Review* 25: 48–63. [CrossRef]

Hultgren, Anna Kristina. 2014. Whose Parallellingualism? Overt and Covert Ideologies in Danish University Language Policies. *Multilingua* 33: 61–87. [CrossRef]

Maringe, Felix, and Nicholas Foskett. 2010. *Globalization and Internationalization in Higher Education: Theoretical, Strategic and Management Perspectives*. New York: Continuum International Pub. Group.

MECD (Ministerio de Educación, Cultura y Deporte, and España Gobierno de). 2014. Estrategia para la Internacionalización de las Universidades Españolas 2015–2020. Available online: http://www.educacionyfp.gob.es/educacion-mecd/dms/mecd/educacion-mecd/areas-educacion/universidades/politica-internacional/estrategia-internacionalizacion/EstrategiaInternacionalizaci-n-Final.pdf (accessed on 13 May 2019).

Pérez-Llantada, Carmen. 2018. Bringing into Focus Multilingual Realities: Faculty Perceptions of Academic Languages on Campus. *Lingua* 212: 30–43. [CrossRef]

SEPIE. 2017. *Internationalisation of Higher Education in Spain: Reflections and Perspectives*. Edited by Adriana Pérez-Encinas, Laura Howard, Laura E. Rumbley and Hans De Wit. Madrid: Spanish Service for the Internationalisation of Education.

Soler-Carbonell, Josep, and Hakan Karaoglu. 2015. English as an Academic Lingua Franca in Estonia: Students' Attitudes and Ideologies. In *Attitudes towards English in Europe*. Edited by Andrew Linn, Neil Bermel and Gibson Ferguson. Berlin: DE GRUYTER, vol. 1, chp. 9. pp. 213–38. [CrossRef]

Spolsky, Bernard. 2012. *The Cambridge Handbook of Language Policy*. Cambridge: Cambridge University Press.
Wächter, Bernd, and Friedhelm Maiworm. 2014. *English-Taught Programmes in European Higher Education: The State of Play in 2014*. Bonn: Lemmens.

 © 2019 by the author. Licensee MDPI, Basel, Switzerland. This article is an open access article distributed under the terms and conditions of the Creative Commons Attribution (CC BY) license (http://creativecommons.org/licenses/by/4.0/).

*Article*

# "Arguments That Could Possibly Be Urged": Modal Verbs and Tentativeness in the *Coruña Corpus*

## Isabel Moskowich * and Begoña Crespo *

Departmento de Letras, Universidade da Coruña, 15071 A Coruña, Spain
* Correspondence: imoskowich@udc.es (I.M.); bcrespo@udc.es (B.C.)

Received: 8 May 2019; Accepted: 5 July 2019; Published: 22 July 2019

**Abstract:** This paper complements previous research into the late Modern English scientific writing uses of the adverbs *possibly* and *perhaps* as manifestations of either subjectivity or intersubjectivity, as presented in the *Coruña Corpus of English Scientific Writing*. In order to have a better understanding of the uses of these adverbs as markers of tentativeness, we will explore their syntagmatic relations with modal verbs. It is widely assumed that scientific discourse has an objective nature, although it has been questioned by its use of hedging and other expressions of stance. In the present study, we will assess how modal verbs accompanying these stance adverbs modulate the expression of tentativeness. The use of stance adverbs shows authorial presence and a covert interaction with the reader. The paper examines different degrees of hesitancy depending on the type of modal verb accompanying these adverbs. The analysis has been carried out on four subcorpora of the *Coruña Corpus of English Scientific Writing*. Our findings will be presented from a more general to a more detailed account for each of the forms under investigation and interpreted taking into account the variables 'date of publication' and 'genre' for the text, and 'sex' for the author.

**Keywords:** modals; late Modern English scientific writing; Coruña Corpus

---

## 1. Introduction

This paper aims to complement previous research into the uses of the adverbs *possibly* and *perhaps* as manifestations of either subjectivity or intersubjectivity, looking specifically at late Modern English scientific writing, as presented in the *Coruña Corpus of English Scientific Writing*.

In the current study, we will be using the same material. However, in order to go a step further, we will explore the syntagmatic relations of these two adverbs and their accompanying modal verbs. Although it is widely assumed that scientific English has shifted from author-centered to object-centered (Atkinson 1998), the presumably objective nature of scientific discourse has in fact been questioned, with the use of hedging (Hyland 1998) and other elements expressing stance (Moskowich and Crespo 2014; Alonso Almeida and Inés 2016; Dossena 2017) cited as evidence here. In the present study, we will continue our description of late Modern English scientific writing by assessing how the modal verbs accompanying these stance adverbs can modulate the expression of tentativeness. *Perhaps* and *possibly* both indicate an author's desire to show tentativeness and uncertainty, as well as being devices that seek the reading public's involvement in the presentation of content (Seoane Posse 2016). The use of stance adverbs of this kind not only shows authorial presence, but also demonstrates a covert interaction with the reader, which makes these texts more engaging for the latter.

We will consider how different shades of meaning and degrees of tentativeness/hesitancy arise depending on the type of modal verb accompanying these two adverbs. To this end, Section 1 will introduce our research questions, and will also deal with a number of considerations that seem to be necessary in order to carry out our analysis. Section 2 provides a description of the linguistic material to be used in the analysis: four subcorpora of the *Coruña Corpus of English Scientific Writing*: *Corpus of*

*English Texts on Astronomy* (CETA), *Corpus of English Philosophy Texts* (CEPhiT), *Corpus of History English Texts* (CHET), and *Corpus of English Life Sciences Texts* (CELiST); this section also includes information on the analysis itself. The findings will be set out in Section 3, from a more general to a more detailed account for each of the forms under investigation. In Section 4, we will interpret and discuss the results in the light of the following variables: time of publication, sex of the author, and genre or discursive format of texts. Finally, some conclusions will be offered in Section 5.

## 2. Previous Considerations and Research Questions

Those engaged in the study of scientific writing in English and its evolution generally accept that there has been a broad shift from an author-centered perspective to one that focuses on the object described or studied. Atkinson's work on the *Philosophical Transactions* (Atkinson 1998) seems to prove this beyond doubt. However, such a claim does not mean that, after three centuries of evolution, present-day scientific writing is entirely dry and objective; indeed, it has been shown that it contains hedging (Hyland 1998) and expressions of stance in different forms (Moskowich and Crespo 2014; Alonso Almeida and Inés 2016; Dossena 2017).

Our first approach to the use of *possibly* and *perhaps* as stance adverbs (in a paper presented at the annual AESLA Conference in 2018) involved an analysis of authorial presence and subjectivity in late Modern scientific discourse. In that paper, we concluded that these adverbs were more often used to express subjectivity than intersubjectivity, and that such use increased over time. In the current paper, we aim to go one step further, asking whether the syntagmatic relations of these adverbs with modal verbs also exhibit traces of tentativeness; this was understood to be one of the manifestations of author subjectivity.

Our starting point will be the definitions for *perhaps* and *possibly* in the *Oxford English Dictionary* (*OED* henceforth). Thus, perhaps is defined as: "Expressing a hypothetical, contingent, conjectural, or uncertain possibility: it may be (that); maybe, possibly" (*OED*). We also know that its origin is Germanic. In turn, *possibly* originates from Romance, and is defined as: "In a possible manner; in accordance with what can or may exist, occur, be done, etc.; within the range of possibility; by any existing power or means, in any possible way. Chiefly, now only, used as an intensifier of *can* or *could*" (*OED*).

> Moreover, as Álvarez-Gil (2019, p. 49) has argued, *possibly* indicates "a low level of authorial commitment to text content by presenting information with doubts and hesitancy". He argued that the authors combine this form with may, might, and could to indicate different levels of likeliness of the events to be true. This combination of the modal and possibly may mean either that the author lacks the necessary evidence for the conclusion presented, or it may be a negative politeness strategy to avoid imposition. The use of this adverb suggests the authors' need to protect their public image rather than a real evaluation of the state of affairs. That is, even if they rely on solid ground to assert a particular conclusion, it possibly adds an extra rhetorical effect to enhance the epistemic meaning as realized by the accompanying modals. (Álvarez-Gil 2019, p. 70)

It also seems in order to offer the meanings of modal verbs in present-day English (see Table 1 below) according to Quirk (1985), bearing in mind that such meanings do not differ extensively from the ones to be found in the late Modern English period (Millward and Mary 2011).

Table 1. Meaning of modal verbs (according to Quirk 1985).

| Modal Verb | Meaning | Paraphrasis |
|---|---|---|
| *May* | epistemic possibility "It denotes the possibility of a given proposition's being or becoming true." | *perhaps* or *possibly* |
| *Might* | epistemic possibility, but more tentative than *may* | |
| *Can/could* | possibility (future possibility) | *it is possible* + inf clause |
| *Shall* | prediction, volition (with first person) | |
| *Should* | obligation | |
| *Will/would* | prediction, volition | |

These meanings are present in the use of modals in late Modern scientific texts, as can be seen in the following examples from the *Coruña Corpus of English Scientific Writing*:

(1) which take place in the maturation of the ovum may <perhaps> be most conveniently displayed by following the history of a... (Balfour 1880, p. 55)
(2) so different from what man at first imagines it may <perhaps> have startled them but in this view there is nothing (Whewell 1858, p. 38)
(3) of secretions that they are the greatest arguments that could <possibly> be urged for the truth of it nothing does more (Keill 1717, p. 132)
(4) causes and effects of several phenomena which future ages may <possibly> discover most of these birds of passage never fail to (Hughes 1750, p. 76)

Although it might be thought that the definitions and uses provided cannot be applied to our findings for late Modern English, given that there is a gap of two centuries between the material in our study and Quirk et al.'s work, the meanings of modals do not seem to have changed, at least in terms of their frequency of occurrence (Leech 2004).

The following section will present the linguistic material for our survey and the methodology used.

## 3. Corpus Material and Methodology

The material used for the present study (see Table 2 below) has been taken from the *Coruña Corpus of English Scientific Writing* (CC). More specifically, we have used four subcorpora: *Corpus of English Texts on Astronomy* (CETA), *Corpus of English Philosophy Texts* (CEPhiT), *Corpus of History English Texts* (CHET) and *Corpus of English Life Sciences Texts* (CELiST). Two of these represent disciplines pertaining to the so-called soft sciences, while the other two represent the hard sciences.

Table 2. Word count per subcorpus.

| Subcorpus | Discipline | Words |
|---|---|---|
| CETA | Astronomy | 409,909 |
| CHET | History | 404,424 |
| CEPhiT | Philosophy | 401,129 |
| CELiST | Life Sciences | 400,305 |
| Total | | 1,615,767 |

Since sex of the author is one of the variables we will be using, the distribution of words by male and female authors in our material is displayed in Figure 1 below. This distribution reflects the situation of scientific text production in the Modern period:

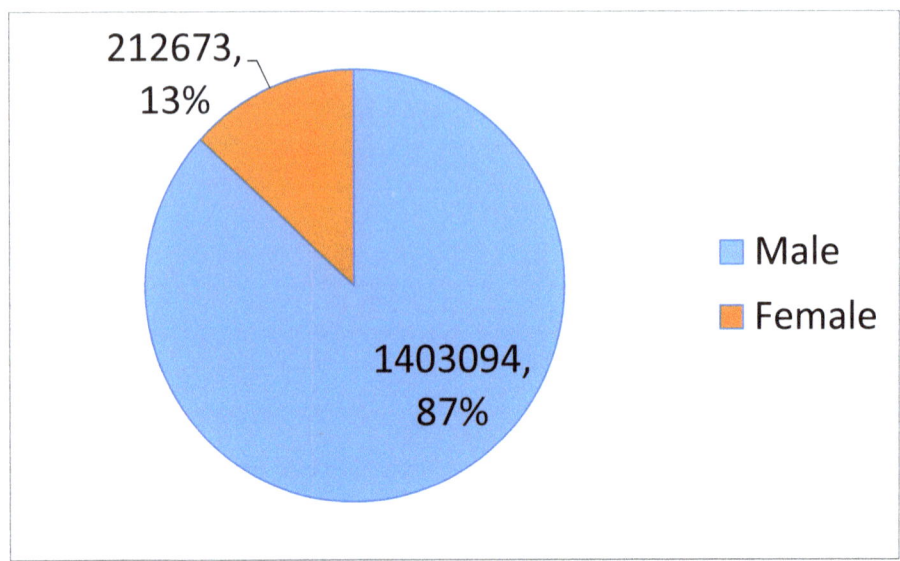

**Figure 1.** Words per sex of author.

Much more variety can be found in terms of genre or communicative format. There are 12 different formats in the four subcorpora, these being unequally represented, in that not all of them were equally popular during the period. This can be seen in Figure 2:

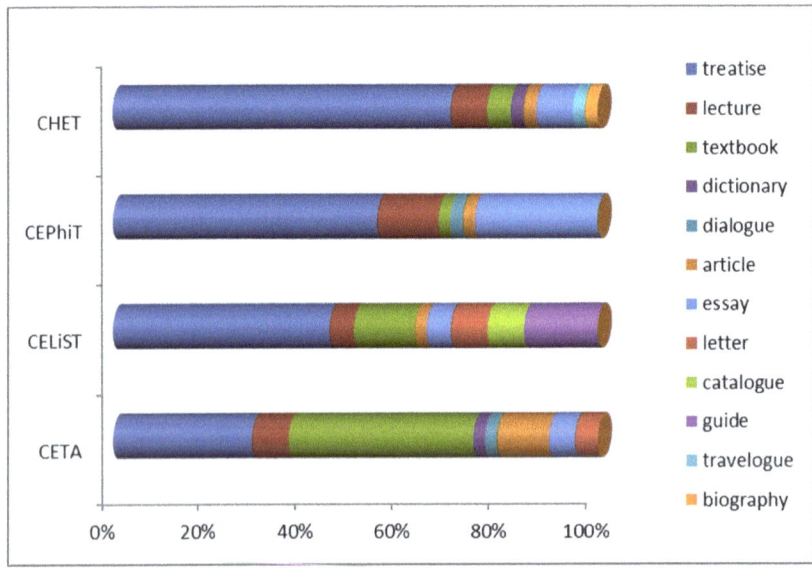

**Figure 2.** Words per genre.

As for the analysis itself, all cases of the adverbs *possibly* and *perhaps* in the subcorpora were considered, but only those containing a modal verb accompanying the adverbs in question were then taken into account. Thus, we focused on examples such as the following:

(5) If the time shall ever arrive, when the facts of natural history are given, without admixture with fable, the world will be more rapidly and satisfactorily advanced in improvement than can <possibly> be hoped for (Godman 1828, p. 29)
(6) rational horizon does not amount to a few seconds or <perhaps> not so much as one second of a minute and (Long 1742, p. 64)
(7) bodies have not so far been satisfactorily observed it is <perhaps> possible that the part removed in the formation of the (Balfour 1880, p. 63)

The *Coruña Corpus Tool* was used to search for all the tokens of the adverbs under survey in the subcorpora. Given that we were interested in looking into the behavior of such adverbs with different types of modals, it was necessary to manually disambiguate each case. This involved a close reading of all the hits, which had previously been collected in a spreadsheet (MS Excel for Mac, version 16.24). Then, the examples that were to be used in the analysis were enriched through the addition of fields including information on the author, his or her sex, the year of publication of the text in question, and the genre to which it belonged.

## 4. Findings and Discussion of Results

The data will be presented here from the more general to the more specific. Starting with the general findings for the adverbs (as set out in Table 3 below), we can see that their use in the four disciplines certainly differs. Totals for the raw numbers have been normalized as a means of making comparisons clearer.

Table 3. Frequency of *possibly* and *perhaps* in the subcorpora.

| Forms | Raw Figures | | | | | Total (NF/10,000) |
|---|---|---|---|---|---|---|
| | CHET | CEPhiT | CETA | CELiST | Total | 3.61 |
| Possibly | 20 | 46 | 24 | 25 | 115 | 0.71 |
| Perhaps | 76 | 212 | 64 | 117 | 469 | 2.90 |

This analysis of the adverbs is enhanced when the accompanying modal verbs are taken into account. Table 4 shows in raw numbers that *may*, with the meaning of possibility, is the most frequent modal verb in all the disciplines apart from History, where *might* is found most often. *May*, as shown in Table 5, repeatedly occurs in combination with *perhaps*, which can be interpreted as a reinforcement of the uncertainty that accompanies "the possibility of something becoming true". This form of strengthening might be taken as the conscious presence of the author, who thus manifests his/her attitude toward a particular statement.

Table 4. Adverbs and accompanying modal verbs.

| | CELiST | CEPhiT | CETA | CHET | TOTAL |
|---|---|---|---|---|---|
| may | 31 | 37 | 20 | 6 | 94 |
| might | 6 | 14 | 0 | 9 | 29 |
| can | 9 | 26 | 9 | 3 | 47 |
| could | 2 | 11 | 7 | 6 | 26 |
| shall | 0 | 3 | 8 | 0 | 11 |
| should | 0 | 2 | 0 | 0 | 2 |
| will | 3 | 13 | 2 | 0 | 18 |
| would | 3 | 9 | 4 | 0 | 16 |
| TOTAL (modals/subcorpus) | 54 | 115 | 50 | 24 | 243 |

Note: Pink colour has been used to highlight the most frequent results; blue colour highlights the least frequent results.

Table 5. *Perhaps* and accompanying modal verbs.

|        | CELiST | CEPhiT | CETA | CHET | TOTAL |
|--------|--------|--------|------|------|-------|
| may    | 24     | 32     | 15   | 4    | 75    |
| might  | 6      | 10     | 0    | 7    | 23    |
| can    | 3      | 3      | 0    | 2    | 8     |
| could  | 0      | 0      | 0    | 0    | 0     |
| shall  | 0      | 3      | 1    | 0    | 4     |
| should | 0      | 2      | 0    | 0    | 2     |
| will   | 3      | 13     | 1    | 0    | 17    |
| would  | 3      | 9      | 4    | 0    | 16    |
| TOTAL  | 39     | 72     | 21   | 13   | 145   |

It is also interesting to note that it is in the History discipline that the lowest number of modal verbs with the two adverbs in question are found. This is surprising, in that History, together with Philosophy, represents the so-called soft sciences, where more authorial presence is expected to be found (Hyland 2005); such disciplines are considered to be more prone to subjectivity than those of the hard sciences.

Curiously, as set out in Table 5 below, *may* is more frequently used in combination with *perhaps* in Philosophy texts, which are more amenable to the inclusion of the expression of feelings, opinions, or ideas; however, it is also found in CELiST, as a representative of the hard sciences, which is an unexpected finding.

As for the form *possibly*, we have found that, although occasionally used with other modal verbs, it occurs most frequently with *can* and *could* to express the certainty of a possibility (Crespo forthcoming). Table 6 below displays this information in some detail for each subcorpus.

Table 6. *Possibly* and accompanying modals.

|        | CELiST | CEPhiT | CETA | CHET | TOTAL |
|--------|--------|--------|------|------|-------|
| May    | 7      | 5      | 5    | 2    | 19    |
| Might  | 0      | 4      | 0    | 2    | 6     |
| Can    | 6      | 23     | 9    | 1    | 39    |
| Could  | 2      | 11     | 7    | 6    | 26    |
| Shall  | 0      | 0      | 0    | 0    | 0     |
| Should | 0      | 0      | 0    | 0    | 0     |
| Will   | 0      | 0      | 1    | 0    | 1     |
| Would  | 0      | 0      | 0    | 0    | 0     |
| TOTAL  | 15     | 43     | 22   | 11   | 91    |

Once again, History is the discipline that exhibits the fewest cases of modals + *possibly*, which might account for the assertiveness and scant authorial presence in these texts. The collocation modal + stance adverb does not seem to be a mechanism to manifest the author's value judgement or stance on a narrated event or fact.

We believe, along with Biber (1991), that scientific English contains more variation than traditionally believed. Therefore, we have decided to interpret our findings in the light of three extralinguistic variables that have proved very useful in other pieces of research carried out with the CC (Monaco 2016; Puente-Castelo 2017): the date of publication of a text, the sex of the author, and the communicative format of the piece. Each of these variables will be discussed in what follows.

### 4.1. Adverbs, Modals, and Time

As noted above, we have used data from two subperiods—the 18th and the 19th centuries, for all subcorpora, and we have found different behaviors in *possibly* and *perhaps* over these two centuries. As Tables 7 and 8 show, there is an increase in the use of *perhaps* of 36.86% from the 18th century (with 198 tokens) to the 19th (with 271).

**Table 7.** Use of *perhaps* in time.

| *Perhaps* | Period | |
| --- | --- | --- |
| | 18th c. | 19th c. |
| | 198 | 271 |

Table 8, however, shows that *possibly* is used less frequently over time, although this decrease is very moderate:

**Table 8.** Use of *possibly* in time.

| *Possibly* | Period | |
| --- | --- | --- |
| | 18th c. | 19th c. |
| | 59 | 56 |

The fact that *perhaps* is more frequently used in the second subperiod under analysis might confirm greater authorial presence in scientific writing over time. Authors, it seems, are still present in their work, and this contradicts one of the initial assumptions cited in Section 1: that scientific writing moves from an author-centered to an object-centered sphere. Authors always have a voice, to a greater or lesser degree, however necessary or important the description of an object, event, or process might be. This explanation cannot account for the decrease in the use of *possibly* unless we consider it as some kind of complementary distribution—that is, *perhaps* replacing the use of *possibly*.

When we look into how the two adverbs behave and whether they tend to occur in structures with modals or not, we find a very slight decrease in both cases.

Figure 3 shows that *possibly* occurs in the same structure as a modal verb more often in the 18th (54 tokens) than in the 19th century (37), there being a moderate decrease in the latter. By contrast, *perhaps* behaves in practically the same way in both subperiods, with 73 occurrences for the 18th century and 72 for the 19th.

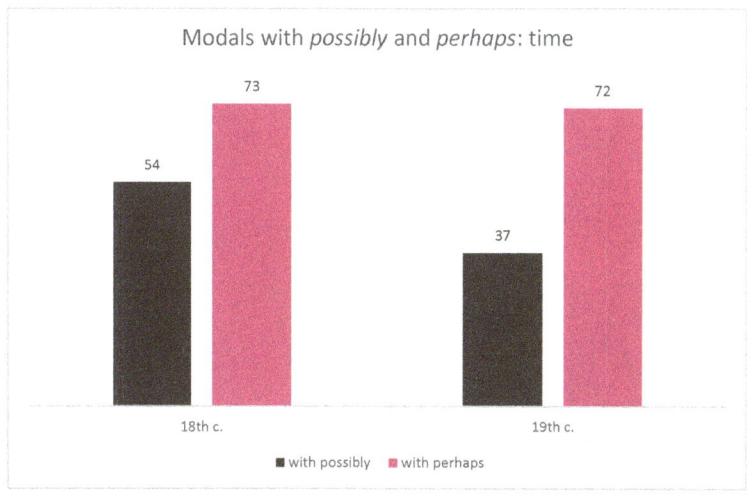

**Figure 3.** Distribution of adverbs with modals in time.

*4.2. Adverbs, Modals, and Sex*

Our expectations regarding the adverbs under discussion here in terms of the sex of the author were that women would probably use them more, as a means of mitigating their claims. Normalized figures were again used here, since there are substantially fewer words produced by women than by men in the CC, this being a matter of representativeness (far more men published scientific works in the late Modern English period). Our results (Figure 4) show—contrary to our initial hypothesis—that female authors tend to use the adverbs *possibly* and *perhaps* more often on their own than when accompanied by a modal verb, which reveals that they do not use mitigation as often as their male peers. This might be explained by them having felt the need to be more assertive if they want to be taken seriously in a highly androcentric world.

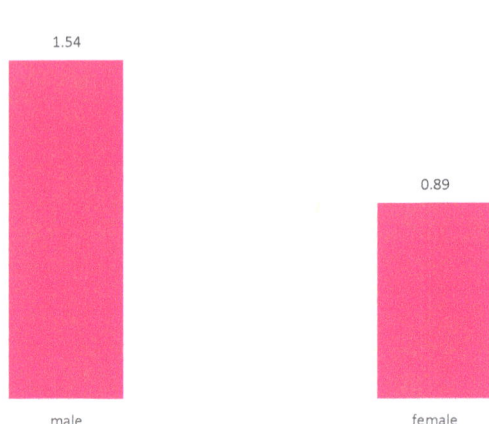

**Figure 4.** Use of adverbs with modals per sex.

On closer inspection, and taking the two adverbs separately, the same pattern is replicated, in that both *possibly* and *perhaps* are used less often by women. This is illustrated in Figure 5, as well as female writers (on the right) using fewer of these forms in general, as we had already noted.

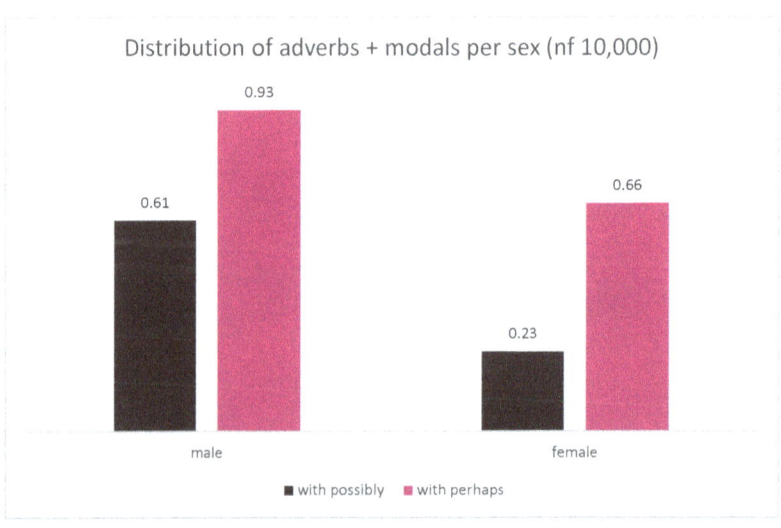

**Figure 5.** Use of *perhaps* and *possibly* per sex.

*4.3. Adverbs, Modals, and Communicative Formats*

Previous research (Crespo and Moskowich 2016; Moskowich 2017) has shown that both subject matter and communicative format or genre exert a great influence on linguistic choice. The genres included in the CC cover different degrees of formality and proximity to the oral register. Thus, we find samples extracted from Lectures, Dialogues, and Letters (speech-based genres) and others such as Textbooks, Treatises, or Travelogues, which are typically written to be read. We have analyzed the behavior of *perhaps* and *possibly* separately, since although the *OED* gives a very similar meaning for both, which might imply similar kinds of use, the results for the previous variables have led us to prefer a separate analysis, this as a means of seeing whether they would also behave differently or not here.

Thus, the adverb *perhaps* was taken first, and a search was made for all those instances in which it was accompanied by modal verbs in the 12 different genres represented in our material. Figure 6 illustrates the very varied distribution that we found. On the one hand, Essay (2.19 nf) and Lecture (1.45 nf) are the two formats that contain the highest number of occurrences of *perhaps* when accompanied by a modal verb. It is to be noted that both formats are close to orality, in that lectures are conceived of as pieces of writing to be read out, and essays were originally the reports of the public demonstrations of experiments. Such characteristics of these formats may explain the preference for an adverb of Germanic origin such as *perhaps*. On the other hand, from the 12 genres, four contained no instances of these constructions, this being the case with Dictionary, Catalogue, Travelogue, and Biography. Curiously, these are discipline-specific genres, in that Biography and Travelogue are exclusive to the History corpus, and Catalogue has thus far only been found in the Corpus of English Life Sciences Texts (under compilation). Meanwhile, Dictionary—a format that can also be found in other disciplines—is represented here by a sample in CETA (Astronomy). It is also true that although the form and function of both Catalogue and Dictionary do not seem to be likely to contain structures such as those we are dealing with, the other two (Travelogue and Biography) might indeed be expected to contain some instances precisely because of their nature.

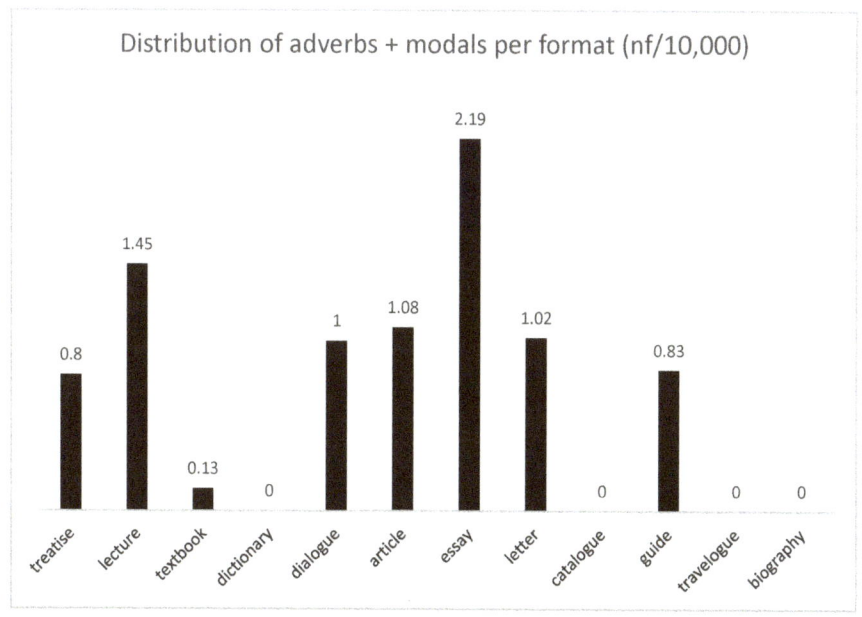

**Figure 6.** Use of *perhaps* with modals per sex.

Our analysis of *possibly* with modal verbs reveals that it also behaves differently depending on the oral-like character of the genres in question. Biography is the format containing most of these structures (1.49 nf), followed by Article (1.35 nf). Conversely, Dialogue and Travelogue contain no cases at all, whereas other, more oral-like genres, such as Lecture and Essay, exhibit only 0.15 nf and 0.8 nf, respectively. The frequent use of *possibly* in genres written to be read (rather than read out orally) may be the result of the word's Romance origins, which is typical of more formal and written texts (Figure 7). Therefore, it seems plausible to assume that both adverbs occur in complementary distribution.

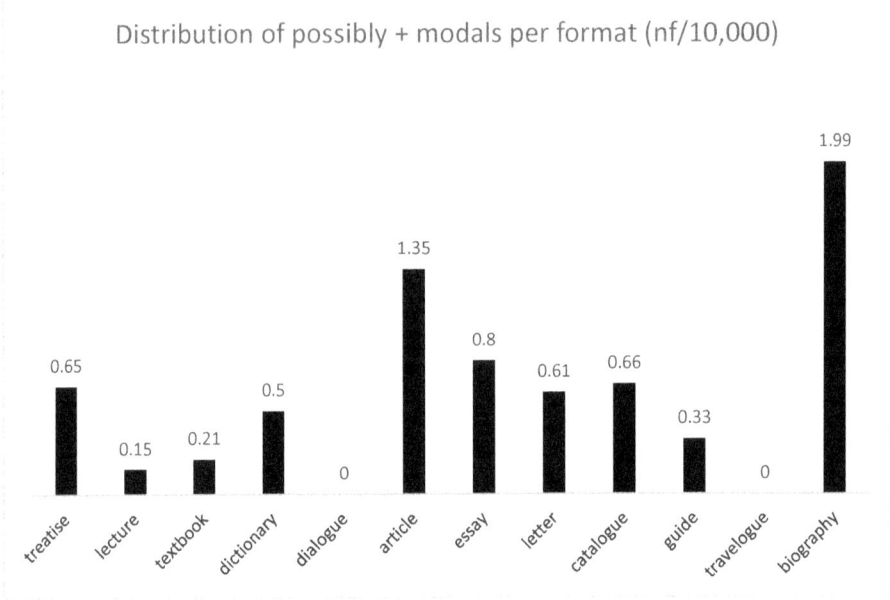

**Figure 7.** Use of *possibly* with modals per communicative format.

All the results presented above—both those of a general nature and those in which the three different extralinguistic variables have been considered—seem to contradict what we know about modal verbs, their meanings, and their uses.

## 5. Conclusions

Our survey of the occurrence of *possibly* and *perhaps* with modal verbs has shown that all the verbs under study are recorded in our material. However, clearly different distributions with the two adverbs have been found: *perhaps* occurs more frequently in constructions with *may*, whereas *possibly* tends to appear with *can* and *could* more often.

As in previous research, we have found that *perhaps* is more abundant in our material than *possibly*. We have also seen that it is more frequently used in oral-like formats, which may be due to its etymology, in that Germanic words are often considered more appropriate for less formal registers. For the same reason, we have seen that *possibly*, of Romance (ultimately Latin) origin, appears more frequently in formats addressed to a specialized reading public, such as Articles.

Incidentally, our study also reveals that, contrary to the *OED*'s definition of *possibly* ("Chiefly, **now** only, used as an **intensifier of can or could**"), the word was already used with this intensifier function as early as the 18th century, at least in scientific writing. The question of whether this is due to its etymological provenance (and perhaps not felt by speakers to be so naturally their own), and also what kind of behavior these adverbs may have in non-scientific writing, must be left for future research.

**Author Contributions:** I.M. has acquired the financial support for the project leading to this publication and has coordinated the research activity planning and execution. Both of them have designed the methodology and conducted the research by collecting and analyzing the data. B.C. has prepared the presentation of the data in the published work, and has reviewed and edited the paper specifically what concerns to critical review, commentary or revision—including pre- or post-publication stages.

**Funding:** The research here reported on has been funded by the Spanish Ministerio de Economía, Industria y Competitividad (MINECO), grant number FFI2016-75599-P and Xunta de Galicia, grant number ED431D2017/1. These grants are hereby gratefully acknowledged.

**Conflicts of Interest:** The authors declare no conflict of interest. The funding sponsors had no role in the design of the study; in the collection, analyses, or interpretation of data; in the writing of the manuscript, or in the decision to publish the results.

**List of Corpora:** Coruña Corpus of English Scientific Writing formed by Corpus of English Texts on Astronomy (CETA), Corpus of English Philosophy Texts (CEPhiT), Corpus of History English Texts (CHET) and Corpus of English Life Sciences Texts (CELiST).

## References

Alonso Almeida, Francisco, and Lareo Inés. 2016. The status of seem in the nineteenth-century Corpus of English Philosophy Texts (CEPhiT). In *"The Conditioned and the Unconditioned": Late Modern English Texts on Philosophy*. Edited by Isabel Moskowich, Gonzalo Camiña Rioboo, Inés Lareo Martín and Begoña Crespo. Amsterdam: John Benjamins Publishing.

Álvarez-Gil, Francisco J. 2019. *Adverbs Ending in -LY in Late Modern English. Evidence form the Coruña Corpus of History English Texts*. Valencia: Universitat Politècnica de València.

Atkinson, Dwight. 1998. *Scientific Discourse in Sociohistorical Context: The Philosophical Transactions of the Royal Society of London, 1975–1975*. London: Routledge.

Biber, Douglas. 1991. *Variation Across Speech and Writing*. Cambridge: Cambridge University Press.

Crespo, Begoña. Viewpoint and subjectivity in scientific discourse: The Coruña Corpus as a case in point. Forthcoming.

Crespo, Begoña, and Isabel Moskowich. 2016. At close range: prefaces and other text types in the Coruña Corpus of English Scientific Writing. *Revista de lenguas para fines específicos* 22/1: 213–37.

Dossena, Marina. 2017. A matter of opinion: Stancetaking in Late Modern English historiography. In *Stancetaking in Late Modern English Scientific Writing. Evidence from the Coruña Corpus Essays in Honour of Santiago González y Fernández-Corugedo*. Edited by Francisco Alonso-Almeida. Valencia: Universitat Politècnica de València, pp. 27–39.

Hyland, Ken. 1998. *Hedging in Scientific Research Articles*. Amsterdam and Philadelphia: Benjamins.

Hyland, Ken. 2005. Stance and engagement: A model of interaction in academic discourse. *Discourse Studies* 7: 173–92. [CrossRef]

Leech, Geoffrey. 2004. Recent grammatical change in English: Data, description, theory. In *Advances in Corpus Linguistics. Paper presented at 23rd International Conference on English Language Research on Computerized Corpora (ICAME 23), Göteborg, Sweden, May 22–26*. Edited by Ajmer Karin and Altenberg Bengt. Amsterdam: Rodopi, pp. 61–81.

Millward, Celia M., and Hayes Mary. 2011. *A Biography of the English Language*. Boston: Wadsworth, Cengage learning.

Monaco, Leida Maria. 2016. Was late Modern English scientific writing impersonal? *International Journal of Corpus Linguistics* 21: 499–526. [CrossRef]

Moskowich, Isabel, and Begoña Crespo. 2014. Stance is present in scientific writing, indeed. Evidence from the Coruña Corpus of English Scientific Writing. *Token: A Journal of English Linguistics* 3: 91–114.

Moskowich, Isabel. 2017. Genre and change in the Corpus of History English Texts. *NJES (Nordic Journal of English Studies)* 16: 84–106.

Puente-Castelo, Luis. 2017. "If I mistake not" Conditionals as stance markers in Late Modern English scientific discourse. In *Stancetaking in Late Modern English Scientific Writing. Evidence from the Coruña Corpus. Colección Scientia [Applied Linguistics]*. Edited by Francisco Alonso-Almeida. Valencia: Servicio de Publicaciones de la Universidad Politécnica de Valencia, pp. 111–29.

Quirk, Randolph. 1985. *A Comprehensive Grammar of the English Language.* London: Longman.

Seoane Posse, Elena. 2016. Authorial presence in Late Modern English philosophical writing: Evidence from CEPhiT. In *'The Conditioned and the Unconditioned': Late Modern English Texts on Philosophy.* Edited by Isabel Moskowich, Gonzalo Camiña Rioboo, Inés Lareo Martín and Begoña Crespo. Amsterdam and Philadelphia: Benjamins, pp. 123–44.

© 2019 by the authors. Licensee MDPI, Basel, Switzerland. This article is an open access article distributed under the terms and conditions of the Creative Commons Attribution (CC BY) license (http://creativecommons.org/licenses/by/4.0/).

Article

# Law and Business Students' Attitudes towards Learning English for Specific Purposes within CLIL and Non-CLIL Contexts

Candela Contero Urgal

Department of French and English Philology, University of Cadiz, 11002 Cadiz, Spain; candela.contero@uca.es

Received: 15 May 2019; Accepted: 20 June 2019; Published: 25 June 2019

**Abstract:** English for Specific Purposes (ESP) courses are present within most non-linguistic undergraduate studies offered in Spain. In particular, the University of Cádiz has a wide range of ESP teaching being delivered in the four campuses of the institution. Whereas this ESP instruction is thought as a way to help students develop language skills to be applied to their career paths, this very practical and useful goal may not be easily recognized by certain students. While previous research has revealed students' attitudes towards learning ESP were generally positive, little has been said on their progression throughout the whole course. The aim of the present paper is to identify Law students' approaches to a Legal English course taught through a specific methodology. Certain teaching strategies, which are also characteristic of the Content and Language Integrated Learning approach, were applied. For that purpose, the opinions of 88 respondents were collected and analysed during the second phase of their ESP course. Results revealed that although students showed a certain level of rejection before the course started, once they became well aware of the teaching methodology, their opinion changed positively. This would definitely be influenced by promoting students' motivation, as well as the teaching methodology applied.

**Keywords:** English for Specific Purposes; Content and Language Integrated Learning (CLIL); business English; legal English; teacher training; foreign language teaching; Integrating Content and Language in Higher Education (ICLHE); English as a medium of instruction (EMI); teaching methodologies in Higher Education; internationalization of the curriculum

## 1. Introduction

English for Specific Purposes (ESP) courses are offered in most undergraduate programmes in Spanish universities. A good example of this is the University of Cádiz, where the Department of French and English Philology is the second largest in this institution, with approximately 50% of its teaching staff committed to delivering ESP courses.

Particularly, in the case of Law students studying in our institution, they are required to pass an ESP course during the last semester of their degree. With this being thought as a way to foster the internationalization of their curriculum once there are about to finish their studies and start their professional career, a considerable number of students have identified this insertion of ESP teaching in their undergraduate programme as an obstacle to terminating their degree. This controversial situation has made teachers concerned about the rationale behind these specific students' negative attitude towards what was intended to be a benefit rather than a disadvantage.

In previous studies, ESP students showed to have positive attitudes towards the teacher, the evaluation method and the learning of English as a Foreign Language (Martinović and Poljaković 2010). It is a fact that students getting into university in recent years are enjoying a progressively more international environment, as some of them have already participated in bilingual or plurilingual academic programmes. They may also have a minimum level of the Foreign Language (FL) certified[1]. Most of them are also used to travelling abroad, therefore communicating in a FL in an international context. Nevertheless, having acquired a certain level of the FL, students may show some reluctance to having ESP courses when their studies are not directly related to linguistic content. One of the main reasons for including ESP teaching in undergraduate study programmes is the internationalization of the curriculum, as studying ESP is intended to help students develop the competences their degree offers in international contexts, with international clients and colleagues. Having appreciated the reluctance of a number of students in the Law Degree at the University of Cádiz towards ESP, the present paper is aimed at studying if there is a change in these students' attitudes at the end of the course, and analysing the possible reasons for that change.

The aforesaid reluctance to ESP courses is explained by the students themselves as a consequence of the process of setting aside certain credits (and therefore, academic schedule) to be employed in a language rather than a content course. In most Spanish universities, as ESP courses are present in non-linguistic undergraduate studies through an individual course in isolation during the whole programme, students perceive ESP teaching as anecdotal content and skills to develop.

While this study was conducted within a monolingual undergraduate programme, results will be compared to those obtained in a bilingual teaching scheme in the Degree in Business Administration. As the rejection level in bilingual programmes seems to be less than in monolingual programmes, we wonder whether Content and Language Integrated Learning (CLIL)[2] is offering our students a unique opportunity through which learning ESP can become a motivating challenge.

## 2. Materials and Methods

The survey was conducted during the last sessions of the course under the name "Basic Legal Terminology in English" which is located in the Spring semester of the fourth year of the Law Degree. It must be mentioned that the exams had not been held yet and that the survey was circulated under two specific circumstances which might have shortened the number of responses collected, including the following ones: the lesson chosen was one particularly devoted to theory analysis, which prevents a considerable number of students from attending the lesson, as students' attendance is rather prevailing in seminars. This fact is a consequence basically originating from the student/teacher ratio. As the number of students per theory group reaches 76 (in previous years it surpassed 180 students per group), students feel more motivated to attend the seminars in which the 152 students are divided into smaller groups. During the course of 2017–2018, there were no more than 38 students per seminar group. It is also quite revealing to comment on the consequences of dividing lessons between theory and practice, as it provokes a general belief that theoretical lessons are delivered in the form of lectures, thus avoiding the interaction between students and the teacher. As taking part in such big groups of students definitely does not facilitate a student-centred teaching methodology in which the student can play an active role in class, seminars are considered a better context to get trained, particularly in the productive language skills as well as in the field of listening comprehension.

Our survey was conducted in a population of 152 students[3], out of which 88 were the final participants in the sample. In total, 69% of the participants were female while the remaining 31% were male students (this gender gap reflects the disparity that can accurately be observed in Law students at the university we are analysing). They were aged from 19 to 51 years old and they were all studying

---

[1] In a study carried out at the Business Faculty in the University of Cádiz in 2017, 50% of the students said to have a B1 or higher level of English certified before coming into tertiary education.
[2] CLIL is compared by many researchers to "English as a medium of instruction" (EMI) as well as the term "Integrating Content and Language in Higher Education", ICLHE (Bradford 2016). We will be using the CLIL approach as applied by the project "Quality assurance in Andalusian plurilingual programs in Higher Education" (P12-SEJ-1588) and Pavón and Gaustad (2013).
[3] All subjects gave their informed consent for inclusion before they participated in the study. The study was conducted in accordance with the Declaration of Helsinki of 1975 and revised in 2013.

the Law Degree in the Faculty of Law at the University of Cádiz[4]. Regarding their English language proficiency, most surveyed students reported an accredited an English level which ranged from A1 to B1 (54%) according to the Common European Framework of Reference for Languages (CEFR). From the remaining percentage, 9% had a B2 accreditation and only 1% reached C1. No one had more than a C1 accredited and there were 36% of the surveyed students who still had no FL certificate (Figure 1). At this point, it is significant to highlight that all students at the University of Cádiz (and most universities around Andalusia and Spain) must certify a B1 level of English or any other FL (certain studies require specific languages, as it is the case of the Degree in Business) before obtaining their diploma upon graduation. That implies that 36% of students who, being in the last semester of their undergraduate studies, need to be particularly interested in developing their English language skills, as they will soon be asked to certify their B1 level of English.

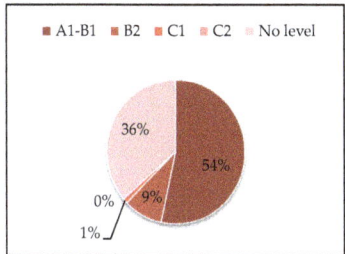

**Figure 1.** Respondents' level of English certification.

Students were given a list of nine statements (see Table 1) selected and adapted from a previous validated study carried out in the State University of Kashan in Iran (Eshghinejad 2016) and applied to the sample shown in Contero's study (forthcoming).

**Table 1.** Set of statements adapted from Esghinejad's 2016 work for Contero's forthcoming study.

| | Statements to Be Analyzed by the Students Surveyed |
|---|---|
| 1. | Speaking English in class makes me feel worried. |
| 2. | When I hear a student in my class speaking English well, I like to practice speaking with him/her. |
| 3. | I am not relaxed whenever I have to speak in English. |
| 4. | I feel embarrassed to speak English in front of other students. |
| 5. | I feel enthusiastic to come to classes taught in English. |
| 6. | Frankly, I study in English just to pass the exams. |
| 7. | I can apply the knowledge from the subjects taught in English in my real life. |
| 8. | I prefer studying in my mother tongue rather than any other foreign language |
| 9. | Studying in English is enjoyable. |

## 3. Results

The results obtained from our study can be classified into the following three main topics: (1) skills expected to be developed by the students in an ESP course; (2) students' positive attitude towards an ESP course which has already been delivered; and (3) students' awareness of the usefulness of ESP in real life. These findings will be described in detail in the subsequent sections.

---

[4] While the results show us a considerable disparity in the age of the respondents, we must clarify that only seven students out of the 88 respondents were older than 30. That means more than the 90% of the students were in their twenties.

*3.1. Skills Students Expect to Develop in an ESP Course*

The surveyed students were asked whether they were expecting to develop law-related or language-related skills throughout this legal English course, as this course seems to help students acquire cross curricular competences.

However, before analysing the students' expectations towards the competences to be acquired in this course, we might need to examine what the course description says regarding this item of the syllabus. In fact, in the description of the course the University of Cádiz[5] offers for its students, the section referring to competences presents no additional information regarding the general skills mentioned in the main description of the Degree. It is only the section related to cross curricular competences which specifically makes reference to the "understanding of legal language in the foreign language" (Official record of the Law Degree as verified by the (Andalusian Agency of Evaluation and Accreditation 2016, p. 73)).

Nevertheless, other institutions make a more precise description of the competences law students are expected to acquire in the legal English courses offered within their undergraduate or even postgraduate law studies. The following five institutions offer different perspectives towards apparently similar courses, at least, according to the content they cover.

The first of the cases to examine is the University of Granada[6] which focuses its attention on two main skills, namely, "getting to know contrastive legal terminology in English, French, Italian or German", as well as "communicating and writing legal texts in English, French, Italian or German". This implies that studying legal English is basically offering the possibility to students to learn legal terminology in a FL, and, additionally being able to communicate in legal contexts with non-Spanish speakers.

When observing the cases of the following institutions, we came across these same two competences in institutions like the Distance University of Madrid (*Universidad a Distancia de Madrid*). The course "English for jurists"[7] is said to help the students develop the following competences:

- To develop the capacity of analysis and synthesis.
- To acquire organizational skills and planning ability.
- To communicate in English in both its written and oral forms.
- To encourage interpersonal relationship skills and manage communication techniques.
- To work in multicultural environments and international contexts.
- To improve the flexibility of the student's communicative capacity to produce specific discourse for different functions, contexts, means, activities and situations in her/his work environment, which will allow her/him to adapt to new situations.

Another institution to mention in the region of Madrid is the University Carlos III de Madrid, as it offers a course titled "Legal and Business English". This course is part of a postgraduate programme, in particular, the Master's Degree in Business Legal Consultancy[8], which is described in its syllabus by having the following objectives:

- To learn the basic concepts of the Anglo-American legal system.
- To master the basic English legal terms regarding the six aforementioned branches of law.
- To know the peculiarities of Anglo-American legal language, including the differences between British English and American English about legal matters, above all, on so-called false friends which, despite their apparent similarity, may have opposite meanings in English and Spanish.

---

[5] https://derecho.uca.es/docs/Centros/Derecho/Oferta_academica/9045.pdf.
[6] http://masteres.ugr.es/negocios/pages/info_academica/asignaturas-pdf/inglesjuridico/!.
[7] https://www.udima.es/es/ingles-juristas.html.
[8] https://aplicaciones.uc3m.es/cpa/generaFicha?est=317&asig=16821&idioma=1.

- To be able to use these skills to explain (oral and written forms) basic aspects of Spanish Law in English in the six areas of Law covered in the course.

In the Andalusian context, it is worth mentioning the course "Introduction to legal English", offered in the Law Degree at the University Pablo de Olavide (Seville)[9], which incorporates the following competences:

- Resolution of legal issues within the context of English law.
- Management and understanding of the main institutions of the English Legal System.
- Knowledge and interpretation of legal texts within the framework of English law.
- Development of teamwork synergy to solve problems.
- Acquisition of skills in the management of a proper legal language vis-à-vis the basic institutions of the Legal English System.

Finally, the last institution we will be commenting on is the University of Jaen, where their legal English course[10] does not specify the competences to be acquired by the students in its syllabus but presents the following objectives which may refer to certain skills:

1. To encourage students to acquire competence in reading skills to facilitate the reading of legal texts in English.
2. To develop speaking skills to improve oral communication skills on topics in their field of expertise.
3. To become familiar with the historical and conceptual singularity of the legal system that is applied in the U.K, since this has influenced Civil Law.
4. To become familiar with the basic terminology of the sources of the U.K Legal System and the organization and administration of justice.
5. To become familiar with the distinctive morphosyntactic features of legal language.
6. To improve oral competence through debate technique, which will be based on reading informative texts in the field of Law.
7. To acquire vocabulary from different didactic activities.
8. To apply strategies to infer the meaning of unknown words from reading activities considering the context in which they appear.
9. To know when and how to use a dictionary.
10. To become familiar with the different strategies of extensive and intensive reading.

This observation of the descriptors of the legal English courses present in Law Degrees in similar contexts to the one of the University of Cádiz suggests there is a very close tie established between law-related and language-related skills. This was confirmed by the results obtained in our survey (Figure 2), as most law students (75%) were expecting to develop both legal as well as language skills. Whereas, only 15% of the students predicted they would only be trained in language skills. If we compare these results to the ones obtained in previous studies (Contero forthcoming), there is a slightly higher proportion of business students (83%) that agreed to state that they were expecting to develop both content-related and language-related skills[11] (Figure 3).

---

[9] https://www.upo.es/cms2/export/sites/facultades/facultad-derecho/es/oferta-academica/grados/grado-en-derecho/descargas/guias-docentes/2015-2016/opt-semestre1/101039-Introduccion-al-Ingles-Juridico.pdf.
[10] http://www4.ujaen.es/~{}avcasas/programa_ingles_juridico.pdf.
[11] It must be mentioned that by content-related skills we are making reference to skills to be developed when acquiring content knowledge, that is to say, facts, concepts, theories, and principles that are taught and learned in specific academic courses (The Glossary of Education Reform 2016: https://www.edglossary.org/content-knowledge/). In the case of language-related skills, we are essentially covering the four basic language skills (speaking, listening, writing and reading).

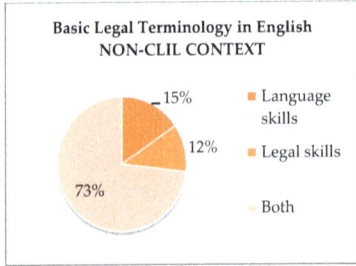

**Figure 2.** Law students' expectations towards the skills to develop in their English for Specific Purposes (ESP) course.

**Figure 3.** Business students' expectations towards the skills to develop in their ESP course.

*3.2. Students' Positive Attitudes towards ESP*

The participants in the survey were given a list of statements so as to identify their degree of agreement with them by using a Likert scale. Such a scale ranged from 1 to 5, where 1 was "strongly disagree", 2 "disagree", 3 "neutral", 4 "agree" and 5 "absolutely agree". It must be highlighted that the use of an odd number of options hindered the possibility of obtaining meaningful results and most students avoided to decide upon agreement or disagreement by locating their opinion in the neutral zone. Nonetheless, we would like to draw attention to the statement whose results were closer to 1, meaning strong disagreement. This statement made reference to the surveyed students' attitude towards learning legal English, as they indicated passing the final exam was not the only motivation they had to study, to come to class and to play an active role in it. This positive attitude towards learning ESP was considerably higher when compared to the results seen in previous studies (Contero forthcoming). As it can be seen in Figure 4, business students were clearly convinced that they had other prevailing motivations to take part in the ESP course which were much more important to just passing the final exam.

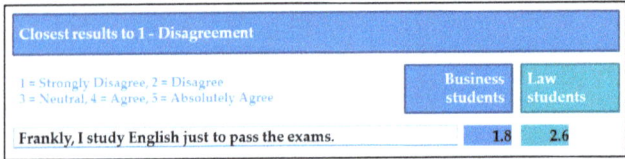

**Figure 4.** Business students' and Law students' motivations to study ESP.

*3.3. Usefulness and Applications of ESP in Real Life*

Although the previously mentioned neutrality was leading the results of our survey regarding the nine statements displayed to our students, we can also emphasize the statement whose results were closer to 5, that is, to total agreement. It was the assertion that they noticeably saw the application of their legal English course in their own life. Law students stated their level of agreement was 3.6, which was located in our scale from neutrality to agreement (Figure 5). However, results were more driven towards total agreement when in previous studies (Contero forthcoming) most business students appreciated a clear usefulness of the ESP course they were taking part in in their real life.

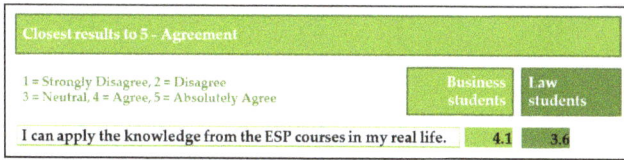

**Figure 5.** Business students' and Law students' opinions towards the application of ESP in real life.

## 4. Discussion and Conclusions

The following three main ideas can be derived from our study: Law students who are in the second semester of their fourth year at the University of Cádiz, that is to say, those who are bound to finish their undergraduate studies in the forthcoming months, believe that in a legal English course: (1) they will be trained in both language-related and content-related skills; (2) there are real motivations for them to have an active role in the course rather than just trying to get the required qualifications; and (3) they see learning legal English will be particularly useful for climbing the career ladder.

The reasoning behind the identification of these three ideas can be found in the teaching methodology applied in the ESP course. As it has formerly been pointed out in recently conducted research (Contero 2018), a new role of the FL teacher is emerging in the spread of CLIL programmes at university. Three were the main functions attached to FL teachers who started teaching in the context of CLIL programme implementations[12], namely, the coordinator of the bilingual programme, a member of the CLIL teacher training team, and the model for the teaching style of emerging CLIL programmes.

If we focus on the third aforesaid function, it is the ESP teacher who can offer a model to the CLIL teacher on how to develop specific language-related skills by means of an appropriate and modern teaching methodology. It is the Foreign Language Acquisition Teaching Method (Haidl Dietlmeier 1993) which can be suggested as a teaching approach used by FL teachers suitable to be combined with the CLIL teaching approach, so as to put forward certain key methodological strategies which might facilitate the integrated learning of the FL and the content. The reason why both teaching approaches can be easily and fruitfully combined (Contero 2017) is that both teaching methods share a major focus on authenticity. From the linguistic point of view, as Haidl Dietlmeier (1993) pointed out, it is the spontaneous and natural use of a language which fosters the acquisition of a language. That implies language acquisition means authentic exposure to it, thus being able to face real challenges from a linguistic perspective. Besides, CLIL researchers also accentuate the importance of authenticity in this particular teaching approach (Pinner 2013), maintaining the CLIL resources used in class are expected to be authentic (Papaja 2014). It is the ESP teacher that can foster authenticity in class so as to combine the effectiveness of both teaching approaches.

In her study, Contero (2017) presented the CLILUT Pentagon as a proposal for systematizing the five main methodological areas which should be covered in all CLIL Teacher Training schemes for University Teachers (CLILUT). One particular methodological area to be tackled is precisely authenticity, as it can facilitate the applicability of the content in real life, it can be a way to link academic teaching to the students' environment and it can help teachers start addressing concrete concepts in order to progressively incorporate abstract concepts into their teaching, consequently fostering acquisition.

---

[12] We may always bear in mind both content and FL teachers' worries on the spread of CLIL due to its implications in their roles (Pavón and Rubio 2010).

The final results of our survey demonstrate students' attitudes towards learning ESP are rather positive. However, we should take into account that this study was conducted at the very end of the course. As we explained in the introduction to this paper, students' attitudes were not that positive at the beginning of the course, in which certain preconceptions of what the ESP course would consist of lead students be rather skeptic towards this module of their degree. One of the causes which might have provoked this skepticism is the scarcity of information offered to students regarding the course's competences to be developed and goals to be achieved. If students are convinced from the very first lesson of the purpose for the inclusion of that course in the last phase of their undergraduate studies, they will probably be taking the course in a much more positive attitude.

The reason why this survey was compared to the results obtained in a previous study conducted in the Business and Administration Degree within the same institution is that the business students were also studying ESP. However, this ESP course had the characteristic of being located within the framework of a CLIL context. Students immersed in a CLIL programme are certainly more used to the integration of content and language in a natural way. This suggests they are more accustomed to acquiring and using a FL in an authentic context in which the connection between the teaching goals and their real life is highly perceptible. That made the data obtained in this prior study more positive regarding the students' attitudes towards the course.

The generation of an authentic context in which the acquisition of a FL is facilitated is recommended both within CLIL and non-CLIL contexts. Developing a positive attitude towards an ESP course can be stimulated by a clear recognition of the competences expected to be acquired by the students. This can be done by means of teaching strategies which can be used by the ESP teacher both within CLIL and non-CLIL programmes in order to foster authentic exposure to the FL, therefore creating a real necessity and willingness in the students to learn.

**Funding:** This research received no external funding.

**Conflicts of Interest:** The author declares no conflict of interest.

## References

Andalusian Agency of Evaluation and Accreditation. 2016. *Official record of the Law Degree as verified by the Andalusian Agency of Evaluation and Accreditation*. Cadiz: University of Cadiz.

Bradford, Annette. 2016. CBI, CLIL & EMI: Differing Approaches and Goals. Paper presented at Conference: JALT 2016: Japan Association for Language Teaching 42nd Annual International Conference on Language Teaching and Learning & Educational Materials Exhibition, Nagoya, Japan, November 25–28.

Contero, Candela. Forthcoming. From teaching English for International Business to teaching International Business in English. Considerations for an ESP teacher to start providing CLIL teacher training. In *Language and Communication: Strategies and Analyses in Multilingual and International Contexts*. Newcastle upon Tyne: Cambridge Scholar.

Contero, Candela. 2017. Técnicas didácticas y metodológicas para el perfeccionamiento de la gestión del aprendizaje del profesor AICLE en la enseñanza superior. Ph.D. Thesis, University of Cádiz, Cádiz, Spain.

Contero, Candela. 2018. The key role of Foreign Language teachers in Content and Language Integrated Learning at University. *The International Journal of Learning in Higher Education* 25: 7–16. [CrossRef]

Eshghinejad, Shahrzad. 2016. EFL students' attitudes toward learning English language: The case study of Kashan University students. *Cogent Education* 3: 1236434. [CrossRef]

Haidl Dietlmeier, Anton. 1993. La 'Teoría de la Relevancia' y los procesos de adquisición en la enseñanza de idiomas extranjeros. *Pragmalingüística* 1: 367–98.

Martinović, Anna, and Ivan Poljaković. 2010. Attitudes toward ESP among university students. *Fluminensia* 22: 145–61.

Papaja, Kasia. 2014. *Focus on CLIL. A Qualitative Evaluation of Content and Language Integrated Learning (CLIL) in Secondary Education*. Newcastle upon Tyne: Cambridge Scholars.

Pavón, Víctor, and Fernando D. Rubio. 2010. Teachers' Concerns about the Introduction of CLIL Programmes. *Porta Linguarum* 14: 45–58.

Pavón, Víctor, and Martha Gaustad. 2013. Designing Bilingual Programmes for Higher Education in Spain: Organisational, Curricular and Methodological Decisions. *International CLIL Research Journal* 2: 81–94.

Pinner, Richard. 2013. Authenticity and CLIL: Examining Authenticity from an International CLIL Perspective. *International CLIL Research Journal* 2: 44–54.

© 2019 by the author. Licensee MDPI, Basel, Switzerland. This article is an open access article distributed under the terms and conditions of the Creative Commons Attribution (CC BY) license (http://creativecommons.org/licenses/by/4.0/).

Article
# Extraction of Terms Related to Named Rivers

Juan Rojas-Garcia * and Pamela Faber

Department of Translation and Interpreting, University of Granada, 18002 Granada, Spain
* Correspondence: juanrojas@ugr.es

Received: 16 May 2019; Accepted: 15 June 2019; Published: 27 June 2019

**Abstract:** EcoLexicon is a terminological knowledge base on environmental science, whose design permits the geographic contextualization of data. For the geographic contextualization of landform concepts, this paper presents a semi-automatic method for extracting terms associated with named rivers (e.g., *Mississippi River*). Terms were extracted from a specialized corpus, where named rivers were automatically identified. Statistical procedures were applied for selecting both terms and rivers in distributional semantic models to construct the conceptual structures underlying the usage of named rivers. The rivers sharing associated terms were also clustered and represented in the same conceptual network. The results showed that the method successfully described the semantic frames of named rivers with explanatory adequacy, according to the premises of Frame-Based Terminology.

**Keywords:** named river; conceptual information extraction; geographic contextualization; text mining; Frame-Based Terminology

## 1. Introduction

EcoLexicon (http://ecolexicon.ugr.es) is a multilingual, terminological knowledge base (TKB) on environmental science that is the practical application of Frame-Based Terminology (Faber 2012). Since most concepts designated by environmental terms are multidimensional (Faber 2011), the flexible design of EcoLexicon permits the contextualization of data so that they are more relevant to specific subdomains, communicative situations, and geographic areas (León-Araúz et al. 2013). However, the geographic contextualization of landform concepts depends on knowing which terms are semantically related to each landform and how these terms are related to each other.

This paper presents a semi-automatic method of extracting terms associated with named rivers (e.g., *Nile River*) as a type of landform from a corpus of English coastal engineering texts. The aim is to represent that knowledge in a semantic network in EcoLexicon according to the theoretical premises of Frame-based Terminology.

The following subsections provide the motivation for the research and the background on distributional semantic models. The rest of this paper is organized as follows. Section 2 explains the materials and methods applied in this study, namely, the automatic identification of named rivers, the selection procedure for terms in distributional semantic models, and the clustering technique for rivers sharing associated terms. Section 3 shows the results obtained. Finally, Section 4 discusses the results and presents the conclusions derived from this work as well as plans for future research.

### 1.1. Motivations for the Research

Despite the fact that named landforms, among other named entities, are frequently found in specialized texts on the environment, their representation and inclusion in knowledge resources has received little research attention, as evidenced by the lack of named landforms in terminological resources for the environment such as DiCoEnviro[1], GEMET[2], or FAO Term Portal[3]. In contrast, AGROVOC[4] basically contains a list of named landforms with hyponymic information, whereas ENVO[5] provides descriptions of the named landforms with only geographic details and minimal semantic information consisting of the relation *located_in* (and *tributary_of* in the case of named rivers and bays).

Until now, knowledge resources have limited themselves to representing concepts such as BAY, RIVER, or BEACH, on the assumption that the concepts linked to each of them are applicable, respectively, to all named bays, rivers and beaches in the real world. To cope with this type of situation, TKBs should include the semantic representation of named landforms.

To achieve this aim in EcoLexicon, regarding named rivers, the knowledge should be represented in a semantic network according to the theoretical premises of Frame-Based Terminology, which propose knowledge representations with explanatory adequacy for enhanced knowledge acquisition (Faber 2009). Hence, each named river should appear in the context of a specialized semantic frame that highlights both its relation to other terms and the relations between those terms. The construction of these semantic networks and the semi-automatic extraction of terms from a specialized corpus are described in this paper. As far as we know, this framework has not been studied in the context of specialized lexicography, which is an innovative aspect of this work.

*1.2. Distributional Semantic Models*

Distributional semantic models (DSMs) represent the meaning of a term as a vector, based on its statistical co-occurrence with other terms in the corpus. According to the distributional hypothesis, semantically similar terms tend to have similar contextual distributions (Miller and Charles 1991). The semantic relatedness of two terms is estimated by calculating a similarity measure of their vectors, such as Euclidean distance, or cosine similarity.

Depending on the language model (Baroni et al. 2014), DSMs are either count-based or prediction-based. Count-based DSMs calculate the frequency of terms within a term's context (i.e., a sentence, paragraph, document, or a sliding context window spanning a given number of terms on either side of the target term). The Correlated Occurrence Analogue to Lexical Semantic (COALS) (Rohde et al. 2006) is an example of this type of model.

Prediction-based models exploit neural probabilistic language models, which represent terms by predicting the next term on the basis of previous terms. Examples of predictive models include the continuous bag-of-words (CBOW) and skip-gram (SG) models (Mikolov et al. 2013).

DSMs have been used in combination with clustering. Work on lexical semantics applying DSMs and clustering techniques includes the identification of semantic relations (Bertels and Speelman 2014), word sense discrimination and disambiguation (Pantel and Lin 2002), automatic metaphor identification (Shutova et al. 2010), and classification of verbs into semantic groups (Gries and Stefanowitsch 2010).

## 2. Materials and Methods

*2.1. Materials*

2.1.1. Corpus Data

The terms related to named rivers were extracted from a subcorpus of English texts on coastal engineering, comprising roughly seven million tokens and composed of specialized and

---

[1] http://olst.ling.umontreal.ca/cgi-bin/dicoenviro/search_enviro.cgi.
[2] https://www.eionet.europa.eu/gemet/en/themes/.
[3] http://www.fao.org/faoterm/en/.
[4] http://aims.fao.org/en/agrovoc.
[5] http://www.environmentontology.org/Browse-EnvO.

semi-specialized texts. This subcorpus is part of the English EcoLexicon corpus (23.1 million tokens) (see León-Araúz et al. (2018) for a detailed description).

2.1.2. GeoNames Geographic Database

The automatic detection of the named rivers in the corpus was performed with a GeoNames database dump. GeoNames (http://www.geonames.org) has over 10 million proper names for 645 different geographic entities, such as bays, beaches, rivers, and mountains. For each entity, information about their normalized designations, alternate designations, latitude, longitude, and location name is stored. A daily GeoNames database dump is publicly available as a worldwide text file.

*2.2. Methodology*

2.2.1. Pre-Processing

After compilation and cleaning, the corpus texts were tokenized, tagged with parts of speech, lemmatized, and lowercased in R programming language. The multi-word terms in EcoLexicon were then automatically matched in the lemmatized corpus and joined with underscores.

2.2.2. Named River Recognition

Both normalized and alternate names of the rivers in GeoNames were searched in the lemmatized corpus. Since various designations can refer to the same river because of syntactic variation (e.g., *Nile River* and *River Nile*), and orthographic variation (e.g., *Yangtze* and *Yangtse River*), a procedure was created to identify variants and give them a single designation in the corpus. Because of space constraints, the procedure is not described.

The variants were normalized in the lemmatized corpus and joined with underscores. The 250 rivers with the highest number of mentions in the corpus are shown on the map in Figure 1. Their latitudes and longitudes were retrieved from the GeoNames database dump. This reflects the representativeness of the corpus in reference to river locations.

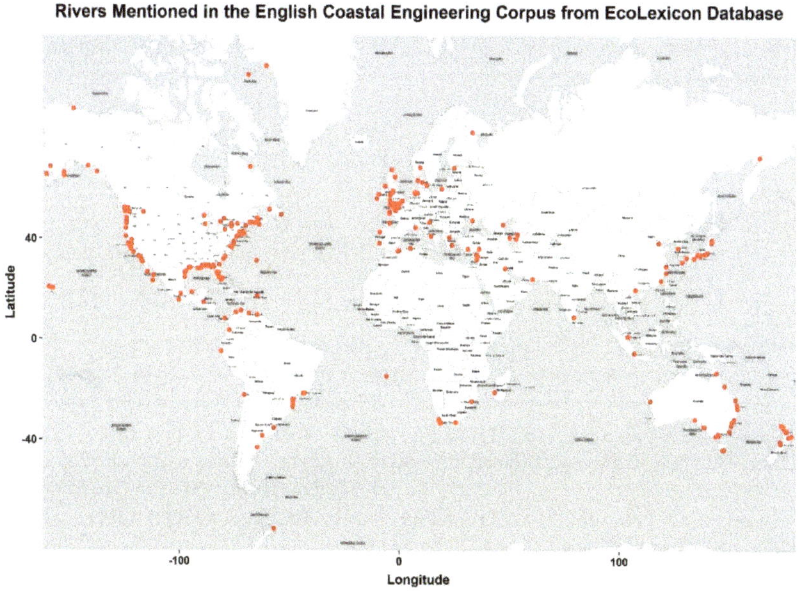

**Figure 1.** Map with the location and color-coded frequency of the named rivers.

The occurrence frequency of the named rivers ranged from 118 to 1 mention. In our study, only those rivers with a frequency greater than 9 were considered. Figure 2 shows the 55 named rivers that fulfilled this condition, along with their numbers of mentions.

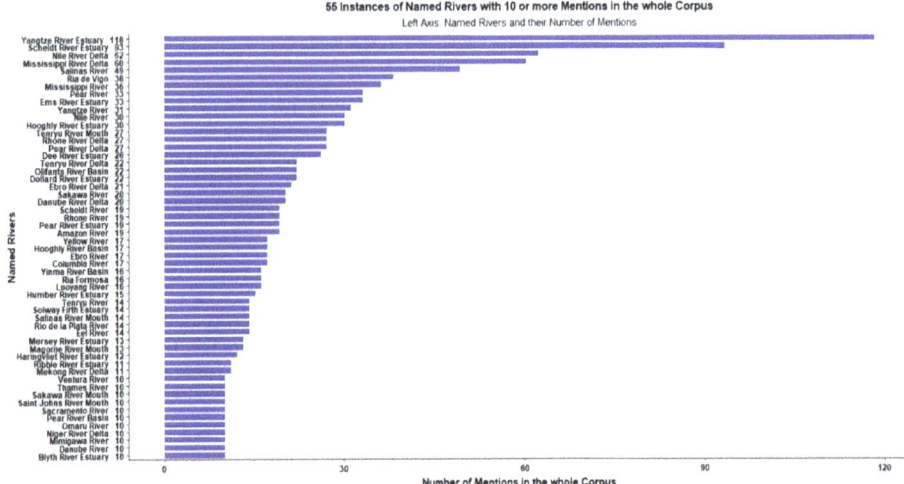

**Figure 2.** Designations and number of mentions of the 55 named rivers whose occurrence frequency was higher than 9.

### 2.2.3. Term-Term Matrix Construction

A count-based DSM was selected to obtain term vectors since this type of DSM outperforms prediction-based ones on small-sized corpora (Ars et al. 2016; Sahlgren and Lenci 2016).

For the construction of the DSM, terms with fewer than three characters, numbers, and punctuation marks were removed. Additionally, the minimal occurrence frequency was set to 5 (Evert 2008). The sliding context window spanned 30 terms on either side of the target term because large windows improve the DSM performance for small corpora (Rohde et al. 2006; Bullinaria and Levy 2007) and capture more semantic relations (Jurafsky and Martin 2017). We followed standard practice and did not use stopwords (i.e., determiners, conjunctions, relative adverbs, and prepositions) as context words (Kiela and Clark 2014). Since only nouns are represented in the semantic networks, adjectives, adverbs, and verbs were also disregarded as context words.

The resulting DSM was a 4705 × 4705 matrix, whose row vectors represented the 55 named rivers plus the 4650 terms inside the context windows of 30 terms on either side of those rivers.

### 2.2.4. Term Selection Procedure and Weighting Schemes

Subsequently, a 55 × 4650 submatrix was extracted, where the rows represented the 55 named rivers, and the columns represented the 4650 terms co-occurring with them. To cluster rivers sharing associated terms, the terms that best discriminated different groups of rivers were selected. This was done by applying Moisl's (2015, chp. 3) statistical criteria, whereby only the column vectors with the highest values in raw frequency, variance, variance-to-mean ratio (vmr), and term frequency-inverse document frequency (tf-idf) were retained. Figure 3 shows the co-plot of the four criteria in descending order of magnitude. A threshold of 2000 was set. This meant that only 1858 column terms fulfilled all criteria.

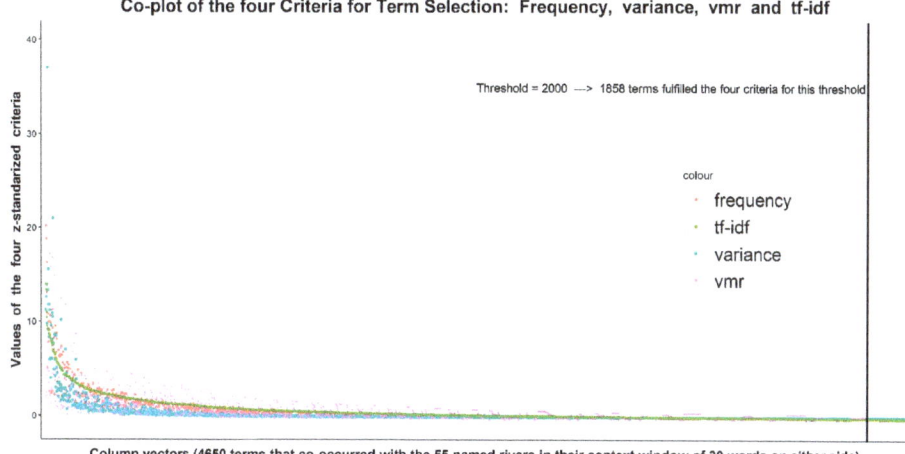

**Figure 3.** Co-plot of the four criteria for term selection.

Accordingly, a reduced matrix of 1913 × 1913 dimensions (1858 terms plus 55 named rivers) was obtained. The matrix was then subjected to three weighting schemes. First, the statistical log-likelihood measure calculated the association score between all term pairs, since it captures syntagmatic and paradigmatic relations (Bernier-Colborne and Drouin 2016; Lapesa et al. 2014) and achieves better performance for small-sized corpora (Alrabia et al. 2014). Secondly, the scores were transformed by applying logarithms to reduce skewness (Lapesa et al. 2014). Finally, the row vectors were normalized to unit length.

2.2.5. Clustering of Named Rivers

A hierarchical clustering technique was applied to the weighted 55 × 1858 submatrix. The cosine distance was used as the intervector distance measure, and the Ward's method as the clustering algorithm, namely, a criterion for choosing the pair of clusters to merge at each step, based on the minimum increase in total within-cluster variance.

Since it was not clear how strongly a cluster was supported by data, a means for assessing the certainty of the existence of a cluster in corpus data was devised. Multiscale bootstrap resampling (Suzuki and Shimodaira 2004) is a method for this in hierarchical clustering, which was implemented in the R package *pvclust* (Suzuki and Shimodaira 2006). For each cluster, this method produces a number ranging from zero to one. This number is the approximately unbiased probability value (AU *p*-value), which represents the possibility that the cluster is a true cluster. The greater the AU *p*-value, the greater the probability that the cluster is a true cluster supported by corpus data. An AU *p*-value equal to or greater than 95% significance level is most commonly adopted in research.

Thirteen groups of rivers with *p*-values higher than 95% were strongly supported by corpus data, as marked by the red rectangles in the dendrogram in Figure 4.

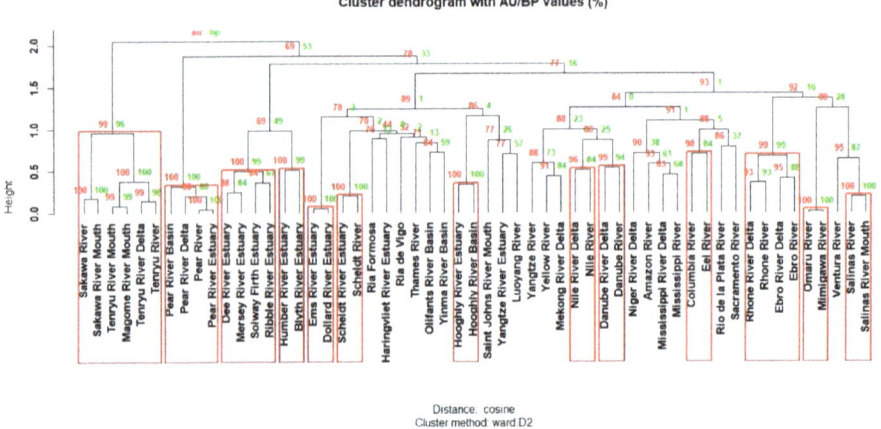

**Figure 4.** Dendrogram of the hierarchical clustering of the 55 named rivers with 13 clusters.

2.2.6. Terms Characterizing each Cluster

To ascertain the terms strongly associated with each of the 13 clusters, the following procedure was used:

1. For each of the named rivers in the 13 clusters, a set of the top 30 terms, most semantically related to each river, was extracted from the DSM using cosine similarity.
2. For each cluster, the mathematical operation set intersection was applied to the sets of the top 30 terms, most semantically related to the rivers in the same cluster. Only the shared terms with a cosine similarity higher than 0.55 were selected.

A reduced set of terms was thus obtained for each cluster to describe the named rivers.

## 3. Results

Because of space constraints, only the results for the first and twelfth clusters in Figure 4 (numbering the clusters from left to right) are presented in this paper. As shown in Figure 4, the first cluster is formed by the *Sakawa* and *Tenryu* rivers, *Sakawa*, *Tenryu*, and *Magome* river mouths, and the *Tenryu River* delta, all located in Japan. The *Omaru* and *Mimigawa* rivers, also located in Japan, comprise the twelfth cluster (see Table 1). These clusters were selected because both contain different rivers, and they all flow in Japan. We found it interesting to explore the reasons why different rivers were grouped together, and why there were two groups of Japanese rivers in the dendrogram, rather than only one.

**Table 1.** Designations and locations of the rivers in the first and twelfth clusters.

| Cluster 1 (Japan) | Cluster 12 (Japan) |
| --- | --- |
| Sakawa River | Omaru River |
| Sakawa River Mouth | Mimigawa River |
| Tenryu River | |
| Tenryu River Mouth | |
| Tenryu River Delta | |
| Magome River Mouth | |

For the description of the frames, the semantic relations were manually extracted by querying the corpus in Sketch Engine (Kilgarriff et al. 2004), and analyzing knowledge-rich contexts, namely, "a context indicating at least one item of domain knowledge that could be useful for conceptual analysis"

(Meyer 2001, p. 281). The query results were concordances of any elements between the river in a cluster and related terms in a ±40 span. The semantic relations were those in EcoLexicon (Faber et al. 2009), with the addition of *supplies*, *prevents*, *accumulates_in*, *inputs*, and *simulates*.

The semantic networks described in the following subsections reflect that most terms related to named rives are complex nominals (e.g., *longshore sand transport*, *beach nourishment*). English complex nominals are multi-word terms (MWTs) with a head noun preceded by a modifying element (i.e., nouns or adjectives) (Levi 1978). The abundance of MWTs is due to at least three reasons: specialized language units are mostly represented by such compound forms (Nakov 2013); complex nominals provide relevant information for the conceptual structuring of a specialized domain (Meyer and Mackintosh 1996), and they are frequently used to designate specialized concepts in English (Sager et al. 1980). For these reasons, complex nominals should be included in the semantic networks and in TKBs such as EcoLexicon (Cabezas-García and Faber 2018).

### 3.1. First Cluster: Sakawa, Tenryu and Magome Rivers

After the construction of dams and coastal protection structures (i.e., breakwaters, jetties, etc.), and extensive *riverbed excavation* for sand mining, the sediment supplied from the *Sakawa* and *Tenryu* rivers markedly decreased, resulting in *beach erosion* on both the *Seisho* and *Enshu-nada* coasts, into which the *Sakawa* and *Tenryu* rivers discharge, respectively. Additionally, since *submarine canyons* have developed very close to the shoreline on the *Seisho Coast*, most *river sediment* from the *Sakawa River* sinks into them because of the *fluvial fan* at its mouth, thus causing *sand loss*. Since urgent measures were required to protect both coasts, beach topography changes were predicted. For that reason, the beach modifications were simulated using the *contour-line-change model* considering the following: the variation in grain size of the beach sediments, the *longshore sand transport* through the *submarine canyons*, and the sediment supply from both rivers.

In the case of the *Sakawa River* (see Figure 5), the most favourable result was obtained when nourishment was performed using fine- and coarse-sized materials, known as *mixture materials*, because the *Seisho Coast* advanced, and the *seabed erosion* near the *submarine canyons* was prevented.

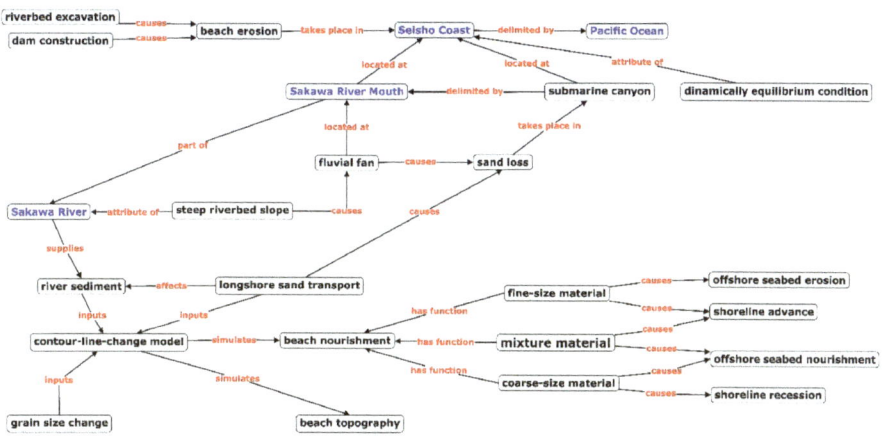

**Figure 5.** Semantic network of the terms associated with the *Sakawa River*.

In the case of the *Tenryu River* (see Figure 6), *sand bypassing* (i.e., man-induced transfer of sand from a given distance landwards of the coast line, to a beach) at *Sakuma Dam* as a measure against *beach erosion* on the *Enshu-nada Coast* was taken to recover the sandy beach, but *breakwaters*, previously constructed as a measure against *beach erosion*, were a barrier to the movement of sand by *longshore sand transport*.

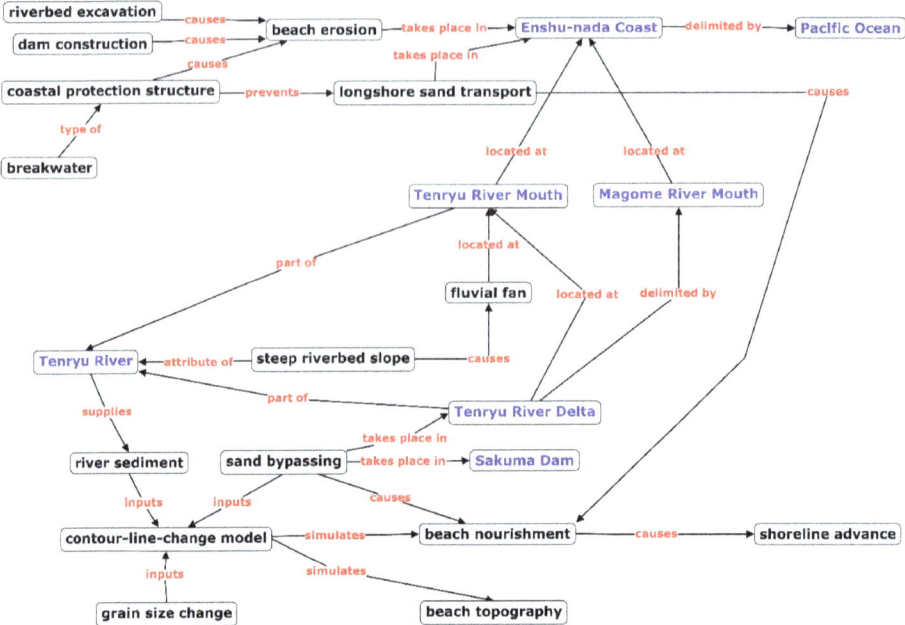

**Figure 6.** Semantic network of the terms associated with the *Tenryu* and *Magome* rivers.

## 3.2. Twelfth Cluster: Omaru and Mimigawa Rivers

Owing to the interruption of sediment flow at dams, degradation of the riverbed was observed downstream of the *Omaru*, *Mimigawa*, *Hitotsuse*, and *Ooyodo* rivers. Sediment discharge through these four rivers was thus considered to decrease considerably, causing *coastal erosion* on the *Miyazaki Coast*. The *Sumiyoshi Beach*, located on this coast, is thus a severely eroded beach because of the decrease in sediment supply from the four rivers, and the blocking of *longshore sand transport* by the *breakwater* of the *Miyazaki Port* (see Figure 7).

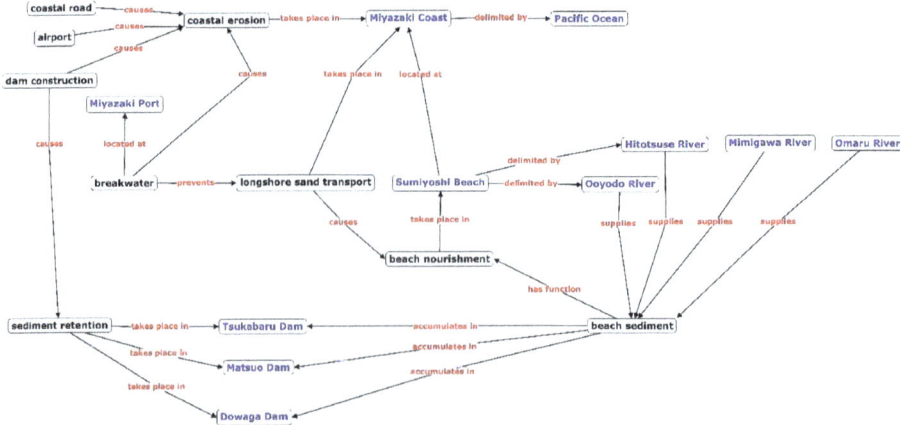

**Figure 7.** Semantic network of the terms associated with the *Omaru* and *Mimigawa* rivers.

## 4. Discussion

To extract knowledge for the semantic frames or conceptual structures (Faber 2012) that underlie the usage of named rivers in coastal engineering texts, a semi-automated method for the extraction of terms and semantic relations was devised. The semantic relations linking concepts in the semantic frames were manually extracted by querying the corpus in Sketch Engine, and analyzing knowledge-rich contexts. The query results were concordances of any elements between the river in a cluster and related terms in a ±40 span. It was a time-consuming task, although essential for the explanatory adequacy of frames (Faber 2009). In future research, the automatic extraction of semantic relations for named rivers by means of knowledge patterns (KPs) (Meyer 2001) will be tested. KPs are lexico-syntactic markers that generally convey semantic relations in real texts. For instance, examples of generic-specific KPs are *such as*, *is a kind of*, and *other*. In (León-Araúz et al. 2016), a KP-based sketch grammar for Sketch Engine was developed, which automatically provides a list of terms that hold a specific semantic relation with a target term. In future work, these KPs will be applied to our corpus, as already done in Rojas-García and Cabezas-García (forthcoming) for other purposes.

The method for the extraction of terms closely associated with named rivers combining, on the one hand, the use of a count-based DSM, weighted by the log-likelihood association measure, and on the other hand, a selection procedure for terms based on four statistical criteria. Although this term selection procedure offered successful results to construct the semantic frames, Topic Modelling (Blei et al. 2003), a domain-specific dimension reduction technique for texts, will be also applied, and a comparison of both methods will be carried out.

The semantic frames presented in the previous section reflect that most terms related to named rives are multi-word terms (MWT) since specialized language units are mostly represented by such compound forms (Nakov 2013). MWT extraction was possible because they were previously matched and joined by means of underscoring in the lemmatized corpus, thanks to the list of MWTs stored in EcoLexicon. This confirms that EcoLexicon is a valuable resource for any natural language processing tasks related to specialized corpora on environmental science. Furthermore, the profusion of MWTs underlines the importance of applying methods (automatic, semi-automatic, or manual) to recognize them for the knowledge representation of a specialized domain.

Finally, the conceptual structures also highlighted that coastal engineering texts attach great importance to the study of the processes that each named river triggers, the processes that affect a certain named river, and the crucial role that a named river plays in preventing coastal erosion. The effective acquisition of this specialized knowledge about named rivers is necessary in communicative situations, such as specialized translation of coastal engineering texts to appropriately render terms into another language (Faber 2012). The semantic networks that underlie the usage of named rivers provide this background knowledge and make the semantic and syntactic behavior of terms explicit by means of the description of conceptual relations and term combinations (Faber 2009).

**Author Contributions:** Conceptualization, J.R.-G.; methodology, J.R.-G.; validation, J.R.-G. and P.F.; formal analysis, J.R.-G.; investigation, J.R.-G.; resources, P.F.; data curation, J.R.-G. and P.F.; writing—original draft preparation, J.R.-G.; writing—review and editing, P.F.; visualization, J.R.-G.; supervision, P.F.; project administration, P.F.; funding acquisition, J.R.-G. and P.F.

**Funding:** This research was carried out as part of project FFI2017-89127-P, Translation-Oriented Terminology Tools for Environmental Texts (TOTEM), funded by the Spanish Ministry of Economy and Competitiveness. Funding was also provided by an FPU grant given by the Spanish Ministry of Education to the first author Juan Rojas-García.

**Conflicts of Interest:** The authors declare no conflict of interest.

## References

Alrabia, Maha, Nawal Alhelewh, AbdulMalik Al-Salman, and Eric Atwell. 2014. An Empirical Study on the Holy Quran Based on A Large Classical Arabic Corpus. *International Journal of Computational Linguistics* 5: 1–13.

Ars, Fatemeh, Jon Willits, and Michael Jones. 2016. Comparing Predictive and Co-occurrence Based Models of Lexical Semantics Trained on Child-directed Speech. Paper presented at 38th Annual Conference of the Cognitive Science Society, CogSci, Austin, TX, USA, August 10–13; pp. 1092–97.

Baroni, Marco, Georgiana Dinu, and Germán Kruszewski. 2014. Don't count, predict! A systematic comparison of context-counting vs. context-predicting semantic vectors. Paper presented at 52nd Annual Meeting of the Association for Computational Linguistics, ACL, Baltimore, MD, USA, June 22–27; vol. 1, pp. 238–47.

Bernier-Colborne, Gabriel, and Patrick Drouin. 2016. Evaluation of distributional semantic models: A holistic approach. Paper presented at 5th International Workshop on Computational Terminology, CompuTerm, Osaka, Japan, December 12; pp. 52–61.

Bertels, Ann, and Dirk Speelman. 2014. Clustering for semantic purposes: Exploration of semantic similarity in a technical corpus. *Terminology* 20: 279–303.

Blei, David M., Andrew Y. Ng, and Michael I. Jordan. 2003. Latent Dirichlet Allocation. *Journal of Machine Learning Research* 3: 993–1022.

Bullinaria, John A., and Joseph P. Levy. 2007. Extracting semantic representations from word co-occurrence statistics: A computational study. *Behavior Research Methods* 39: 510–26. [CrossRef] [PubMed]

Cabezas-García, Melania, and Pamela Faber. 2018. Phraseology in specialized resources: An approach to complex nominals. *Lexicography* 5: 55–83. [CrossRef]

Evert, Stefan. 2008. Corpora and Collocations. In *Corpus Linguistics. An International Handbook*. Edited by Anke Lüdeling and Merja Kytö. Berlin: Mouton de Gruyter, chp. 58.

Faber, Pamela. 2009. The cognitive shift in terminology and specialized translation. *MonTI. Monografías de Traducción e Interpretación* 1: 107–34. [CrossRef]

Faber, Pamela. 2011. The Dynamics of Specialized Knowledge Representation: Simulational Reconstruction or the Perception action Interface. *Terminology* 17: 9–29.

Faber, Pamela, ed. 2012. *A Cognitive Linguistics View of Terminology and Specialized Language*. Berlin and Boston: De Gruyter Mouton.

Faber, Pamela, Pilar León-Araúz, and Juan Antonio Prieto. 2009. Semantic Relations, Dynamicity, and Terminological Knowledge Bases. *Current Issues in Language Studies* 1: 1–23.

Gries, Stefan, and Anatol Stefanowitsch. 2010. Cluster analysis and the identification of collexeme classes. In *Empirical and Experimental Methods in Cognitive/Functional Research*. Edited by Sally Rice and John Newman. Stanford: CSLI, pp. 73–90.

Jurafsky, Daniel, and James Martin. 2017. Vector Semantics. In *Speech and Language Processing*. Unpublished Draft of August 28.

Kiela, Douwe, and Stephen Clark. 2014. A Systematic Study of Semantic Vector Space Model Parameters. Paper presented at 2nd Workshop on Continuous Vector Space Models and their Compositionality (CVSC), EACL, Gothenburg, Sweden, April 26–30; pp. 21–30.

Kilgarriff, Adam, Pavel Rychlý, Pavel Smrz, and David Tugwell. 2004. The Sketch Engine. Paper presented at 11th EURALEX International Congress, Lorient, France, July 6–10; pp. 105–15.

Lapesa, Gabriella, Stefan Evert, and Sabine Schulte im Walde. 2014. Contrasting Syntagmatic and Paradigmatic Relations: Insights from Distributional Semantic Models. Paper presented at 3rd Joint Conference on Lexical and Computational Semantics, SEM'2014, Dublin, Ireland, August 23–24; pp. 160–70.

León-Araúz, Pilar, Arianne Reimerink, and Pamela Faber. 2013. Multidimensional and Multimodal Information in EcoLexicon. In *Computational Linguistics*. Edited by Adam Przepiórkowski, Maciej Piasecki, Krzysztof Jassem and Piotr Fuglewicz. Berlin: Springer, pp. 143–61.

León-Araúz, Pilar, Antonio San Martín, and Pamela Faber. 2016. Pattern-based Word Sketches for the Extraction of Semantic Relations. Paper presented at 5th International Workshop on Computational Terminology, CompuTerm, Osaka, Japan, December 12; pp. 73–82.

León-Araúz, Pilar, Antonio San Martín, and Arianne Reimerink. 2018. The EcoLexicon English corpus as an open corpus in Sketch Engine. Paper presented at 18th EURALEX International Congress, Ljubljana, July 17–21; pp. 893–901.

Levi, Judith. 1978. *The Syntax and Semantics of Complex Nominals*. New York: Academic Press.

Meyer, Ingrid. 2001. Extracting knowledge-rich contexts for terminography: A conceptual and methodological framework. In *Recent Advances in Computational Terminology*. Edited by Didier Bourigault, Chistian Jacquemin and Marie-Claude L'Homme. Amsterdam and Philadelphia: John Benjamins, pp. 279–302.

Meyer, Ingrid, and Kristen Mackintosh. 1996. Refining the terminographer's concept-analysis methods: How can phraseology help? *Terminology* 3: 1–26. [CrossRef]

Mikolov, Tomas, Kai Chen, Greg Corrado, and Jeffrey Dean. 2013. Efficient estimation of word representations in vector space. Paper presented at International Conference on Learning Representations, ICLR, Scottsdale, AZ, USA, May 2–4.

Miller, George, and Walter Charles. 1991. Contextual correlates of semantic similarity. *Language and Cognitive Processes* 6: 1–28. [CrossRef]

Moisl, Hermann. 2015. *Cluster Analysis for Corpus Linguistics*. Berlin: De Gruyter Mouton.

Nakov, Preslav. 2013. On the interpretation of noun compounds: Syntax, semantics, and entailment. *Natural Language Engineering* 19: 291–330. [CrossRef]

Pantel, Patrick, and Dekang Lin. 2002. Discovering Word Senses from Text. Paper presented at ACM Conference on Knowledge Discovery and Data Mining, KDD-02, Edmonton, AB, Canada, July 23–26; pp. 613–19.

Rohde, Douglas, Laura Gonnerman, and David Plaut. 2006. An Improved Model of Semantic Similarity Based on Lexical Co-Occurrence. *Communications of the ACM* 8: 627–33.

Rojas-García, Juan, and Melania Cabezas-García. forthcoming. *Use of Knowledge Patterns for the Evaluation of Semiautomatically-Induced Semantic Clusters*. Serie Forum für Fachsprachen-Forschung; Berlin: Frank & Timme.

Sager, Juan C., David Dungworth, and Peter F. McDonald. 1980. *English Special Languages. Principles and Practice in Science and Technology*. Wiesbaden: Brandstetter Verlag.

Sahlgren, Magnus, and Alessandro Lenci. 2016. The Effects of Data Size and Frequency Range on Distributional Semantic Models. Paper presented at 2016 Conference on Empirical Methods in Natural Language Processing, Austin, TX, USA, November 1–5; pp. 975–80.

Shutova, Ekaterina, Lin Sun, and Anna Korhonen. 2010. Metaphor identification using verb and noun clustering. Paper presented at 23rd International Conference on Computational Linguistics, COLING, Beijing, China, August 23–27; vol. 2, pp. 1002–10.

Suzuki, Ryota, and Hidetoshi Shimodaira. 2004. An application of multiscale bootstrap resampling to hierarchical clustering of microarray data: How accurate are these clusters? Paper presented at Fifteenth International Conference on Genome Informatics, GIW2004, Yokohama, Japan, December 13–15.

Suzuki, Ryota, and Hidetoshi Shimodaira. 2006. Pvclust: An R package for assessing the uncertainty in hierarchical clustering. *Bioinformatics* 22: 1540–42. [CrossRef] [PubMed]

© 2019 by the authors. Licensee MDPI, Basel, Switzerland. This article is an open access article distributed under the terms and conditions of the Creative Commons Attribution (CC BY) license (http://creativecommons.org/licenses/by/4.0/).

MDPI  
St. Alban-Anlage 66  
4052 Basel  
Switzerland  
Tel. +41 61 683 77 34  
Fax +41 61 302 89 18  
www.mdpi.com  

*Languages* Editorial Office  
E-mail: languages@mdpi.com  
www.mdpi.com/journal/languages  

www.ingramcontent.com/pod-product-compliance
Lightning Source LLC
LaVergne TN
LVHW071956080526
838202LV00064B/6764